THE FRACTURED REPUBLIC

THE FRACTURED REPUBLIC

Renewing America's
Social Contract in the Age
of Individualism

YUVAL LEVIN

BASIC BOOKS
A Member of the Perseus Books Group
New York

Published by Basic Books,
A Member of the Perseus Books Group

Books published by Basic Books are available at special discounts for bulk purchases in
the United States by corporations, institutions, and other organizations. For more information,
please contact the Special Markets Department at the Perseus Books Group, 2300 Chestnut
Street, Suite 200, Philadelphia, PA 19103, or call (800) 810–4145, ext. 5000, or
e-mail special.markets@perseusbooks.com.

Library of Congress Cataloging-in-Publication Data

Names: Levin, Yuval, author.
Title: The fractured Republic : renewing America's social contract in the age
    of individualism : how America can overcome nostalgia, revive civil
    society, and thrive in the twenty-first century / Yuval Levin.
Description: New York : Basic Books, [2016] | Includes bibliographical
    references and index.
Identifiers: LCCN 2016002304| ISBN 9780465061969 (hardcover) | ISBN
    9780465098606 (electronic)
Subjects: LCSH: Civil society—United States. | United States—Politics and
    government—21st century. | United States—Social conditions—21st
    century. | United States—Economic conditions—21st century. | United
    States—Civilization—21st century.
Classification: LCC E893 .L48 2016 | DDC 306.20973--dc23 LC record
available at http://lccn.loc.gov/2016002304

10 9 8 7 6 5 4 3 2 1

For Cecelia, with love

Christian nations in our day appear to me to offer a frightening spectacle: The movement that carries them along is already strong enough that it cannot be suspended, and it is not yet rapid enough to despair of directing it. Their fate is in their hands, but soon it will escape them. To instruct democracy, if possible to reanimate its beliefs, to purify its mores, to moderate its movements, to substitute little by little an understanding of affairs for its inexperience, and knowledge of its true interests for its blind instincts; to adapt its government to time and place; to modify it according to circumstances and men—such is the first duty imposed on those who would guide society in our day. A new political science is needed for a world altogether new. But that is what we hardly dream of: Placed in the middle of a rapid river, we obstinately fix our eyes on some debris we still perceive on the bank, while the current carries us away and takes us backward toward the abyss.

—ALEXIS DE TOCQUEVILLE,
Democracy in America

CONTENTS

INTRODUCTION

LIFE IN AMERICA IS ALWAYS getting better and worse at the same time. Progress comes at a cost, even if it is often worth that cost. Misery beckons relief, so that our virtues often turn up where our vices have been. Decay and decadence almost always trail behind success, while renewal chases ruin. And in a vast society like ours, all of this is always happening at once. That means there are no simple stories to tell about the state of our country, and that upbeat and downcast social analyses are often just partial descriptions of one complex whole.

That complexity is a constant annoyance for people in my line of work. I am the editor of a journal of public affairs and a scholar at a think tank in Washington, DC, where I write about policy and politics. I am therefore in the business of trying to understand our public problems and proposing solutions. That would be easier to do if our public life were, as we all sometimes imagine it is, the scene of simple struggles between the righteous and the wrong, and if the recipe for flourishing were obvious and within our easy reach if only our political opponents were cleared away.

American politics is frequently paralyzed by the illusion that things might be that easy. But in our time, in particular, our politics is overwhelmed by an unusually intense and often debilitating frustration that is rooted in a form of that illusion, but runs deeper. Liberals and conservatives both frequently insist not only that the path to the America of their (somewhat different) dreams is easy to see, but also that our country was once on that very path and has been thrown off course by the foolishness or wickedness of those on the other side of the aisle. Liberals look back to the postwar golden age of midcentury America, which they believe embodied the formula for cultural liberalization amid economic security and progress until some market fanatics threw it all away. Conservatives look fondly to the late-century boom of the Reagan era, which they say rescued the country from economic malaise while recapturing some of the magic of the confident, united America of that earlier midcentury golden age, but was abandoned by misguided statists.

Each side wants desperately to recover its lost ideal, believes the bulk of the country does, too, and is endlessly frustrated by the political resistance that holds it back. The broader public, meanwhile, finds in the resulting political debates little evidence of real engagement with contemporary problems and few attractive solutions. In the absence of relief from their own resulting frustration, a growing number of voters opt for leaders who simply embody or articulate that frustration.

This book begins from that widespread frustration, which I take to be a function in large part of a failure of diagnosis, and so a failure of self-understanding. American life in the decades since the end of World War II has not been, on the whole, a story of finding the right course and then falling away from it. We have actually held fairly steadily to something like a single complex but coherent trajectory, which has turned out to bring us progress at a cost.

In our cultural, economic, political, and social life, this has been a trajectory of increasing individualism, diversity, dynamism, and liberalization. And it has come at the cost of dwindling solidarity, cohesion, stability, authority, and social order.

The America that emerged from World War II and the Great Depression was exceptionally unified and cohesive, and possessed of an unusual confidence in large institutions. But almost immediately after the war, it began a long process of unwinding and fragmenting: over the subsequent decades, the culture liberalized, the economy was deregulated, and an exceptional midcentury elite consensus in politics gave way to renewed divisions. In time, this fracturing of consensus grew from diffusion into polarization—of political views, of incomes, of family patterns and ways of life. There was no sharp break in this process, and no change of direction midway. We have grown less conformist but more fragmented; more diverse but less unified; more dynamic but less secure.

Both progressives and conservatives are conflicted about this combination of gains and losses. Progressives tend to treasure the social liberation, cultural diversification, and expressive individualism of our time, but they lament the economic dislocation, the loss of social solidarity, and the rise in inequality and fragmentation—and their consequences for the most vulnerable Americans, in particular. Conservatives tend to celebrate the economic liberalization, dynamism, and prosperity, but they lament the social instability, moral disorder, cultural breakdown, and weakening of fundamental institutions and traditions—and their consequences for the most vulnerable Americans, in particular.

Some exceptionally brooding traditionalists bemoan it all, of course, but only by ignoring the genuine progress modern America has made. Some exceptionally gleeful libertarians celebrate all of it, but only by ignoring the human costs we have paid. Most progressives and conservatives see good and bad, but each group believes not only that we could have what it values without what it deplores but also that Americans once had the recipe for such a feat, whether in the mid-1960s or the early 1980s.

As a result, our political life is now exceedingly nostalgic. The ambitions of most of its various partisans begin with calls for a reversal of some portion of the great diffusion of our national life that has defined the American experience for more than half a century. This nostalgia is at the core of the frustration that so overwhelms our politics now. If we could see our way past it, we might gain a much better grasp of the nature of the problems we face and the shape of potential solutions.

Some of the most considerable challenges we now confront are actually the logical conclusions of the path of individualism and fracture, dissolution and liberation that we have traveled since the middle of the twentieth century. And some of the most considerable resources at our disposal for addressing those challenges are also the products of our having traveled this path. Our problems are the troubles of a fractured republic, and the solutions we pursue will need to call upon the strengths of a decentralized, diffuse, diverse, dynamic nation.

The state of our politics makes it terribly difficult to see any of this or to act on it, however. The structure of our key debates suggests to us that politics must be a choice between collectivism and atomism—between empowering a central government to impose solutions and liberating isolated citizens to go their own ways. These debates therefore often devolve into accusations of socialism and social Darwinism, libertinism and puritanism, and they encourage us to think that we must either double down on dissolution and radical individualism or return to mass consolidation and centralization.

But if we considered the lessons of our postwar history, and the lessons of what preceded and precipitated it, we might come to grasp a truth that some perceptive friends of American democracy have long sought to call to our attention: collectivism and atomism are not opposite ends of the political spectrum, but rather two sides of one coin. They are closely related tendencies, and they often coexist and reinforce one another—each making the other possible. It is when we pursue both together, as we frequently do in contemporary America, that we most exacerbate the dark sides of our fracturing and dissolution.

There is an alternative to this perilous mix of over-centralization and hyper-individualism. It can be found in the intricate structure of our complex social topography and in the institutions and relationships that stand between the isolated individual and the national state. These begin in loving family attachments. They spread outward to interpersonal relationships in neighborhoods, schools, workplaces, religious communities, fraternal bodies, civic associations, economic enterprises, activist groups, and the work of local governments. They reach further outward toward broader social, political, and professional affiliations, state institutions, and regional affinities. And they conclude in a national identity that among its foremost attributes is dedicated to the principle of the equality of the entire human race.

Our society is thus like a set of concentric rings, beginning with the most concrete and personal of human connections and concluding in the most abstract and philosophical of human commitments. Each ring, starting from the innermost sanctum of the family and the individuals who compose it, anchors and enables the next and is in turn protected by it and given the room to thrive. The outermost ring of society is guarded and sustained by the national government, which is charged with protecting the space in which the entire society can flourish and enabling all Americans to participate in and benefit from what happens there.

This understanding of society, this picture of our social compact, is itself what is most threatened by the fracture and fragmentation of our era. But it is at the same time what holds the key to balancing diversity with cohesion, and dynamism with moral order. The middle layers of society, where people see each other face to face, offer a middle ground between radical individualism and extreme centralization. Our political life need not consist of a recurring choice between having the federal government invade and occupy the middle layers of society or having isolated individuals break down the institutions that compose those layers. It can and should be an arena for attempting different ways of empowering those middle institutions to help our society confront its problems.

There will be no simple or universal formulas for doing that, but there are never simple or universal formulas for revitalizing a complex society. Indeed, the absence of easy answers is precisely a reason to empower a multiplicity of problem-solvers throughout our society, rather than hoping that one problem-solver in Washington gets it right.

This book therefore ultimately argues that the frustration that defines our time should lead us not to seek an impossible return to a half-remembered golden age, but instead to work toward a modernized politics of subsidiarity—that is, of putting power, authority, and significance as close to the level of the interpersonal community as reasonably possible. That is what the modernization we now so badly need would look like.

Our country has a long tradition of contending with its vastness and its multiplicity in this way. And our politics has resources for the task as well. Progressives can draw upon a deep reserve of experience in populist community and labor activism, a history of intellectual dalliances with a communitarian liberalism, and a lively elite culture of localist consumerism.

But they must also resist their own instincts toward both administrative centralization and moral individualism. Conservatives can call upon a profound intellectual tradition and a rich philosophy of society rooted in the preeminence of the mediating institutions, a commitment to constitutionalism and federalism, and vast experience with a host of different forms of bottom-up problem solving in the church, the market, and the charitable enterprise. But they must also resist a long-honed inclination to express their objections to centralization in radically individualist terms. And countless Americans of all parties and no party are practical, experienced experts in putting family, faith, and community first and helping one another in hard times.

A modernized ethic of subsidiarity would therefore not yield a radical revolution in American life but an incremental revival. And it would not involve a checklist of public programs and policy steps. It would begin, instead, with an instinct for decentralization in our public affairs, a tendency toward experimentation and bottom-up problem solving, a greater patience for variety in our approaches to social and economic problems and priorities, more room for ingenuity and tolerance for trial and error, and more freedom for communities to live out their moral ideals, and so to each define freedom a little differently.

It would involve greater attentiveness to the near at hand, and so a lesser emphasis on immense national battles—lowering the stakes, and therefore the temperature, of our national politics. It would surely bring much change to the institutions of our entitlement state and welfare system over time, but by enabling salutary competition rather than replacing one set of centralizing assumptions with another. It would not call upon some revanchist fantasy of a premodern age of voluntarism, but rather would seek to modernize our public institutions to bring them into line with a decentralizing society where choice and competition are the norm. It would, in other words, work to turn our very fracture and diversity into tools for addressing some of their own worst consequences.

THIS BOOK IS STRUCTURED AS an effort to show why such an ethic might be necessary, and what it might involve. It begins by suggesting that the acute frustration that characterizes twenty-first-century America is closely linked to an intense nostalgia that can teach us something but that also blinds us to the nature of our contemporary strengths and weaknesses and must be overcome.

It then offers a cursory overview of some key historical trends of the past century that our nostalgia might particularly incline us to ignore or misunderstand, and that therefore could be particularly useful for putting the midcentury golden age that so beckons to us into perspective. These trends suggest that we cannot hope to address our problems by reversing course. And they argue, in particular, that it is especially implausible to imagine that we might recapture the dynamics of midcentury America. Our society was then precariously suspended between an era of consolidation and conformity, on the one hand, and an age of liberalization and fracture, on the other—benefiting from the best of both, but in a way that could not last.

Rather, we should strive to understand the problems that our fragmentation and fracturing have posed for us, and the ways that our diversity and dynamism might help us to address them. We should look for ways to thrive that are suited to the nation we have become and are still becoming. The book concludes by considering where such a search might lead us—in economic, cultural, and political terms.

What follows is thus part diagnosis and part prescription. But it is mostly a fumbling for clarity—not a comprehensive picture of our circumstances and prospects, but a guided tour of some key elements of each that we might be particularly prone to miss.

In light of that, a few brief caveats about your guide are in order before we begin. First, I am a conservative, and not a bashful or half-hearted one. I have worked for a Republican president (George W. Bush) and several Republican members of Congress, and I deeply identify with the ends and means of the American Right. I would not pretend to put my most basic political views to the side in advancing the arguments that follow. On the contrary, they are drawn from my experience working to refine and elevate conservative ideas in our politics in various ways, and they reflect my convictions and views, as they must.

This book contains a fair amount of criticism of the contemporary Right. But it is, I freely acknowledge, criticism rooted in shared commitments and goals, which points to places where we on the Right now fall short of what American conservatism could be at its best. It is a form of self-criticism, and so is unavoidably prone to the ever-present tendency of self-criticism to meld into self-congratulation. I have tried to avoid that, needless to say, but I am certain I have sometimes failed. The book also contains a fair amount of criticism of the contemporary Left. But it is criticism from the outside, and so is inevitably different in character—less intimate and so less nuanced, fair, and forgiving—than anything I might have to say about the Right. I have tried to correct for this, too, but it likely matters most where it was not obvious enough to me to have been remedied.

Such partiality is the lot of any writer on public questions. Anyone who tells you otherwise is asking to be disbelieved, and ought to be. And I submit that this is not a reason to dismiss social and political writing but to value it. There is no perch above society from which we can see more clearly than the people living in it. There are only perches within society, and we can elevate our sights by considering how things might look from those of others. So I imagine that some readers will not nod their heads approvingly at every judgment in these pages—because they don't see things my way, and also because they see things I do not. I only hope they might ask themselves whether the reverse might also be true—and so that what follows in these pages, by exposing something I have seen to someone with eyes to see it differently from me, might spark some insights that would not have otherwise occurred to either of us.

And this points to the final proviso I would offer: this book is an essay, in the original sense of the term. An essay is an attempt to understand. It is not a legal brief, or a treatise, or a manifesto of some kind, but an effort to grasp what isn't easy to reach, and to see what isn't perfectly clear. An essay gropes and grapples. So the arguments that follow are not intended to be delivered in a tone of confident authority but in a mode of questioning and trying out. That kind of tone can be impossible to sustain in the course of a book-length essay, and constant recurrence to it through qualification and throat-clearing would quickly grow tiresome. I will do some of that, where it seems especially needful. But know that I offer the whole of the case that follows, and each of its parts, as but one man's observations from a particular vantage point on our politics.

That vantage point has left me endlessly impressed with our extraordinary country, but also concerned for its future. That mix of confidence and worry, what Alexis de Tocqueville called "that salutary fear of the future that makes one watchful and combative, and not that soft and idle terror that wears hearts down and enervates them," should guide our thinking about the nation's challenges. I have tried to make it the dominant tone of what follows.[1]

PART I

OUT OF ONE, MANY

I

BLINDED BY NOSTALGIA

The first decade and a half of the twenty-first century has been a frustrating time for Americans. Opinion polls and election results attest to exceptional levels of pessimism and unease. We have not been happy with the state of our economy, our politics, and our culture—or, in other words, with our common public life as a nation.

At first glance, this unease seems fairly easy to explain. Our economy has been sluggish since this century began, and not only during the economic crisis and recession of 2008–2009. The country's *strongest* year of economic performance in the twenty-first century so far, 2004, saw a level of growth (3.8 percent) that barely reached the *average* of any of the prior four decades. The century also began with the worst terrorist attack in American history, which shattered our hope for a peaceful post–Cold War world. The globe has since seemed to stumble from one perilous crisis to another, with no real prospect of a stable order yet in sight. Meanwhile, our politics has been polarized and intensely divisive. And our cultural battles about sensitive subjects—from stem cells to marriage, religious liberty to national identity—have been fought at a fever pitch that has left all sides feeling besieged and offended.

Some key indicators that cross economics, culture, and politics—such as family breakdown and inequality—have also persistently pointed in troubling directions for quite some time. And these may be especially pertinent to the curse of entrenched poverty and low social mobility in America, which has been with us for decades now but has made itself felt more forcefully in this century.

The opening years of the twenty-first century have thus given Americans real reasons to worry. And yet, there has plainly been more to the frustration of this era than a straightforward response to challenging circumstances. Our problems are real, but the ways in which we discuss them often seem disconnected from reality, so that the diagnoses attempted by politicians, journalists, academics, and analysts have tended only to contribute to a marked disorientation in our public life.

That disorientation has itself been a defining feature of American public life in this century so far. It's as if we cannot quite figure out where we stand, and therefore where we're headed. We live in a period of profound transformation, but we have been thinking and talking about it in a peculiar way: we have tended to understand this era of uncertainty not so much as a *transition* but as an *aberration*, and so we have spent the past decade and more waiting for a return to normal that has refused to come.

We have been inclined to judge every new economic datum in recent years by whether it offers signs of our finally getting back to what we assume is our natural course—but in fact has not been our course in this century at all. Our best social analysts have assessed the implications of vast cultural and economic trends more by how far they suggest we have strayed from mid-twentieth-century benchmarks than by what they might tell us about contemporary America and its future path.

The political system has shared in this tendency and reinforced it. The Right and Left alike have seen the challenges of this century as consequences of our abandoning a favored path that once served us well (though, of course, they disagree about just what that path involved). The Republican and Democratic parties have each portrayed our country as the victim of a malicious interruption perpetrated by the other, and so each has seen the challenges of this century as reasons to double down on its own long-standing agenda rather than for trying to apply enduring principles to novel circumstances.

Democrats talk about public policy as though it were always 1965 and the model of the Great Society welfare state will answer our every concern. And Republicans talk as though it were always 1981 and a repetition of the Reagan Revolution is the cure for what ails us. It is hardly surprising that the public finds the resulting political debates frustrating.

Even though our leaders are often just reflecting our own anxiety and wistfulness, voters can sense as a general matter that the politicians' diagnoses are wrong, and that their prescriptions are therefore deficient. This suspicion has given us the feeling that our politics has become inept and rudderless, which drives a further loss of faith in leaders and institutions—and even greater frustration with how things are changing and how our country just doesn't seem to function as well as it used to.

We have spent the beginning of this century drenched in nostalgia. And while we might sometimes be nostalgic because we find today's circumstances frustrating, the opposite is also frequently the case, especially in our politics: we are frustrated because we are so nostalgic. And the particular form that our nostalgia has taken renders us incompetent, or at least badly confused.

We have grown so accustomed to the ubiquity of a particular kind of nostalgia in our public life that we barely stop to notice it anymore. But listen to how we speak to one another about the state of the country, and you will quickly be struck by the sheer power that a certain understanding of our fairly recent past has over us. It is a kind of living specter that looms over our sense of the present and the future. It serves as a reference point for our most important judgments. And it emerges with particular force when we analyze our dissatisfaction—when we try to explain what is wrong.

Describing the economic anxieties of many Americans in his 2011 State of the Union Address, for instance, President Barack Obama sought to evoke that common memory of loss:

Many people watching tonight can probably remember a time when finding a good job meant showing up at a nearby factory or a business downtown. You didn't always need a degree, and your competition was pretty much limited to your neighbors. If you worked hard, chances are you'd have a job for life, with a decent paycheck and good benefits and the occasional promotion. Maybe you'd even have the pride of seeing your kids work at the same company. That world has changed. And for many, the change has been painful.[1]

Here we find all of the archetypal elements of the nostalgic appeal: Obama called upon personal recollections of a lost ideal, described that bygone time as possessing everything we now take ourselves to lack, and defined progress as a recovery of what that earlier age had to offer.

It is unlikely that very many people watching that night actually did *remember* the world the president described, or even that such unadulterated opportunity ever really prevailed in America. But even if it is not a very accurate recollection, this vague collective reminiscence of a prelapsarian America is a defining feature of our own era. And just as in the president's speech, it often serves to root our aspirations in remembrance—to argue that great things are achievable in America because we once achieved them.

Nostalgia serves this purpose for conservatives no less than liberals. Obama's opponent in the following year's presidential election, former Massachusetts governor Mitt Romney, appealed to the same sort of shared congenial memory. Speaking to the 2012 Republican National Convention upon winning the party's nomination for the presidency, Romney began by telling his audience that he had seen the promise of America:

I was born in the middle of the century in the middle of the country, a classic baby boomer. It was a time when Americans were returning from war and eager to work. To be an American was to assume that all things were possible.[2]

A recovery of that eagerness, that attitude, that lost assumption, he told the nation that night, was the essential prerequisite to a flourishing future for America. Others at that convention delivered the same basic message to the public: we can do it again because we did it back then.

The Republican who had effectively come in second to Romney in the primaries that year, former Pennsylvania senator Rick Santorum, made this case especially powerfully, putting it at the center of his vision of American renewal. In his book *Blue Collar Conservatives*, Santorum began his assessment of the country's problems this way:

There was a time not long ago when Americans without college degrees could expect to earn a decent and steady income in exchange for hard work. This income and job stability provided a foundation for families and communities that, with their churches, Little Leagues, Boy Scout troops, and a hundred other civic organizations, fostered the strong values and the work ethic that underpinned American life. Millions of Americans came of age in these communities and took those values with them as they started their own families and thanked God for his blessings. With good incomes, Americans could afford new cars, kitchen appliances, and trips to Disneyland. Demand for such new goods kept others working and employment strong. With stable marriages, children enjoyed the gift of security and neighborhoods where values were taught at home and in church and enforced by parents. This is how I grew up.[3]

At the Democrats' 2012 national convention later that same summer, US Senate candidate (and now senator) Elizabeth Warren of Massachusetts, like several other prominent speakers, articulated a progressive version of the same basic point, personalizing it just as Romney and Santorum had:

I grew up in an America that invested in its kids and built a strong middle class; that allowed millions of children to rise from poverty and establish secure lives. An America that created Social Security and Medicare so that seniors could live with dignity; an America in which each generation built something solid so that the next generation could build something better. But for many years now, our middle class has been chipped, squeezed, and hammered.[4]

Whatever the argument being advanced about America's challenges in our politics in recent years, it is a pretty good bet that it has been rooted in an understanding of that lost era of American greatness—that it has been an argument for understanding our challenges as functions of an unfortunate detour.

Recourse to a glorious past is of course nothing new in political rhetoric. But these kinds of appeals do not hearken to America's Founders and their principles, or to some heroic peaks of achievement and greatness that might inspire us now to live boldly. They hearken to a living memory so powerfully present for many Americans as to seem like the natural state of American life. And they suggest that a return to that state—that getting back on that track—should be the goal of American politics.

The lost golden age at the center of these stories occurred in the decades that followed World War II. A great many of our current political, economic, and cultural debates are driven by a desire to recover the strengths of that period. As a result, they are focused less on how we can build economic, cultural, and social capital in the twenty-first century than on how we can recover the capital we have used up. That distinction makes an awfully big difference.

This kind of analysis is by no means limited to politicians. In fact, it is precisely because such nostalgia characterizes the thinking of so many of our most able and important scholars, journalists, commentators, and social analysts that it poses a problem for our capacity for self-diagnosis. Politicians and intellectuals across the political spectrum articulate what we are missing by pointing to what they miss about midcentury America. This inclination is understandable, but its ubiquity means that its blind spots risk becoming our collective blind spots as a nation.

ALTHOUGH LIBERALS AND CONSERVATIVES BOTH frequently look back to midcentury America with fondness, they long for different things about it, and their distinct nostalgias now frequently give our politics its shape.

Liberals are especially nostalgic for the economic and political order of that era. Government was growing, the labor movement was powerful, and large corporations in key sectors seemed content to work with government and labor to manage the affairs of the nation. This combination seemed to deliver broadly shared prosperity for a generation. Meanwhile, a surge in confidence in government led to the Great Society agenda and to a managerial politics that offered a public program to cure every public problem.

Economic analysis on the Left now frequently consists of arguments depicting the past forty years as an era of almost uninterrupted decline from that high point—with wages stagnating or falling, inequality climbing, worker protections diminishing, and the middle class getting squeezed. As we will see (especially in chapters 3 and 5), this depiction of key economic trends over that period leaves a lot to be desired. But it often seems like not so much a narrative history as a form of yearning to return.

That yearning is sometimes made remarkably explicit. In 2007, the progressive economist and commentator Paul Krugman, a leading voice on the Left in this century, published a book entitled *The Conscience of a Liberal*, laying out his basic views of America's challenges. The book begins with a chapter called "The Way We Were," which opens with a characteristic example of the sort of homesickness, or longing for a time that got it right, that so pervades many analyses throughout our politics. Krugman's opening words were: "I was born in 1953. Like the rest of my generation, I took the America I grew up in for granted—in fact, like many in my generation, I railed against the very real injustices of our society, marched against the bombing of Cambodia, went door to door for liberal political candidates. It's only in retrospect that the political and economic environment of my youth stands revealed as a paradise lost, an exceptional episode in our nation's history."[5]

Krugman then framed his economic and political analysis and his prescriptions as a recipe for a recovery of what that lost era had to offer—understanding its prosperity and promise as functions of the political and economic order of the time, and therefore as recoverable through efforts to reestablish key components of that order in our own day. An extraordinary number of the most prominent works of social analysis in recent years have followed the same pattern—positing the postwar decades as a standard of excellence against which to assess how America is doing by one important measure or another.

Many, for instance, point to the relatively low levels of inequality in the United States during the postwar years. In 2015, Robert Putnam, a Harvard political scientist known for tracking key social trends, published a book called *Our Kids: The American Dream in Crisis* that sought to illustrate how things have changed on that front. The book begins with the same now-familiar brand of nostalgia. Here are his opening words: "My hometown was, in the 1950s, a passable embodiment of the American Dream, a place that offered decent opportunity for all the kids in town, whatever their background. A half-century later, however, life in Port Clinton, Ohio, is a split-screen American nightmare." But also crucial to what Krugman and many others on the Left want to recover from the postwar era is the political vision that gave shape to public policy through much of the 1960s—a robust faith in the potential of welfare-state liberalism to address the nation's problems.[6]

Another important progressive book of recent years, sociologist Lane Kenworthy's *Social Democratic America*, published in 2014, argues for a recovery of the belief in that promise even in the face of the undeniable costs and political difficulties it would entail. Kenworthy seeks to salvage an old vision of the future. "From the 1940s to the 1970s," he writes, "Americans up and down the income ladder enjoyed improved economic security, expanding opportunity, and steadily rising incomes." The years that followed embodied a loss of faith in the approach to public policy that had made such progress possible, in his analysis. But that faith can be recovered, and the upward trajectory regained.[7]

And when Democrats translate their aspirations into policy, they tend to follow just that model—seeking to add more rooms onto the mansion of the Great Society through massive legislation that creates large, centralizing, new programs empowering the federal government to manage portions of the private economy and provide benefits to individuals. Thus even the policy innovations, such as they have been, in our twenty-first-century politics have been shaped by a hearkening to the great postwar model. When the House of Representatives voted on final passage of the

Affordable Care Act (often called Obamacare) in March 2010, House Speaker Nancy Pelosi gaveled the vote closed using the same gavel that Congressman John Dingell had used when presiding over the passage of Medicare in 1965, highlighting the party's allegiance to the approach to public policy that characterized the Great Society and its era.

When liberals have confronted political resistance to those efforts in this century, they have again tended to return to memories of a lost paradise—this one characterized by political consensus and bipartisan comity. In his 2006 book, *The Audacity of Hope*, then senator Barack Obama remarked on how powerful the memory of that time was among critics of twenty-first-century Washington. It is, he wrote, "one of the few things that liberal and conservative commentators agree on, this idea of a time before the fall, a golden age in Washington when, regardless of which party was in power, civility reigned and government worked."[8]

In fact, liberals and conservatives agree about more than that. They both approach our challenges nostalgically today, even if conservatives yearn for different facets of the postwar golden age. On the Right, it is often not so much the economic consensus of that era that beckons as the cultural or moral consensus—and it, too, has been fading for decades.

Another of the most important books of this still-new century, Charles Murray's superb *Coming Apart*, published in 2012, evinces this same melancholy sentiment. Murray, like Krugman and Putnam, opens his book with a look back at the America of his youth, describing some key features of our national life in the early 1960s as a standard against which to measure the subsequent decline of important cultural indicators. He posits a particular day, the day before the assassination of President John F. Kennedy in 1963, as symbolizing the apex of the old American order, a height from which we have since fallen. "This book," he writes, "is about an evolution in American society that has taken place since November 21, 1963, leading to the formation of classes that are different in kind and in their degree of separation from anything that the nation has ever known." The rest of the book is filled with tables and charts that carefully measure how America has changed (in most respects for the worse) by various social and cultural indicators since 1960.[9]

Not all on the Right consider the mid-1960s the crowning glory of America's twentieth-century golden age, though. For many, that honor belongs to the Reagan years. Ronald Reagan tried to draw upon (and revive) some elements of the same American consensus that had characterized the early postwar decades, but with a different sense of the proper role and scope of government in mind and with a greater emphasis on the role of free and open markets. He believed the promise of postwar America could be realized without the expansion of the welfare state it had engendered, and (although he did not ultimately succeed in rolling back prior expansions of federal power) his economic reforms were crucial to bringing back the roaring growth that had characterized that period and so helped extend the golden age, at least for a while.

The 1980s also saw a resurgence of confidence and national pride, and the decade was witness to something of a cultural revival. All of this lasted through (and was extended in) the 1990s, and therefore contributed, as we shall see in greater detail in the coming chapters, to the "double-peak" trajectory of postwar America—with a boom in the 1950s and 1960s, a decline in the 1970s, and a resurgence in the 1980s and 1990s. This double-peak story is an important part of why we have spent the beginning of the twenty-first century waiting for another return of the boom years—and why many conservatives, in particular, believe that the formula that enabled such a resurgence to occur in the 1980s could work the same magic in our time.[10]

Key to what Reagan achieved, in the eyes of conservatives, was that he recaptured something of the magic of the midcentury decades. So in a sense the Right is awaiting a second renaissance while the Left awaits a first one, but both have in mind the postwar decades as the original model to be recovered—the model of America in its prime.

Of course, no one could deny that the postwar decades in America were the scene of much trouble, too. Alongside the cohesion and the dynamism we yearn to restore also came epic battles over communism, civil rights, Vietnam, Watergate, and countless other fronts: the burning cities, the political assassinations, the campus radicalism, and the social breakdown of that time. But even these conflicts and protests are frequently digested into our nostalgic politics—reenacted as responses to our own problems in ways that sometimes verge on the absurd.

Among activists of all stripes in our politics, there is a palpable wistfulness about the protest movements of the 1960s and early 1970s. Younger liberals, in particular, have frequently sought to replay those days on college campuses. Thus the war in Iraq that began in 2003 was forced into the box of Vietnam, and the Occupy Wall Street movement that arose in response to the financial crisis of 2008 was a sort of farcical pantomime of 1960s sit-ins—the same look, but with none of the substance. Students in many universities in more recent years have sought to re-create something of the atmosphere of midcentury campus protests, even if their substantive concerns hardly approach the scale of those struggles. Asked if she identified with these contemporary student protests during a Democratic presidential debate in the fall of 2015, candidate Hillary Clinton spoke to precisely the nostalgia they evoke, saying, "I come from the '60s, a long time ago. There was a lot of activism on campus—Civil Rights activism, antiwar activism, women's rights activism—and I do appreciate the way young people are standing up and speaking out."[11]

Meanwhile, every major political scandal of our time is sooner or later given a name that ends in "gate," in an ironic tribute to the Watergate scandal, and every movement for social change (be it for gay rights or for an end to abortion) takes on the particular trappings of the civil rights movement. Our bipartisan language of protest and dissension draws upon midcentury memories and myths.

In a great many ways, then, American politics in the twenty-first century has been shaped by these distinct nostalgias of the Left and Right. And, to be sure, there is plenty to be nostalgic for. The social, political, and economic forms of American life at midcentury made possible a degree of prosperity and cohesion that in turn enabled many Americans to flourish and improve their circumstances. But what *specifically* enabled such flourishing, and what has changed? What was exceptional or valuable about those forms, and what was not? To what extent are those factors that shaped midcentury life specific to that era, and to what extent might they be generalized and applied to our current age? The pervasiveness and intensity of our nostalgia make it hard to achieve the kind of analytic distance that would allow us to address these questions seriously.

That pervasiveness is especially peculiar when it comes to Americans under age fifty or so. Most Americans are simply too young (as I am) to have had any actual experience of that putative midcentury bliss. And yet our national understanding of the postwar decades is shot through with a deeply personal sense of longing and recollection. The nature of that passion reveals a further barrier to diagnosis and analysis that ought to be of concern. The objects and the flavor of our national nostalgia are not random. They draw on the memories of a particular group of Americans who have exercised an extraordinary power over the nation's self-image. They are in large part a function of the enormous cultural dominance of the baby boomers—a dominance that, like the power of nostalgia itself, we too often now take for granted.

THE BABY BOOMERS ARE THE children of the World War II generation. They are generally defined as Americans born between 1946 and 1964, so they are now in their fifties and sixties; the oldest among them are entering their seventies.

They are a generation that has always stood out, first and foremost, for its sheer size: about 75 million Americans were born in those years, an era when the constraints of depression and then war gave way to an unprecedented economic expansion, and with it a sharp increase in rates of marriage and childbearing. In the twenty years before the baby boom began, the number of births in America hovered around 2.6 million per year, according to the US Census Bureau. During the baby-boom years, this figure climbed to 4 million per year.[12]

The baby boomers transformed the age structure of American society. If you were to chart the nation's population by age at different times over the past seven decades, you would find in each case a large bulge representing the baby boomers at different stages of life—what demographers have often playfully called "the pig in the python."[13]

The demographic dominance of the baby boomers has always translated into economic and cultural dominance, too. Because they were born into a postwar economic expansion, they have been an exceptionally middle-class generation, targeted as consumers from birth. Producers and advertisers have flattered this generation for decades in an effort to shape their tastes and win their dollars. And the boomers' economic power has only increased with time as they have grown older and wealthier. Today, baby boomers possess about half the consumer purchasing power of the American economy, and roughly three-quarters of all personal financial assets, although they are only about one-quarter of the population.[14]

All of this has also made the baby boomers an unusually self-aware generation. Bombarded from childhood with cultural messages about the promise and potential of their own cohort, they have conceived of themselves as a coherent group to a greater degree than any generation of Americans before them. Since the middle of the twentieth century they have not only shaped the course of American life through their preferences and choices but also defined the nation's self-understanding.[15]

Indeed, the baby boomers now utterly dominate our understanding of America's postwar history, and in a very peculiar way. To see how, let us consider an average baby boomer: an American born in, say, 1950, who has spent his life comfortably in the broad middle class. This person experienced the 1950s as a child, and so remembers that era, through those innocent eyes, as a simple time of stability and wholesome values in which all things seemed possible.

By the mid-1960s, he was a teenager, and he recalls that time through a lens of youthful rebellion and growing cultural awareness—a period of idealism and promise. The music was great, the future was bright, but there were also great problems to tackle in the world, and he had the confidence of a teenager that his generation could do it right.

In the 1970s, as a twenty-something entering the workforce and the adult world, he found that confidence shaken. Youthful idealism gave way to some cynicism about the potential for change, recreational drugs served more for distraction than inspiration, everything was unsettled, and the future seemed ominous and ambiguous. His recollection of that decade is drenched in cold sweat.

In the 1980s, in his thirties, he was settling down. His work likely fell into a manageable groove, he was building a family, and concerns about car loans, dentist bills, and the mortgage largely replaced an ambition to transform the world. This was the time when he first began to understand his parents, and he started to value stability, low taxes, and low crime. He looks back on that era as the onset of real adulthood.

By the 1990s, in his forties, he was comfortable and confident, building wealth and stability. He worried that his kids were slackers and that the culture was corrupting them, and he began to be concerned about his own health and fitness as fifty approached. But on the whole, our baby boomer enjoyed his forties—it was finally his generation's chance to be in charge, and it looked to be working out.

As the twenty-first century dawned, our boomer turned fifty. He was still at the peak of his powers (and earnings), but he gradually began to peer over the hill toward old age. He started the decade with great confidence, but found it ultimately to be filled with unexpected dangers and unfamiliar forces. The world was becoming less and less his own, and it was hard to avoid the conclusion that he might be past his prime.

He turned sixty-five in the middle of this decade, and in the midst of uncertainty and instability. Health and retirement now became prime concerns for him. The culture started to seem a little bewildering, and the economy seemed awfully insecure. He was not without hope. Indeed, in some respects, his outlook on the future has been improving a little as he contemplates retirement. He doesn't exactly admire his children (that so-called "Generation X"), but they have exceeded his expectations, and his grandchildren (the youngest Millennials and those younger still) seem genuinely promising and special.

As he contemplates their future, he does worry that they will be denied the extraordinary blend of circumstances that defined the world of his youth. The economy, politics, and the culture just don't work the way they used to, and frankly, it is difficult for him to imagine America two or three decades from now. He rebelled against the world he knew as a young man, but now it stands revealed to him as a paradise lost. How can it be regained?

This portrait of changing attitudes is, of course, stylized for effect. But it offers the broad contours of how people tend to look at their world in different stages of life, and it shows how Americans (and, crucially, not just the boomers) tend to understand each of the past seven decades of our national life. This is no coincidence. We see our recent history through the boomers' eyes.

Were the 1950s really simple and wholesome? Were the 1960s really idealistic and rebellious? Were the 1970s aimless and anxious? Did we find our footing in the 1980s? Become comfortable and confident in the 1990s? Or more fearful and disoriented over the past decade and a half? As we shall see in the coming chapters, the answer in each case is not simply yes or no. But it is hard to deny that we all frequently view the postwar era in this way—through the lens of the baby-boomer experience.

The boomers' self-image casts a giant shadow over our politics, and it means we are inclined to look backward to find our prime. More liberal-leaning boomers miss the idealism of the flower of their youth, while more conservative ones, as might be expected, are more inclined to miss the stability and confidence of early middle age—so the Left yearns for the 1960s and the Right for the 1980s. But both are telling the same story: a boomer's story of the America they have known.

The trouble is that it is not only the boomers themselves who think this way about America, but all of us, especially in politics. We really have almost no self-understanding of our country in the years since World War II that is not in some fundamental way a baby-boomer narrative. That is why younger Americans so often find themselves reenacting memories they do not actually possess, and why our nation increasingly behaves like a retiree.

Understood in this way, our national mood over the past fifteen years begins to make sense: it's a mood of fatigue, of an unwillingness to accept the fact that changes and challenges are always coming and going, and that the moment of hope and achievement so cherished in memory by the boomers did not in fact resolve anything in a permanent way. How can we still be fighting these fights and facing these problems? Why could our glory days not last?

This is not quite to say that our mood has been detached from reality. The concerns we express through nostalgia speak to very real problems. And yet that nostalgia is not the best way to understand those problems. That the baby boomers so dominate our national memory and self-image means that we don't think enough about what came before the golden age of the boomers' youth, and that we don't think clearly about just how things have changed since that time. We use the era of their youth as a benchmark for normality, which keeps us from seeing how very unusual it actually was.

America needs to be careful not to let aging baby boomers define its outlook. We cannot afford to farm out our vision of the future to a retiring generation. We can already see some indications of where that will lead: our political, cultural, and economic conversations today overflow with the language of decay and corrosion, as if our body politic is itself an aging boomer looking back upon his glory days.[16]

We must resist this narrative of decline, which leads us to attribute the economic growth and social cohesion that characterized midcentury America to a kind of youthful energy, and the contemporary diminution in both to something like senescence. The median age of the US population is certainly older now (roughly thirty-seven years old) than it was in the 1960s (just over twenty-nine years old), and a growing proportion of Americans are elderly. This demographic fact bears on the state of the country, of course, but it is not the essence of the problems that most trouble us.

Far greater changes are afoot. And they are changes that we must strive to understand as creating circumstances that are in some important ways new, and fresh, and full of possibility, rather than just a kind of winding down. The world is always new for the young, and we do young Americans a great disservice to understand it only through the eyes of their elders. We are living in a time of change, and therefore a time that is as much a beginning as an end. But we will only be able to think clearly about what is beginning, and about how we can make the most of it, if we can pull ourselves away from lamentations for a lost youth.

The baby boomers' grip on our national self-image will surely loosen in the years to come. The boomers are no longer as numerically dominant as they once were. In 2015, they constituted 24 percent of the population, while members of Generation X (born between the mid-1960s and early 1980s) made up 21 percent and the Millennials (born after the early 1980s) 27 percent, according to census data. Rising generations of Americans will

soon need to look around and build their own understanding of the present, and sense of the future, that do not take mid-twentieth-century
America as their benchmark.[17]

IF WE ARE TO DO that successfully, we will need to begin by understanding
the particular distortions to which the dominance of the boomers has left
us prone. Otherwise we risk not only failing to come to terms with the
present, but also failing to properly learn from the past—and even from
nostalgia itself.

Nostalgia, after all, is by no means all bad. And the analysts, scholars,
journalists, and politicians who bemoan how things have changed in this
half-century are pointing at some important truths about both the past
and the present. We must be careful not to dismiss what they see, but also
not to ignore what they miss. As the political theorist Peter Augustine
Lawler has put it, "all reputable social and political analysis deploys selective nostalgia." The trouble is that ours is frequently selective in the wrong
ways, and is so intense as to be blinding.[18]

To learn from nostalgia, we must let it guide us not merely toward "the
way we were," but toward just what was good about what we miss, and
why. Political scientist Mark Henrie has put it this way:

> In the face of loss, the human good is vividly revealed to us. We lament
> the loss of goods, not the loss of evils, which is why lament *illuminates*.
> Is it not striking that whereas antebellum Southern writers championed
> both the economic and moral superiority of the "peculiar institution,"
> postbellum Southern conservatives typically did not *lament* the loss of
> slavery? Rather, the latter lamented the loss of gentility, gallantry, do-
> mesticity, and the virtues of yeomen agriculturalists. Although it may be
> true that nostalgia views the past through rose-colored glasses, such a
> criticism misses the point. To see the good while blinkered against evils
> is, nevertheless, *to see the good*.[19]

Many of those who assess our contemporary circumstances through
various nostalgic lenses understand this facet of their own thinking.

Robert Putnam laments the loss of opportunity in the decades since his childhood in Ohio, but he does not ignore the dark sides of that era. Having laid out the exceptional degree of opportunity available in his hometown in the 1950s, he takes note of those left behind or pushed to the margins. "Few of us, including me, would want to return there without major reforms," he concludes (though he does not mention the possibility that those "major reforms" might be a big part of the reason why the era he misses cannot be recovered).[20]

Charles Murray similarly notes that although the America of the 1960s that is his benchmark was extraordinarily cohesive, it was also a nation starkly divided by race, one in which the status of women left "much to be outraged about," and a culture with far less diversity of options and paths than ours now affords.[21]

But for all these caveats, the prescriptions of these writers are nonetheless fundamentally backward looking, because their standard is a particular point in time. It is a time from which today's America has much to learn, but also a time that was the actual scene of their own youth: a time when they believe they and their country both reached a peak.

That time existed. It was not a dream. But it was not the paradise that some now suggest, and it was made possible by a set of circumstances—historical, social, economic, political, and cultural—that are no longer with us. As we will see in the next several chapters, those midcentury circumstances constituted an inevitably fleeting transition: a highly consolidated society in the process of liberalizing. No combination of public policies could re-create them. No amount of moral hectoring will, either.

Instead, we should consider how they came to be, how and why America has changed, and what this might mean for what America is becoming. And we should apply the lessons we learn to the essential work of economic, social, and political reform.

To begin to escape our overpowering frustration, then, we should try first to better appreciate the real strengths and weaknesses of the midcentury America that still so beckons to us, and to better grasp the nature of the transformation that was then beginning and is still underway.

2

THE AGE OF
CONFORMITY

At home and abroad, the United States found itself in a unique position
after World War II. The other developed nations—not only those defeated
in the war but also most of America's victorious allies—took a great deal
of time to recover from the terrible toll of that struggle. Many of them
never did regain their prior stature. America, in contrast, emerged as a
strong, unified, global colossus. It embarked on a period of extraordinary
economic growth accompanied by impressive cultural dynamism and liberalization. At the same time it enjoyed relative cultural cohesion, low
economic inequality, high confidence in national institutions, and widespread optimism about the nation's prospects.

It is not surprising, therefore, that the postwar years now seem like a
golden age to so many Americans. Our nation in that era appears like the
very model of a successful America, one that we must strive to recapture.
In reality, however, postwar America was a nation in flux, and it was never
the stable model of our imagination that could be made permanent if only
we could implement the right policies. The postwar era turns out to have

been an unstable and therefore unavoidably temporary inflection point in our national life—a kind of bridge between two quite different Americas. And as such, it was a time when many Americans could benefit from the best of both while avoiding the worst of either.

In very broad terms, the first half of the twentieth century (and the final decades of the nineteenth) can be seen as an age of growing *consolidation* and *cohesion* in American life. As our economy industrialized, the government grew more centralized, the culture became more aggregated through mass media, and national identity and unity were frequently valued above personal identity, individuality, and diversity. In those years, a great many of the most powerful forces in American life were pushing every American to become more like everyone else. The second half of the twentieth century and the opening years of the twenty-first have instead been marked by growing *deconsolidation* and *decentralization*. The culture has become increasingly variegated, the economy has diversified and become more deregulated, and individualism and personal identity have triumphed over conformity and national unity. In these years, a great many of the most powerful forces in American life have been pushing every American not to become more like everyone else, but to be more fully himself or herself.

Keeping one foot in each of these two distinguishable eras, midcentury America combined cohesion and dynamism to an exceptional degree. That precarious balance made possible an extraordinary era, and it surely has a lot to teach us about what we should value today. But we cannot hope to replicate it—certainly not now, well over half a century into an age of profound disaggregation in nearly every arena of American life. And if we see that special time for what it was, we would almost certainly conclude that we don't actually want to bring it back.

The shift from conformity to diversity, from unity to fracturing, is just one thread of our history. It is not the whole story, and it cannot give us a comprehensive explanation of the last century, of course. But following this thread can help us better understand what we miss about midcentury American life, and why we have such trouble naming our anxieties and addressing them today. It offers us a way to learn from our nostalgia, rather than being blinded by it.

AN ASPIRATION TO NATIONAL UNITY has always been part of the American story, as it must be part of the self-understanding of any genuine nation. But for Americans, that aspiration has always existed alongside a recognition of our exceptional diversity. In 1776, a committee of the Continental Congress assigned to design an official seal for the United States settled on the Latin phrase "E pluribus unum," meaning "Out of many, one," as a motto. It referred both to the unity of the several newly independent states and to the coming together of a population that even in the late eighteenth century was remarkably diverse and disparate.

America's early leaders often found it necessary to minimize or sidestep this incorrigible multiplicity. In making the case for adoption of the US Constitution in the fall of 1787, the statesman and diplomat John Jay argued (in Federalist No. 2) that a tightknit union should naturally appeal to the American public, given the common character and background of so many Americans: "Providence has been pleased to give this one connected country to one united people—a people descended from the same ancestors, speaking the same language, professing the same religion, attached to the same principles of government, very similar in their manners and customs, and who, by their joint counsels, arms, and efforts, fighting side by side throughout a long and bloody war, have nobly established general liberty and independence."[1]

This was awfully wishful thinking even then, and it only grew to be further from the truth over time. Millions of men and women brought forcibly from Africa or descended from those who had been were enslaved and savagely mistreated in half the country. Large numbers of immigrants, mostly from Europe, entered the American fold, though under more welcoming circumstances. The nation began its westward expansion into a lawless wilderness, where ways of life, mores, and norms differed dramatically in different regions. By the middle of the nineteenth century, a civil war threatened to rip America in two, and unprecedented numbers of additional immigrants arrived. Waves of expansion and modernization washed over the continent, and John Jay's "one connected country" was no more. Many wondered if this immense and varied society could hold together at all.

Ultimately, and uneasily, it did hold together. As it happens, the process of modernization—economic, cultural, and political—was itself a primary consolidating force, in America as throughout the developed world.

In his important 1997 book *Modernization and Postmodernization*, political scientist Ronald Inglehart summarized the findings of decades of scholarship in the social sciences about how cultural and economic changes take shape in industrializing societies. In economics, he argued, modernization generally involves the growth of large, industrial manufacturers at the expense of small, local producers. This process vastly increases the scale of economic activity and worker specialization and introduces great distances between employers, employees, and consumers. It is also often associated with movements of workers from the country to the city in search of opportunities, and hence growing urbanization. In government, modernization means bureaucratization, which follows a similar pattern wherever it occurs: an increasingly centralized and uniform set of rules and institutions replaces ad hoc, often localized practices, and the scale of government action increases. On the cultural front, modernization tends to replace localism and traditional attachments with mass culture. It displaces the small and near-at-hand with larger, often more distant entities, and it causes a rapid increase in the scale of national institutions.[2]

These are general patterns. No two societies are identical, and in many ways the American experience was, as we shall see, unique. But these general tendencies nonetheless offer some important insights—especially about how American society was drawn together during the nation's second century.

The US economy began to industrialize in earnest following the Civil War. Mechanization of both agricultural and industrial production accelerated. The transportation and communication infrastructure that had been developed in the course of the war began to be used for commerce. Large manufacturing firms started to replace small producers, especially in the Northeast, as owners of factories began to use new management and production techniques. They employed hundreds of workers at once through mechanized production processes and put out increased volumes of many goods. At the same time, agricultural mechanization reduced the demand for labor on farms, driving workers to search for employment in more industrialized urban areas. According to the US Census Bureau, about a quarter of Americans lived in urban areas in 1870; by 1920, roughly half did.

Immigration also increased dramatically in this period, bringing in a large pool of low-skilled workers who could be employed at relatively low pay. More than 25 million immigrants came to America in the last three decades of the nineteenth century, and the nation's population in that period nearly doubled.

Meanwhile, the nation's transportation system grew, linking Americans together and enabling the products of the new industrial economy to be sold and distributed across the country. That growth was perhaps best symbolized by the completion of the transcontinental railroad in 1869, but it involved far more dramatic expansions in interior point-to-point transportation between American cities. The country had about 9,000 miles of railroads in 1850, 53,000 in 1870, and 200,000 in 1900.[3]

This economic expansion generated extraordinary growth in the American financial system. Large numbers of local and regional banks rose to meet the demand for credit and to provide opportunities for saving and investment. This burgeoning banking system didn't always work smoothly, of course: the United States experienced a series of painful recessions at the end of the nineteenth century, including, in 1893, the most severe depression the nation had experienced up to that point. But these downturns took place against the backdrop of enormous long-term economic growth. In every key sector of the economy, the last three decades of the nineteenth century saw what can only be described as massive modernization.

The industrial era thus involved an immense increase in the *scale* of the American economy. Everything got bigger, and the economy seemed increasingly to be a function of vast interactions among large players. In the lives of many Americans, this new scale of change did not at first present itself as a consolidating force. On the contrary, it took the form of dislocation and disruption. Industrialization meant the concentration of power and wealth in the hands of a few and the emergence of large numbers of impoverished urban workers. And the political system, still dominated by the corrupt party machines of post–Civil War America, seemed unable to adjust to the new realities.

But these dislocations, driven by economic consolidation, created pressure for corresponding political reforms to take place. America's government needed to keep pace with its growing, changing economy. The call for such reforms became the rallying cry of a new "progressive" movement in American politics that would further press the cause of national unity and consolidation.

PROGRESSIVISM BEGAN AS AN URBAN social movement led by intellectuals and social activists who were eager to alleviate the plight of industrial workers. They sought to document that plight—both journalistically and artistically—and to build support for new laws that would limit the power of the wealthiest Americans and increase the power of the population at large.

Progressives did not seek to return America to a preindustrial way of life; rather, they sought to respond to the consolidation of economic and political power in the hands of the wealthy few by consolidating democratic political power, workers' economic power, and popular cultural power. They believed that the growing scale of the economy demanded growth in the scale of government, unionized labor, and mass culture. A coherent national identity was needed, but based in the masses instead of an economic elite: they would answer consolidation with consolidation, gigantism with gigantism.

When it came to politics, this meant both increasing the democratic character of American government and increasing the power of government experts to manage the economy. The progressives were simultaneously populist and technocratic. These two tendencies may at first seem contradictory, but in fact both are ways of making government stronger. The early progressives believed that populism and technocracy would be in harmony, since if people were given the power to control their government, they would choose expert governance over rule by nefarious economic interests.[4]

The progressives argued that joint social action could only be effective at the national level, and that such national action was needed to protect the individual from the threats posed by powerful economic forces beyond the control of the common man. They were far less interested in the mediating layers of society—local authority, for instance, or private associations—which they considered unequal to the task of helping Americans handle the increasingly massive scale of the nation's life. This binary emphasis—on the individual, on the one hand, and on the national state, on the other—would ultimately cause enormous problems. At the time, however, the progressives were confident that it was both necessary and just.[5]

That confidence soon ran into an obstacle—the American constitutional system itself, which places stringent restrictions on both populism and technocratic power at the federal level. Direct democracy—wherein power is in the hands of the people though general, direct voting—is different from, for instance, the electoral college system, which channels the power of the people to elect a president through a complicated (and elitist) mechanism. Until the progressive reforms of the early twentieth century, US senators were generally chosen by state legislators rather than directly by the public. At the same time, the Constitution avoids empowering expertise, whether in the executive branch, in the judiciary, or in some independent power center, and instead sets different elected and appointed institutions against one another in an endless struggle for power, which we refer to as our system of checks and balances. The Constitution rejects the populist view that the people have the knowledge required to rule, and it rejects the technocratic view that a body of experts has the knowledge required to rule. Instead, it embodies the view that no one has the requisite knowledge, and that government should therefore be designed to force different groups in society to bargain and cooperate. Restraining public power enables society to avoid the large mistakes that would ensue if too much power were wielded by any one group.

The progressives therefore saw themselves from the first as chafing at constitutional constraints. They argued that the Constitution was a preindustrial anachronism that had been built to protect the privilege of America's elites by preventing change, and that it was therefore unsuited to governing a modern nation. America, they said, should give the federal government far more power in relation to the states, and should give the executive branch far more power in relation to the legislative and judicial branches. In both cases, their objective was a centralizing consolidation intended to enable the government to take decisive action in the name of the nation.[6]

Indeed, "the nation," for the progressives, was a crucial concept too often missing from American political thought. Like other modernizing movements throughout the West in the same period, progressivism was a nationalist movement: it sought to link the disparate elements of a large society more tightly together. To do this, progressives aimed to break up subnational commitments that might complicate the individual's attachment to the nation as a whole.

When it came to national unity, these efforts were starting from a low base. At the end of the nineteenth century, Americans were a diffuse and in some respects a bitterly divided people. The Civil War was a not-so-distant memory (the average soldier had been just under twenty-five years old during the war, and so was in his sixties in 1900), Reconstruction had gone poorly, and regional differences were vast. Moreover, racial stratification was rigid and often backed by violent force, ethnic divisions ran deep, mass immigration was undermining cultural cohesion, and economic inequalities, already stark, were growing more so.

Theodore Roosevelt, the first president to be deeply influenced by progressive ideas, sought to forge in response a "new nationalism" to take the place of the old federalism. "The national government belongs to the whole American people," he said in a speech presaging his attempt to return to the White House in 1912, "and where the whole American people are interested, that interest can be guarded effectively only by the national government." And he was blunt in asserting his impatience with the complexity and slowness of the federal constitutional system and in insisting on the resulting need for consolidation:

The New Nationalism puts the national need before sectional or personal advantage. It is impatient of the utter confusion that results from local legislatures attempting to treat national issues as local issues. It is still more impatient of the impotence which springs from overdivision of governmental powers, the impotence which makes it possible for local selfishness or for legal cunning, hired by wealthy special interests, to bring national activities to a deadlock. This New Nationalism regards the executive power as the steward of the public welfare.[7]

By the same logic, Roosevelt and other progressives argued for an unprecedented degree of national control over the economy—and even over the growth of personal wealth. "We grudge no man a fortune in civil life if it is honorably obtained and well used," Roosevelt said. But being "well used" was to have a social definition. Wealth should benefit what Roosevelt called "the national community":

It is not even enough that it should have been gained without doing damage to the community. We should permit it to be gained only so long as the gaining represents benefit to the community. This, I know, implies a policy of a far more active governmental interference with social and economic conditions in this country than we have yet had, but I think we have got to face the fact that such an increase in governmental control is now necessary.[8]

Herbert Croly, a scholar, a journalist, one of the founders of the progressive *New Republic* magazine, and perhaps the chief theorist of progressivism in the early twentieth century, put the matter just as bluntly in 1909: "In economic warfare, the fighting can never be fair for long, and it is the business of the state to see that its own friends are victorious." To carry out that business, the progressives said, the state needed to develop and expand in two areas in particular: bureaucratization and regulation.[9]

By building out government bureaucracy—especially, but not exclusively, at the federal level—progressives aimed to eradicate the corrupt spoils system that had dominated government employment and administration in late nineteenth-century America. They were also impressed by the industrial management techniques that had given rise to large manufacturers in the private sector, thinking that it might be possible to import these techniques into the public sector to make government run more efficiently on the large scale they believed was necessary. They sought a massive increase in the scale and scope of federal agencies, the power of which would be wielded through modern methods of institutional organization, information management, and personnel coordination, all with an emphasis on uniformity and rational efficiency.

Mass production and factory organization were everywhere the models. Progressives wanted many existing institutions, from the postal service to the growing networks of local public schools, to mimic the structures and forms of modern industry: think of the modern public school with its regimentation, its bells breaking the day into uniform portions, and even its appearance and construction, modeled since the progressive era on urban factories.

But regulation would prove to be a far more significant tool for consolidation and control than even bureaucracy was. The progressives argued that, in order to direct the power of the emerging industrial economy for the public good, rather than simply for the benefit of a fortunate few, government regulators would need to manage key sectors of the economy. Open competition and wild market forces should not be permitted to determine economic outcomes. These efforts, they said, should focus especially on the sectors undergirding the growth of the industrial economy: manufacturing, transportation, communication, and finance. They sought to give regulators broad discretion rather than making them subject to strict legislative control.

The Interstate Commerce Act of 1887 created the first modern "independent" regulatory agency, the Interstate Commerce Commission (ICC), which became the model for much of the regulatory state that followed. The ICC's purpose was to regulate the railroads and other sectors of the transportation infrastructure (bus lines, for example). It was to ensure "reasonable and just" rates by common carriers and nondiscriminatory pricing and terms of service—small companies and farmers, for example, were not to be charged higher rates than large firms (although this requirement was left exceedingly and intentionally vague). The progressives then imposed regulations in numerous other industries in subsequent decades. They enacted measures to manage economic concentration, to place controls on labor conditions and terms, and to regulate food and drugs, the lumber industry, and new sectors of the economy made possible by the technological advances of the early twentieth century (for example, aviation and mass communication).

Although these regulatory measures all took shape in response to the consolidating power of the industrial economy, they functioned not by pushing back against that aggregating tendency, but by further consolidating American society—in the process often reducing economic competition to increase government control over the economy and expanding the scope and scale of the state itself. The federal government, as Herbert Croly put it, was to become "responsible for the subordination of the individual to the demand of a dominant and constructive national purpose." Croly's comment was a stark summary of the ethic of consolidation emerging in early twentieth-century America.[10]

ALL THE WHILE, TECHNOLOGICAL INNOVATIONS seemed only to further press this consolidation, extending it from the economy and politics to American culture. The rise of mass media—starting especially in the second decade of the twentieth century (and so just as progressivism was picking up steam), when commercial radio and cinema began to reach larger audiences—worked to homogenize public cultural experiences and tastes and draw the nation together. Mass mobilization for World War I did much the same, uniting Americans around common concerns and against common enemies.

This unity had a nasty and dark side, of course. American progressivism was far from immune to the tendencies toward fascism that characterized nationalist movements in Europe around the same period, and indeed it was much influenced by them. National unity did not generally mean breaking the barriers between races, for instance, or the long-standing norms that left black citizens badly disadvantaged at every turn. In fact, these norms tended to be reinforced and hardened, and to be made part of what was understood to constitute the nation's cohesive identity. They were at times even exacerbated by explicitly eugenic policies championed by many progressives. These policies were intended, among other things, to restrict the growth of ethnic and minority populations.[11]

And in just the way that nationalist movements in Europe used national emergencies as opportunities to advance the kind of consolidation they sought, World War I seemed, to some progressives, to offer a chance for government to take decisive national action to advance the cause of political and social consolidation and restructuring. Writing in the *New Republic*, the progressive thinker John Dewey pointed to the "immense impetus to reorganization afforded by this war." And the progressive president, Woodrow Wilson, leapt at the opportunity.[12]

Wilson used the war to advance the cause of centralization and public management of the economy. He created a panoply of commissions and boards to bring various industries—from food producers to steel manufacturers to railroad companies—into the service of the national cause. A powerful War Industries Board was established to oversee the process. The board acted, as one of its members, Grosvenor Clarkson, would later write, as "a dictatorship by force of necessity and common consent which step by step and at last encompassed the nation and united it into a coordinated and mobile whole." The Wilson administration also established a Committee on Public Information to make the case for all these entities to the public using the new mass media.[13]

Making that case inevitably meant advancing arguments for greater national unity, and these frequently elided into arguments for censorship (which the government pursued intensely against many organs of the press) as well as mistrust of dissenters and immigrants. American culture was becoming a culture of conformity, restraint, and homogenization. Opposition to immigration was by no means universal among progressives, though it was prevalent in the labor movement, which had become an important part of the progressive coalition. Throughout World War I, however, opposition to immigration—based in both economic concerns and ethnic animosities—spread and strengthened. It was undoubtedly an element of the nationalizing spirit of the age.[14]

In the years after the war, Congress codified this emerging consensus in a series of laws that set strict national and ethnic quotas on immigration and dramatically curtailed the number of immigrants permitted to enter the United States each year. These laws served to further restrain the diversity and cultural flux that had accompanied industrialization and to enforce an ethic of consolidation in American life.

From the late nineteenth century through World War I, all of these trends—economic, political, and cultural—pushed hard against America's earlier traditions of decentralization and localism. Not only were our national institutions increasingly cohesive, but cohesion was increasingly the *substance* of our cultural self-understanding. At the core of this unity was not just a common set of ideals, but also the notion of commonality itself as an ideal. Solidarity was in important respects becoming a fundamental American virtue.

There was certainly something of a counter-reaction, especially in the 1920s, as Americans sought some relief from the regimentation of the war years and the collective-minded moralism that had followed (embodied, for instance, in Prohibition). The culture of the Jazz Age and the economics of the Roaring Twenties chafed against conformity and constraint. But the ethic of national unity and centralization nonetheless remained dominant. The era of consolidation was far from over, and events would soon conspire to reinforce it.

THE GREAT DEPRESSION, WHICH BEGAN in earnest in 1929, would draw the nation even closer together, further consolidating the economy, government, and culture. Most of the New Deal initiatives pursued by Franklin Roosevelt's administration to combat the economic collapse amounted to crude, if well intentioned, cartel-building exercises. They were intended to protect incumbent businesses and workers while restraining production (as overproduction was then widely believed to be at the core of the catastrophe), limiting competition, and propping up prices. The result was a highly centralized economy characterized by an unprecedented degree of corporatism—cooperation between large public and private institutions in the management of the nation's affairs—that would remain a defining feature of American life for decades.

The economic slowdown itself, and the increase in income taxes that accompanied the government's massive response, also brought on a significant reduction in the income inequality that had accompanied the rise of

industrialism, and that had been especially pronounced in the 1920s. Income disparities had certainly been a glaring exception to the ethic of consolidation. By 1928, nearly 25 percent of the nation's income was in the
hands of the top 1 percent of earners, according to Internal Revenue Service
data analyzed by economists Thomas Piketty and Emmanuel Saez. But
beginning in the 1930s, and accelerating dramatically in the war years of the
early 1940s, wages, too, began to compress, so that the income share of the
top 1 percent was reduced to 16 percent in 1940 and 11 percent by 1944.[15]

At the same time, the New Deal reinforced the pressure for cultural
cohesion and for deemphasizing individualism and diversity in favor of
national unity and solidarity. The case for many New Deal programs rested
largely on the same arguments for taking national action used during
World War I. Roosevelt and his supporters routinely compared the Depression to a war, saying it was a national emergency that required exceptional
levels of centralized authority and national spirit. New public employment
programs, in particular, were organized along the lines of a military draft.
The Civilian Conservation Corps, whose members wore military-style uni-
forms, was one prominent example. Americans were encouraged to understand their circumstances and their obligations in terms of their citizenship
in a great nation managed by large, powerful institutions that would help
them through the risks and instabilities of modern life.

In a sense, the New Deal was proof of the degree to which the idea of
consolidation had become ingrained in American thinking by the fourth
decade of the twentieth century. Franklin Roosevelt was not a hard-edged
ideologue. He understood himself to be acting pragmatically. But by the
time of his presidency, American elites had thoroughly internalized the
notion that modernization amounted to consolidation. They believed that
economies of scale were the essence of modern power. And they accepted
these ideas so thoroughly that they took them to be simply commonsense
pragmatism.

The process of consolidation intensified enormously with America's
entry into World War II. The mass mobilization made necessary by the
war put the federal government in charge of the economy as never before.
It now began controlling prices and wages, effectively nationalizing key

manufacturing sectors, and in many respects halting open competition, both for consumers and workers, in parts of the economy. Wage inequality compressed dramatically, with pay at the top declining amid industrial controls, on the one hand, while, on the other, a labor shortage and government policy highly favorable to unionization played a part in increasing compensation for workers.

American individualism went into further abeyance as the culture of wartime service and sacrifice elevated solidarity and commitment to national institutions above all else. At the height of the war, America was unified and mobilized as one—not only as a result of the global emergency, but as the culmination of a half-century process of modernization, centralization, and consolidation.

This was the America that emerged into the postwar years. The global circumstances in which the nation found itself offered immense advantages. All of the major economic competitors of the United States had burned each other's economies to the ground, while the US economy had only grown stronger. America's domestic circumstances—the sum of the trends we have very broadly traced—also played a crucial role: the America that would seek to press its advantage would be a culturally unified (if racially stratified) and economically consolidated nation governed by a sprawling and active national government, and its people would have an exceptional level of trust in the large institutions dominating the country.

But almost as soon as this consolidated America emerged from the war, it began to unwind, and to seek some relief from the intense cohesion that had been building for so long. Cultural liberalization came first, then economic liberalization. Politics would follow even later. But the general trend was unmistakable.

Crucially, however, the liberalization that would characterize the postwar era took place at first against the backdrop of the highly cohesive America that had taken shape in the prior half-century. The country could benefit from the familial, social, cultural, and economic stability made possible by that unity and order, while also benefiting from the dynamism made possible by greater individualism, diversity, and competition. It was an unstable mix, but it allowed the nation, for a time, to enjoy the best of both worlds.

BECAUSE WE TEND TO SEE the second half of the twentieth century through the eyes of the baby boomers, especially those who came of age in the 1960s, we often implicitly assume that the cultural transformation of that era did not begin until that decade. But, in fact, it began almost immediately after World War II.

The boomers might have been children in the 1950s, but America was not childish or simple in those years, as our caricatures of the era now too often suggest. The late 1940s and the 1950s were a time of self-examination and self-criticism and also of cultural liberalization. The intense grip of self-restraint and solidarity that had defined the first half of the century was beginning to loosen. While the decades before the war had been characterized by consolidation, the second half of the century was defined by *diffusion*.

In physics and chemistry, diffusion describes the tendency of particles in certain circumstances to move from areas of high concentration to areas of low concentration. As the particles spread out, the overall cohesion of the matter is reduced. By analogy, in economic, political, and cultural terms, we might think of diffusion as the tendency of a tightly wound body politic to begin to disperse in all directions, becoming more scattered and individuated. The process of societal diffusion therefore involves decentralization, diminishing conformity, declining uniformity, and weakening authority.

Cultural diffusion in America didn't begin all at once: the transition lasted for decades and went through various phases. But the end of the war plainly marked a meaningful turning point. By the summer of 1945, Americans had endured more than fifteen years of almost continuous hardship, first because of economic depression, and then from war. They were ready to ease up, and the postwar environment allowed them to do so. There followed what historian Alan Petigny has aptly called "the renunciation of renunciation." The turn began with an outburst of liberationist pop psychology and philosophy that enjoined Americans to set aside the culture of sacrifice and focus instead on their own individual desires and ambitions.[16]

In 1946—the year the first baby boomers were born—pediatrician Benjamin Spock published *Baby and Child Care*, which advised American parents to relax and raise their young children in less regimented ways that showed more regard for each child's individuality. The book was a runaway best-seller. The best-selling nonfiction book the following year was a kind of self-help manual entitled *Peace of Mind*, written by Rabbi Joshua Liebman. It assured Americans that it was okay to "love thyself." In 1949, the pop-psychology book *The Mature Mind*, by Harry Overstreet, topped the *New York Times* best-seller list for sixteen weeks. It called on Americans to pursue "self-affirmation," rather than submerging their own identities beneath vast cultural codes of behavior rooted in guilt.[17]

Ironically, we think of the culture of the 1950s as being dominated by conformity and uniformity even though that was when these cultural tendencies began to be aggressively challenged—and perhaps in large part *because* of such challenges, for it was the challengers who identified and emphasized conformity as a defining characteristic of their generation. Books like David Riesman's *The Lonely Crowd* (1950) and William Whyte's *The Organization Man* (1956) described conformity as the great curse of the age. And indeed, conformity had been a prominent cultural force in American life for decades—what was unique about the 1950s was not that this force was still prevalent (which it surely still was), but that it was coming under such attack.

Most of the critics saw this conformity, and the almost blind faith in large, national institutions that they observed in the population, as crushing individual initiative and expression. Some also noted the danger these traits posed to the American tradition of localism and civic action, which had already come under strain in the first half of the century. Robert Nisbet, a brilliant sociologist and author of the 1953 classic *The Quest for Community*, raised particular alarms about the dangers such "giantism" could pose to the institutions of family, community, and civil society. He foresaw with extraordinary prescience how a culture of excessive centralization could quickly transform into a culture of excessive individualism.

That transformation, he said, would take place precisely because the middle option, of meaningful localism and community, had been increasingly closed off.

By the mid-1950s, individualism was no longer purely countercultural. The case against conformity was increasingly the content of American popular culture. In popular music, books, and films, the figure of the lone rebel rejecting society's bourgeois consensus came gradually to represent a kind of youthful ideal—as evident throughout much of the culture, from Elvis Presley's music to James Dean's films to popular books like J. D. Salinger's *The Catcher in the Rye*.

Even defenders of American nationalism and traditionalism began to line up on the side of individualism. The anticommunism of the 1950s is a complex example: while it was itself a force for national solidarity, it also tapped into worries about the fate of the individual under the stultifying collectivism of communist ideology. The emerging Cold War, at least in its early stages, would therefore unify Americans in defense of individualism. The burgeoning conservative movement of the 1950s also had its origins in a deep concern about the decline of American individualism in an age of consolidation.

In the inaugural issue of *National Review*, the flagship publication of modern American conservatism, launched in 1955, its editor and founder, William F. Buckley Jr., warned that "there never was an age of conformity quite like this one." He promised that his new magazine would combat the reigning uniformity of opinion. "The largest cultural menace in America is the conformity of the intellectual cliques," Buckley argued. And "the most alarming single danger to the political system lies in the fact that an identifiable team of Fabian operators is bent on controlling both our major political parties—under the sanction of such fatuous and unreasoned slogans as 'national unity,' 'progressivism,' and 'bipartisanship.'" Resistance was especially called for, Buckley insisted, with regard to the consolidating role of the national government. "In this great social conflict of the era," he announced, "we are, without reservations, on the libertarian side."[18]

Of course, another, even greater social conflict was brewing in the 1950s around the question of race. The civil rights movement offered a powerful critique of the consensus politics of previous decades, which had largely suppressed the question of the rights of African American citizens. The movement for racial equality was certainly a movement for integration, but it also fought against the power of mass institutions, which had long undermined full equality. It sought equality for African Americans as individuals.

Martin Luther King Jr., who by the mid-1950s had become the most prominent voice of the civil rights movement, frequently described his work as being part of the struggle against conformism and consolidation in American life more generally. Like Nisbet, King warned that a half-century and more of social consolidation had made Americans too fond of giant institutions. "We are producing a generation of the mass mind," King warned in a famous 1954 sermon. He continued: "Especially in this country many people are impressed by nothing that is not big: big cities, big churches, big corporations. We all are tempted to worship size. We live in an age of 'Jumboism' whose men find security in that which is large in number and extensive in size. Men are afraid to stand alone for their convictions. There are those who have high and noble ideals, but they never reveal them because they are afraid of being nonconformist."[19]

It was time to shake the nation out of this overconfidence in largeness that stood in the way of moral reform, King insisted. The images of peaceful protests for equal rights, and often of violent responses from police and from many whites in the Deep South, also shook the feeling of stability and solidarity that otherwise tended to characterize America in the 1950s, reinforcing the sense that the constricting old consensus was being overturned.

By the early 1960s, that sense was undeniable. The civil rights movement was growing in influence and strength. Women were becoming more vocal in demanding a greater role in the economic, cultural, and political spheres. Many were repudiating conventional female roles they considered oppressive. A liberationist youth culture also became increasingly evident—and hippies and student activists came onto the scene.

The gradual breakdown of common norms had a much darker side, too. Just as solidarity had an underside of repression, so liberalization had an underside of chaos; there are no unmixed goods in the city of man. Families, especially among Americans at the margins of the great cohesive consensus (such as African Americans and the very poor), began to show signs of instability in the postwar years. By 1965, as the rate of out-of-wedlock births among African Americans reached 25 percent, Daniel Patrick Moynihan, then an assistant secretary in the Department of Labor, was warning of a coming crisis of the black family. Violent crime rates also began climbing significantly in the 1960s. And as social upheaval turned at times to outright disorder, Americans began to feel that their society was being torn from its moorings.

But all of this, in both the 1950s and the 1960s, took place against the backdrop of an extraordinarily stable and cohesive social foundation and of what would strike us now as exceptionally limited diversity in every area of American life. Cultural liberalization was a real and powerful force, but the culture being liberalized was highly consolidated and constrained.

There was nothing like the profusion of cultural options we take for granted today. Most Americans had, at most, three or four television stations to choose from, for instance, and a few radio stations playing hits from a single, unified Top-40 list. The average American's diet would now strike us as astonishingly dull, and even in major cities there were few exotic restaurants or international cuisines. Choices in books, magazines, and other sources of entertainment and information were scant.

More important, basic cultural norms were also much more uniform and constrained than they are today. Marriage rates were quite high, and divorce was relatively rare. In 1960, about 75 percent of married women with children in the home were stay-at-home mothers (the figure would decline throughout the 1960s, but from a very high level). Workforce participation rates for men, meanwhile, never fell below 80 percent in that era. Most Americans maintained strong attachments to the traditional institutions of society.[20]

America also remained unusually culturally homogeneous in this period as a result of the severe limitations placed on immigration in the interwar years (which remained in place until 1965). By 1950, the percentage of people residing in the United States who had been born abroad (which had reached nearly 15 percent in 1910) was down to 7 percent. It continued to fall in the following years, reaching 5.4 percent in the 1960 census and 4.7 percent in 1970—almost certainly the lowest level in American history.

But the persistence of prewar consolidation was most evident in the US economy, where the liberalizing currents of the postwar turn took much longer to show their effects.

THE ECONOMY OF THE 1950S and 1960s was exceedingly regulated and constrained. That fact is sometimes hard to remember, because the period was nevertheless marked by strong growth and meaningful dynamism as America demobilized from war. It was during this period that America took its position as the undisputed global economic leader.

America's ascendance had a lot to do with the aftermath of the war itself. Every significant foreign competitor had seen its economy decimated by the fighting. For a time, the United States was the dominant force in essentially every large sector of the global economy. In the 1950s, the nation produced more than half of the world's total manufactured goods—a mind-boggling, if obviously transitory, advantage. This dominance allowed our economy to prosper despite strict regulatory constraints. Over time, the constraints would prove far more problematic.[21]

At the core of the postwar economy, as of the prewar economy, was a corporatist, cartel-based approach to regulation. Its purpose was to stifle competition to help large, incumbent players and to maintain an artificial balance between powerful producer interests and powerful labor interests. The country's commercial infrastructure—from transportation and communication to energy, banking, and finance—remained heavily regulated, so that commercial activity of all sorts, which required these various means of moving people, goods, information, and resources, was far more strictly managed than it is today. Trucking and airline routes; oil, gas, and electricity rates; telephone charges; local, regional, and national banking: all were tightly controlled by federal bureaucracies. Prices and production levels of agricultural goods were subject to regulatory adjustment.[22]

Meanwhile, a highly progressive (and frankly confiscatory) wartime system of federal taxation, with marginal income-tax rates topping out at an astonishing 91 percent, remained in place until the early 1960s. Labor markets, especially in manufacturing, were subject to laws and regulations that heavily favored the interests of the major unions, and so in effect stifled competition in those markets just as federal policy stifled competition in much of the rest of the economy. Roughly 30 percent of American workers were unionized in the 1950s and 1960s, and the unions often worked with employers in their industries to suffocate competition in an implicit mutual-aid pact—making sure that new competitors entering the market had to offer the same pay and benefits as existing giants and couldn't gain advantages over them by cutting costs.

The power of unions also frequently kept both women and African Americans at a disadvantage. In many industries (and especially in unionized manufacturing jobs), men were effectively overpaid in this period relative to their contribution to productivity, at least in part to enable (or induce) women to remain out of the workforce. The Manhattan Institute's Scott Winship has described that pattern of overpayment as a "breadwinner wage premium," predicated on the idea that a husband should be able to support a family on a single salary. And the persistence of racist hiring practices in many of the same industries restricted competition for jobs, leading to artificially inflated wages for working-class whites. Sharply constrained immigration also contributed to the wage inflation by restraining the growth of the labor supply.[23]

This combination of inflated wages, high taxes, constrained competition, and an ethic of national solidarity that prevailed in much of corporate America contributed to the prosperity of many, albeit mostly white, working-class Americans in this period. It also contributed to the persistent compression of wages. The portion of national income held by the top 1 percent of earners averaged just under 11 percent between 1945 and 1970, according to IRS data (in 2014 it was 21 percent).[24]

Although it was a period of robust economic growth and relatively low income inequality, then, this was otherwise a time of much-constrained economic dynamism: that growth, after all, was made possible in large part by peculiar global economic conditions and America's economic momentum coming out of the war, and the low income inequality was a function precisely of restraints on dynamism.

That combination of global circumstances, regulatory restraints, cultural exclusions, and policy controls is not one that we could (or would want to) re-create today. But at the time, it must have seemed to liberals like they could have it all: a consolidated economy that kept workers secure, and a culture that was loosening up and diversifying. For conservatives, the era epitomized exceptional cultural stability and cohesion—what seemed to be a broad and traditionalist moral consensus, but also fairly broadly shared prosperity. The Left was fighting the cultural constriction while reveling in the economic consensus; the Right was fighting the economic constrictions while reveling in the cultural consensus. Both sides today therefore recall that time as offering a stable foundation for a satisfying struggle for necessary liberalization, even if each side has a different idea of what the foundation was and what needed to be liberalized.

This is why conservatives tend to locate the end of the golden age in the early or mid-1960s (recall Charles Murray's choice of November 1963 as his end-point), when the cultural stability of the 1950s truly began to give way, while liberals locate the end of the era a few years later, when, as we shall see, the foundations of the postwar economic order began to weaken. Generally speaking, both can look back to the midcentury decades with genuine nostalgia, even if they don't entirely agree about what made it most worth missing.

BUT THERE IS ANOTHER POWERFUL reason why liberals and conservatives both miss those years, and why they can both think back on them as an era of good feelings. Along with relative cultural and economic cohesion, the postwar decades involved a highly unusual elite consensus on a broad range of issues in American politics.

The politics of the 1950s was dominated by the studied moderation of Dwight Eisenhower. Ike helped some Republicans accommodate themselves to some elements of the New Deal and put the federal government generally on the side of the civil rights movement, but he sought gradual change and emphasized stability and steadiness. Political polarization was relatively low. Each of the major parties contained both liberal and conservative elements. These elements might be laid out in different regional and socioeconomic arrangements, but politics was not marked by deep divisions in ideology.

Even in the early 1960s, an overwhelming consensus on many key issues still stretched across party lines. That consensus was characterized by extraordinary trust in centralized, technocratic management by large, established institutions. This faith in institutions, nurtured by the decades of prewar consolidation and assimilation, was one of the most exceptional features of postwar America.

And this confidence certainly extended to government. When a team from the University of Michigan studying national elections asked Americans in 1964 how much of the time they thought the federal government could be trusted to do the right thing, 76 percent said either "just about always" or "most of the time." (When Gallup asked exactly the same question in 2010, those two options garnered a combined 19 percent of the responses.)[25]

John F. Kennedy's administration sought to ride this wave of confidence, presenting itself as bringing what journalist David Halberstam later termed "the best and the brightest" to Washington to tackle the nation's and the world's greatest problems. After Kennedy's assassination, Lyndon Johnson worked to translate this attitude into an aggressive policy agenda.

Thanks to continuing public grief over Kennedy's death and to a weak Republican candidate, Arizona senator Barry Goldwater, the 1964 election gave Johnson's Democratic Party an enormous mandate to advance its agenda. Johnson won 61 percent of the vote, the highest portion of the popular vote since James Monroe's reelection in 1820, and his party gained two-thirds majorities in both the House and the Senate.

Johnson would not be shy about using these majorities. Dubbing his agenda the "Great Society," he put in place a vast array of new federal laws and programs that reflected the contradictory mix of cohesion and diffusion that had so defined the early postwar decades. The Great Society embodied the unstable dichotomy of the 1950s and 1960s: economic consolidation and cultural liberalization. Squarely behind cultural liberalization were, especially, the Civil Rights and Voting Rights acts of 1964 and 1965. Almost as consequential, the immigration reforms adopted in 1965 put an end to blatantly racist immigration quotas. Other elements of Johnson's Great Society, however—and perhaps most notably the education, antipoverty, and health-care programs enacted in those same years— were expressions of a belief in the consolidation, centralization, and bureaucratization of government power that drew upon the logic of an era that was ending. These programs, many of which are still with us, have functioned by a logic that over time has grown increasingly removed from that of the larger economy and society, and they have therefore become more and more dysfunctional and sclerotic.

The Great Society therefore embodied a prominent paradox of American life long noted by the keenest observers of our society: that administrative centralization often accompanies cultural and economic individualism. As the national government grows more centralized, and takes over the work otherwise performed by mediating institutions—from families and communities to local governments and charities—individuals become increasingly atomized; and as individuals grow apart from one another, the need for centralized government provision seems to grow. As we shall see, this dynamic has been key to many of the problems of our age of fracture.[26]

And it is frequently a cultural as well as an economic and political dynamic that is at work. The architects of the Great Society were plainly aware of the importance of the cultural, even spiritual, dimension of social life. A significant portion of Johnson's agenda sought to provide some purpose or meaning to postwar America in response to a worry about aimlessness in a modernizing society. Many on the Left by the mid-1960s had come to miss the sense of purpose that the Depression and the war had given economic policy. In its own way, the Left was becoming concerned about the breakdown of consolidation in American life.

Johnson spoke to this point when he first labeled his agenda the "Great Society." On May 22, 1964, in a speech at the University of Michigan, he described that agenda as, perhaps above all, intended to give the United States a coherent national purpose. "For a century," he said, "we labored to settle and to subdue a continent. For half a century we called upon unbounded invention and untiring industry to create an order of plenty for all of our people. The challenge of the next half-century is whether we have the wisdom to use that wealth to enrich and elevate our national life, and to advance the quality of our American civilization." He told the assembled college students that it would be up to their generation to determine whether an America no longer held together by the demands of crisis and emergency would be held together at all.[27]

Much of the rhetoric and substance of the Great Society agenda dealt with cultural enterprises, from the creation of a public broadcasting system to the support of the arts and humanities in the academy. The inordinate emphasis on government support for cultural elements of American society now seems striking. As Johnson's rhetoric suggests, there was a sense that the consolidating forces that had pulled America together for much of the twentieth century—the forces that had arisen with the industrial economy, that had empowered the large institutions that dominated every arena of American life, and that had made a centralizing progressivism the default philosophy of American politics—were fading fast. And they were being replaced by forces of individualism and diversity that would exercise a kind of centrifugal force in American life and leave the nation far less united and mobilized than in the past.

Our country would contend with these forces—for good and bad—from that time right through ours. It is plainly apparent that the attempt of Americans in the early postwar decades to combine consolidation and diffusion could not help but be merely transitory. Liberalizing change against a context of consolidation would inevitably change the context in which the opposing forces operated. That is more or less the story of the remainder of the postwar era. But it is a story we have been living while not always quite recognizing. The appeal of the midcentury moment, or at least of what we choose to remember about it, has given shape to our national self-understanding. And the actual remnants of that time in our culture, economy, and politics have been very important.

That appeal and those remnants have defined our domestic politics, in particular. Through the veil of baby-boomer nostalgia, the consensus politics of the mid-1960s often seem to us like an ideal of self-government—a "golden age when Washington worked," as President Obama put it. But, in fact, the Great Society era—especially in the immediate wake of the tidal-wave 1964 election—also marked a temporary failure of our intentionally adversarial and grinding system of government. The consensus around the Great Society allowed for an intense spurt of government activism that our constitutional architecture was not designed to permit.

Our politics fairly soon returned to a more balanced state in which our governing institutions and parties staunchly resisted one another's advances and change took place at its former slow and measured pace. But precisely because of that return to normality, the products of the Great Society have been very hard to undo or reform when change has been called for. A large portion of our domestic politics in recent decades has been a struggle to change or correct what those exceptional midcentury majorities wrought, and the same is very likely to be true in the decades to come.

But the cultural aim of the Great Society—the quest for purpose that Lyndon Johnson prioritized when declaring his ambitions—has largely fallen by the wayside. The Public Broadcasting System, the National Endowment for the Arts, the National Endowment for the Humanities, and some of the other cultural projects of the Great Society are still with us, but the idea that they might help us to resist or reverse the cultural disaggregation of postwar America and supply us with national purpose is no longer part of the equation. Johnson's programs would not be the way to counterbalance America's growing diffusion.

By THE END OF THE 1960s, it was becoming apparent that the midcentury balancing act would be unsustainable. The economic consolidation and restraint of competition that had marked the early postwar decades could be tolerated while America held a position of unique global advantage in the wake of the war. But as the 1970s approached, the nation's economic competitors were well on their way to getting their acts together. And the costs of our consolidated economy were becoming apparent just as the darker sides of the breakdown of the culture of conformity and stability began to show themselves.

The late 1960s and the bulk of the 1970s constituted the darkest, most ominous time in America's postwar path—it was the moment when we could no longer deny that something fundamental was changing and that, in some profound way, America seemed to be coming apart. The transient balance of midcentury was undone not by the nefarious workings of ill-intentioned partisans of one stripe or another, but by the progress of the very forces that—acting on a highly consolidated nation—had brought that balance about to begin with: the forces of individualism, decentralization, deconsolidation, fracture, and diffusion.

These have been the chief sources of many of our deepest problems in modern America, yet they must also be the sources of solutions and reforms. By the 1970s, Americans were increasingly forced to come to terms with what that complicated challenge might entail. Those years ultimately offered us some important lessons about how to make the most of diffusion and diversity. But we were going to have to learn the hard way.

3

THE AGE OF FRENZY

THE LATE 1960S AND EARLY 1970S were defined by disillusionment. The Vietnam War undermined America's image of itself as a benevolent global power, and debates over that conflict shattered the political consensus that had characterized the previous decades. Political assassinations—especially the killing of Martin Luther King Jr., who had embodied the hopes of the civil rights movement, and of Robert F. Kennedy, who had given voice to the liberal idealism of the time—further diminished America's self-assurance. By the early 1970s, the forces underlying the confidence and optimism of the postwar era seemed to be failing all at once.

During this period a series of downturns more severe than anything the country had experienced since the Great Depression shook the US economy. The growing prosperity that Americans had come to take for granted in the postwar years no longer seemed certain. Cultural liberalization, to many, seemed to be descending into cultural chaos. The integrationist promise of the civil rights movement was challenged from within by critics who called on African Americans to separate themselves from the cultural mainstream. And the political optimism that had undergirded the Great Society—the faith that a technocratic government could manage America and endow it with a durable balance of prosperity and liberation—began to quickly melt away, leaving many Americans wondering if the government could do much of anything right.

But it was the collapse of the culture of solidarity that was perhaps most jarring. The spirit of nonconformity that had emerged at the end of World War II, which had morphed in the 1960s into an idealistic quest for self-actualization, had degenerated by the 1970s into a jaded and strident individualism. Rejection of authority had quickly become the reigning spirit of American culture.

In the final three decades of the twentieth century, Americans began to face the implications of these changes—which turned out to be a volatile mix of dynamism and disorder. The price of social progress and the consequences of cultural dissolution were becoming apparent, and they were turning out to be one and the same. The result was at first turmoil and disorder, but over time a real effort to make the most of new circumstances emerged, with decidedly mixed success.

THE TWO DECADES FOLLOWING THE war witnessed multiple forms of liberalization, but always against a broader background of cohesion and stability. But by the 1970s, the change had become the context—deconsolidation itself became an organizing principle of American life. The country was no longer tethered by the forces of cohesion and disaggregation. The center had ceased to hold, and America increasingly defined itself by an ethic of individualism and a culture of diversity and fracture.[1]

Although the transformation ultimately turned out to have its most profound impact on the country in cultural terms, most Americans first felt the breakdown of the 1970s in economic terms. Throughout the US economy, but especially in its core industrial sectors, economies of scale seemed to be giving way to the burdens of scale—rigidity, over-commitment, and an inability to learn and adjust. Growth slowed a bit, and the economy became unpredictable. The United States had experienced no recessions from 1961 until 1969, but then it went through two significant ones over a five-year period. Unemployment rose, too—it had averaged 4.5 percent in the 1950s and 4.8 percent in the 1960s, but it climbed to an average of

6.2 percent in the 1970s. Even that high average masked dramatic highs and lows: in May 1975, the unemployment rate reached 9 percent, its highest level since the Great Depression.[2]

But soaring inflation rates were even more demoralizing for Americans. To many they signaled the end the postwar economic order. Inflation undermined the growth and wealth creation to which Americans had become accustomed and depreciated the value of what they had built up. The inflation rate had begun to creep upward in the mid-1960s, after a full decade of exceptional stability at very low levels. When it reached 5.5 percent in 1969, the newly elected president, Richard Nixon, pledged to make it a priority. By 1974, the inflation rate reached 11 percent.[3]

Meanwhile, the international monetary system developed after World War II also began to come apart. That system involved key Western economies pegging their currencies to the dollar, which in turn was pegged to the value of gold. As America's global dominance waned, our increasingly prosperous allies came to believe the dollar was overvalued and sought to shed their dependence on it. The Nixon administration responded by effectively exiting the postwar monetary arrangement, and began the process of delinking the dollar from gold in 1971. To prevent a sudden burst of inflation in the wake of that move (and to restrain the rise of inflation more generally), the administration put temporary wage and price controls into effect throughout the economy—the first since the end of World War II.

These policies were an attempt to regain some centralized, consolidated control of the economy's pace and performance. They seemed to help in the short term, but by 1973 it had become clear that they had been disastrously ill-conceived. The attempt to control prices set off shortages, black markets, and a sense of instability. These pressures, combined with oil-export limits imposed by Arab oil producers in response to America's support of Israel, in turn allowed inflation to explode. As the inflation rate soared, the unemployment rate rose and economic growth slowed. This dreaded "stagflation" would characterize the economy through the 1970s, and for several years the nation seemed powerless before it.[4]

This sense of powerlessness caused many Americans to gradually lose faith in their government. While the crisis of the Great Depression was much more severe than anything America experienced in the 1970s, most people believed that the Depression had been driven largely by private-sector malfeasance, and that the government ultimately had taken aggressive measures to counteract its effects. Although the New Deal did not succeed in rescuing the US economy (only the war ultimately did that), it strengthened the public's faith in the federal government. Inflation was different. It appeared to have been caused by errors of public policy and exacerbated by reckless decisions in Washington. Americans found themselves parked in long lines at gas stations and facing rising prices for key staples at the supermarket, and they were left with a sense that their leaders had lost control. This crisis of confidence contributed to a broader loss of faith in the authority of the nation's core institutions.

Those institutions didn't help, of course. The Watergate scandal, for example, which unrolled slowly into public view over a period of two years, until President Nixon's disgraced resignation in August 1974, amply confirmed that cynicism was justified. Public trust in Congress fell almost as precipitously, as did faith in big business and big labor—the other components of the exceptional corporatist consensus of the postwar years.[5]

Unionization and large-scale manufacturing—two pillars of economic strength in the postwar era—both grew weaker during this period. Union membership peaked in 1954, when nearly 35 percent of American workers were members of unions. By the 1970s, less than 25 percent of workers were unionized, and unionization ceased to be the norm even in new manufacturing jobs. Meanwhile, the broad-shouldered industries that had symbolized American postwar strength—the automakers, the steel producers, and other large manufacturers—began to lose their momentum and to fall behind foreign competitors in the 1970s.

In the face of these challenges, the first instinct of America's leaders was to double down on the mechanisms of consolidation. Their goal, as Nixon's wage and price controls suggested, was to get things back in hand by restraining competition and change for a time, in the hope that the nation's regulated, consolidated economy would ride out the trouble. But by the late 1970s, leaders in both parties began to recognize that the consolidation of the economy was itself part of the problem. The prewar arrangements at the heart of the implicit contract between America's powerful government and the largest private economic players were not well suited to the dynamism and liberalization of the postwar age. Every other aspect of American culture and society was liberalizing; now the economy needed to liberalize as well.

Thus, in the mid- and late 1970s, a wave of deregulation began to roll through the economy. It represented the unraveling of the prewar economic order that still defined much of the US economy, restraining competition and imposing uniformity. This deconsolidation was very much an extension—rather than a betrayal or reversal—of the changes working their way through the rest of American society in the postwar decades. The government loosened and in places reversed its tight control of the infrastructure of the economy. Barriers to entry were removed, and competition was increasingly encouraged and rewarded. New laws opened trucking, railways, airways, and other transportation sectors to new entrants and innovators. The energy industry was gradually deregulated. AT&T was stripped of its telephone monopoly (a process that began in 1974 but took many years to complete), opening the path to a new age of digital communication. Banking and finance were partially deregulated, too.[6]

In each case, the new openness yielded in time some major innovations that helped to transform American life and vastly increase the nation's prosperity and productivity. Some barriers and consolidating tendencies (most notably the high marginal tax rates of an earlier era) stayed in place for a few more years, but the late 1970s saw an immense deconsolidation in America's economy. A nation of big, powerful institutions was giving way to a nation of smaller, more nimble players competing intensely in a highly dynamic, if therefore also less stable, economy.

The American political system was also decentralizing rapidly during this period. The unusual, broad elite consensus of the mid-1960s had been shattered, and polarization was swiftly on the rise. But even as the political parties were becoming more distinct, they were growing less powerful as institutions. The Republican and Democratic establishments began to lose their control over both the electoral and legislative processes at the national level. In 1972, the Democratic Party replaced its presidential nominating process, which had been controlled by senior party officials, with a far more open, decentralized, primary- and caucus-dominated system. Hubert Humphrey had become the Democratic nominee for president in 1968 without even participating in a single state primary—leading to something of a populist revolt within the party's institutions. A younger generation of activists wanted voters to have more power and established leaders to have less. The reforms of 1972 dramatically demoted party bosses and elevated primary voters. Republicans soon followed suit, adopting essentially the same procedures.

Meanwhile, the congressional class of 1974, elected in the wake of Watergate, moved to weaken the presidency and decentralize Congress. They ended the practice of executive spending impoundment, by which the Nixon administration had given the executive branch of government enormous leeway over the power of the purse. They enacted the War Powers Act to let Congress play more of a role in foreign policy. And they decentralized and opened up the congressional budget process and committee system.

There were, even in that period, some countervailing forces, especially in government. Thanks in particular to the Great Society programs, formal administrative authority was in some respects actually growing *more* centralized in Washington even in the 1970s (and as we shall see, administrative centralization in government often goes hand in hand with individualism and fragmentation throughout the rest of society). Yet even while more authority was being channeled toward some of the institutions of our government, those institutions themselves (like most other American institutions) were losing some of their internal coherence and cohesion, and losing the trust of the public.[7]

BUT WHILE THE DIFFUSION OF power in the economic and political arenas had lasting implications, it was in the cultural arena that the transformation of American life was most visible. Here, the swift, profound, and multifaceted revolution in norms was nothing short of astonishing.

In a 1976 essay in *New York* magazine, the novelist and journalist Tom Wolfe coined the term "the 'me' decade" to describe the 1970s. The decade was defined, Wolfe argued, by an ethic of individualism and atomism. This ethic had arisen in some corners of the culture in the 1950s and 1960s, but by the mid-1970s it had reached society's core. The reasonably broad prosperity of the 1960s, combined with the weakening of traditional cultural institutions and the rise of assorted forms of narcissism (from self-help movements to the use of psychedelic drugs for "self-discovery"), had created "the greatest age of individualism in American history," Wolfe wrote. He paid particular attention to the spiritual lives of Americans, where he thought the implications of this transformation might be the most profound of all.[8]

And without question, there was an unprecedented transformation in spiritual and religious life in this period. It involved, above all, the collapse of the power and stature of the mainline Protestant denominations, which had long played a leading role in American society and culture. Those mainline churches were themselves in important respects creatures of America's prewar consolidation. They emerged as the unified denominations we would now recognize in America—Presbyterians, Methodists, Lutherans—only in the early decades of the twentieth century. Before that, for most of the nineteenth century, American Protestantism had witnessed endless divisions and subdivisions among sects. But a unified response by relatively liberal churches to a wave of fundamentalist energy, combined with the general consolidating character of the age, created several large mainline Protestant sects that by the early 1960s were home to a majority of the US population.[9]

These churches reached their peak in the 1950s, when the nation's core institutions still stood strong and firm. That decade was a high-water mark for America's religious institutions more generally. The mainline churches were culturally dominant as never before; Catholicism was strengthening and growing; evangelicalism was vibrant and engaged with the larger culture; and the black Protestant churches riveted the nation with an astonishing display of moral gravity and courage in the civil rights movement.

But like the other core American institutions in that period, these churches were already being transformed from within just as they reached the apex of their power. Where they might have been expected to act as restraints on the excesses of a liberalizing culture, the mainline churches, in particular, chose instead to serve as accelerants, adopting every fashionable trend and excusing every countercultural tendency of the 1960s. In essence, they were undermining their own authority while they undermined trust in the nation's elite institutions more generally.[10]

That loss of faith had direct consequences for the strength of the churches themselves. Membership in the Lutheran, United Methodist, Episcopalian, and Presbyterian churches all peaked in the late 1960s and began a sharp decline. American Catholicism went into a tailspin, too: although the church's overall membership remained steady (thanks in large part to rising Catholic immigration from Latin America), its institutions fell into deep crisis in the 1970s as Mass attendance and religious vocations plummeted. The authority of the church in the lives of American Catholics correspondingly diminished.

What arose in place of these established institutions was a far more decentralized, personalized, evangelical Christianity. Its teachings were generally more conservative (if also more individualist) than those of the mainline denominations, but its *structure*, in keeping with the spirit of the age, was far more diffuse—with individual and largely unconnected church communities arising nearly independently. The scale of evangelicalism, however, was never sufficient to make up for the decline of mainline Christianity. Therefore, as *New York Times* columnist Ross Douthat argued in his superb 2012 book *Bad Religion*, the 1970s saw a massive movement "away from institutional religion and toward a more do-it-yourself and consumer-oriented spirituality—that endures to the present day."[11]

RELIGION WASN'T THE ONLY ASPECT of American cultural life that was transforming during the 1970s. The same shift—from institutional norms and traditional structures toward a kind of hyper-individualism—was evident throughout the culture, and it unleashed a swift collapse of norms in a number of areas. Illegal drug use rose steeply, for instance, through the decade. In 1973, 12 percent of respondents told a Gallup poll that they had tried illicit drugs; by 1977, the number was nearly 25 percent.[12]

The same tendency toward disorder was evident in a steep rise in violent crime. The national crime rate, as maintained by the Federal Bureau of Investigation, rose from 1,887 crimes per 100,000 Americans in 1960 to 3,985 in 1970 and 5,950 in 1980—a rate of increase unlike anything America had ever experienced before (to our knowledge) or since. This rise was concentrated in urban areas, so that for many Americans living in cities, in particular, the 1970s were a time of great risk and fear.

But it was changing attitudes and practices around sexuality and the family that wrought the most dramatic transformations. Family breakdown, which began to increase with the postwar liberalization of the culture, came into prominence in unprecedented fashion in the 1970s.

Under Governor Ronald Reagan, California enacted the nation's first modern "no-fault" divorce law in 1969, and the great majority of the states followed suit in the 1970s. Divorce rates were already rising, but this legal revolution opened the floodgates. While about 20 percent of couples who married in 1950 ended up divorced, nearly 50 percent of those who married in 1975 did. Approximately half of the children born to married parents in the 1970s saw their parents separate, compared to only about 11 percent of those born in the 1950s.[13]

Acceptance of divorce was due in part to the liberalization of views on the subject among those mainline Protestant denominations noted above, but it resulted even more from the general rise of individualism in the postwar decades. "In this new psychological approach to married life," University of Virginia sociologist W. Bradford Wilcox observed, "one's primary obligation was not to one's family but to one's self; hence, marital success was defined not by successfully meeting obligations to one's spouse and children but by a strong sense of subjective happiness in marriage."[14]

The same shift in attitudes about the family helped to push childbearing rates sharply downward in the 1970s. At the height of the baby boom, in the mid-1950s, the "fertility rate" (that is, lifetime births per woman) had climbed above 3.5. By 1970, it was at 2.3. But it fell much further throughout the 1970s, to a modern low of 1.7 in 1976, where it essentially remained for the rest of the decade. Meanwhile, the US Supreme Court's

1973 *Roe v. Wade* decision (advanced and defended under the banner of personal choice and individualism) left the United States with one of the world's most radically permissive abortion regimes, which effectively allowed abortion all the way through pregnancy and even to the moment of birth. By 1980, more than 1.5 million abortions were taking place in America each year.

The rate of out-of-wedlock births was skyrocketing at the same time. Just over 9 percent of births were out of wedlock in America in 1969, and just under 19 percent were in 1979. These figures varied enormously by race (more than half of black births were out of wedlock in the late 1970s, while a little over 8 percent of white births were), but the rates of increase were intense for both races.[15]

This increase had a lot to do (as both cause and effect) with changing attitudes about out-of-wedlock births: as the stigma around them diminished, pregnancy was less likely to lead to marriage. And it was also part of a larger transformation in attitudes about sexuality in general in American life. That larger transformation brought greater tolerance for homosexuality and a most welcome decline in violence and mistreatment of gays and lesbians. But it also yielded greater tolerance for promiscuity, obscenity, and pornography and a marked coarsening of the culture.

Ultimately, the sexual revolution, which covered much more ground than this, was surely the most culturally transformative of all the waves of change, liberation, and individualism that swept over American life in the postwar era—and in one way or another it was connected to all of the others. In a time of rapid technological progress in many arenas, no technology was as transformative as the birth-control pill, first approved for use in America in the early 1960s. And no other economic, cultural, or social change was as profound as the changing place of women in American society and the changing relations between women and men. Indeed, almost none of the other changes the country experienced in that era, and almost none of the economic and cultural trends (for good and for bad) that we are tracing here, can really be understood apart from the sexual revolution and its implications. It is hard to think of any cultural transformation in human history as simultaneously swift and profound as the changing place of women in the lives of Western societies in the decades after World War II.

A POWERFUL SENSE OF GROWING instability and unraveling, or growing individualism and liberation, thus prevailed in the culture of the 1970s. It was, at least in part, a logical extension of the forces unleashed in America at the end of World War II. But the shift seemed to many to have gone too far, and it set off a conservative reaction that would come to define the subsequent decade and more of American life.

In some respects, the conservative reaction was an attempt to recapture some of the order and stability of the immediate postwar years. This was the law-and-order conservatism that both Richard Nixon and, in time, Ronald Reagan sought to embody. And it was the revived moralism of the rising evangelical movement. But although the backlash was a response to the dark side of postwar liberalization, it did not actually take the form of a return to consolidation, or even quite a hearkening to prewar norms. On the whole, the country's reaction to the excesses of the 1970s actually involved a kind of doubling down on the spirit of postwar individualism. It was an effort to bring some order to America's postwar diffusion, not to repudiate it entirely.

Americans thus sought a cure for the malaise and pandemonium of the 1970s not through the revival of an old consolidating tendency, but through the maturation of the new spirit of individualism and liberation. There was no fighting the core fact of postwar America—the fact of an intensifying deconsolidation—but there could be better ways to live with it. The spirit of individualism, the nation could readily see, had gone too far and grown too wild. America's old norms no longer held sway. But people cannot long abide an absence of norms, and so in the course of the later 1970s and into the 1980s, American society went through what political scientist Francis Fukuyama, in his 1999 book *The Great Disruption,* called a "renorming." This meant not the recovery of old cultural rules and taboos, but the development of new ones. These new norms were rooted in the new ethic of individualism but geared to giving people's lives some stability and structure.

In economics, as we have seen, the reaction to the breakdown of the 1970s tended to point toward a liberation of the private sector and so away from the tight grip of consolidated regulation. It therefore pointed toward an economy disciplined by market competition rather than by a fading nationalist solidarity. In religion, the reaction tended to point to a noninstitutional, disorganized Christianity of personal fulfillment and individual grace in place of the older establishment churches. In the struggle against crime and social disorder, it pointed to a new ethic of personal (rather than communal) responsibility and consequences. By the mid-1980s, this approach would justify a policing revolution and an increasingly bipartisan commitment to combatting violent crime, but for the most part without a recurrence to the vocabulary of social obligation. In the personal, social, and sexual lives of many Americans, the reaction meant a new emphasis on health as an impetus to order and self-discipline—a kind of cold, materialist moralism that counseled against self-destructive narcissism on the grounds of self-preserving narcissism.

This brand of implicit, emergent reaction to disorder took some time to work. In the economy, stagflation persisted right through the 1970s and into the early 1980s. But it was ultimately conquered, and while the new economic order would come with some serious costs, it also brought very real prosperity for the great bulk of the country. In the culture, too, this renorming took its time to show results. But in the course of the 1980s and 1990s, a number of the alarming social indicators of the 1970s did return to more tolerable levels or stabilize—at least for Americans in the middle class and above.

But that caveat, of course, is no small matter. The cultural breakdown that had characterized postwar America began with the economic and cultural elite in the 1960s, but by the middle of the 1970s it had spread throughout our society. The economic breakdown of the 1970s, needless to say, hit the most disadvantaged Americans hardest. And the renorming that began in the late 1970s, and that would characterize the 1980s and 1990s, was much more accessible to better-off Americans than to the poor.

A more competitive, meritocratic economy held more promise for people who were well positioned to hone their skills and take risks. A culture of more ordered individualism was more valuable to people building from a foundation of stability than to those working to rise from entrenched disadvantage, or to overcome the burdens of broken homes and communities. Over and over, the effects of America's diffusion, and then of its efforts to adjust to that diffusion, seemed to reach the wealthy and advantaged as rewards, but hit the poor and disadvantaged as punishments. If the new American ethic pushes every individual to become more like himself or herself, rather than more like everyone else, it will, even at its best, tend to accentuate differences, to increase distances, and to turn a range of distinctions into a set of bifurcations. This is among the more prominent consequences of America's postwar evolution.

The lesson many Americans implicitly learned in the 1970s was that the emergence of a new national ethic of liberation and fracture could not be reversed, and so had to be channeled to the good. This did not mean that we had found an answer to our social challenges, but only that we had more properly defined the question, which became: How can we make the most of the opportunities afforded by the dynamism and the freedom set loose by America's postwar diffusion while mitigating its costs and burdens, especially for the most vulnerable among us?

In the 1980s and 1990s, many Americans (first on the Right and then also on the Left) seemed to understand that this was the question we should wrestle with. The results of their efforts to do so were mixed, to be sure, but the efforts were in many respects very promising. In our own century, however, many Americans (on the Left and Right alike) have lost sight of the question, and sought instead to put aside the hard-earned lesson of the 1970s: the basic fact that you cannot go back to midcentury America.

The result has been our often broken and nostalgic politics, which too often ignores the tools at our disposal, and too easily sells short the mixed achievements of the 1980s and 1990s and the lessons they might offer us. Those lessons, the implications of the great renorming of the last two decades of the twentieth century, are full of both causes for hope and reasons to worry.

THE TWENTIETH CENTURY ENDED BETTER than Americans in the 1970s would have had any reason to expect. In retrospect, we can see how the seeds of renewal were planted in the darkest season of frenzy and despair, but it was surely far from obvious at the time.

Stagflation did not end when the 1970s did. Upon becoming president in 1981, Ronald Reagan pursued an economic program of aggressive tax cuts (both to increase marginal incentives for work and investment and to reduce the tax burdens on American families), sharp monetary tightening (continuing his predecessor's efforts to combat inflation), and increases in defense spending (to better deter and confront the Soviet Union). All of this was balanced by only modest spending reductions elsewhere in the budget.

The tax cuts helped eliminate some of the last remnants of the economic consolidation of the prewar years. When Reagan took office, the top marginal personal-income tax rate was 70 percent; when he left, it was 28 percent. And while it has since risen again, to roughly 40 percent, it seems unlikely to return to 1970s levels in the foreseeable future. Without question, these cuts contributed in time to greater economic growth, innovation, and productivity. But in the near term, they yielded large budget deficits and sharply increased public borrowing. These effects, together with the tight monetary policies instituted in the previous decade, contributed to extremely high interest rates. And the interest rates, in turn, seemed to keep the economy from recovering from its late-1970s slump.[16]

Inflation did begin to decline in the early 1980s (from a postwar high of almost 15 percent in the spring of 1980 to roughly 4 percent by the end of 1982), but the recession persisted through Reagan's first two years. In the fall of 1982, unemployment reached nearly 11 percent, which was higher than it had been at any point in the 1970s (and indeed, since the Depression). Growth remained weak through the end of 1982.

But in the course of 1983, it became clear that the economy had turned a corner. The mix of monetary and tax policies added to the momentum of the business cycle and drove a robust recovery. The economy would not be in recession again until the early 1990s, and unemployment began to gradually work its way down, too, continuing to fall each year for the remainder of Reagan's term in office.

The fiscal, monetary, and regulatory policies pursued in the Reagan years (often with some bipartisan backing) amounted to a kind of turbo-charging of the economic liberalization that America's postwar diffusion had gradually set in motion. It meant that some of the trends of the 1970s would continue—the decline of labor unions, the growth of income inequality—but that some of their negative consequences would be mitigated by stronger economic growth and by a greater market orientation throughout the economy. That orientation also helped set the stage for the information technology revolution, which would power further growth beyond the Reagan years.[17]

The greater prosperity of the 1980s brought about a peculiar change of norms and attitudes about money and wealth in America. Just as public disapproval of out-of-wedlock births and drug abuse had diminished as prewar norms faded, so taboos surrounding public displays of wealth (and even expressions of greed) receded. The recovery of the Reagan years was accompanied throughout the popular culture by a kind of open celebration of wealth among those fortunate enough to possess it, and an open fascination with opulence among those not so fortunate.

GREATER PROSPERITY ALSO TOOK SOME of the sting out of the social transformations the country was experiencing, but those transformations certainly persisted. The growth in rates of divorce, out-of-wedlock births, abortion, and similar measures of family breakdown slowed some from the 1970s, but the breakdown continued nonetheless, and its character (as well as its relationship to the other key social trends of the time) became a little clearer as it did.

The centrifugal forces unleashed in midcentury America were, by the 1980s, working powerfully to pull people apart from the core institutions of our national life: family, work, religion, and community. Many Americans, including especially those in the most vulnerable economic situations, were becoming systematically detached (or dis-integrated) from those institutions, and thereby increasingly isolated. Declining rates of marriage and rising rates of divorce were very much connected to falling rates of workforce participation (among men), religious observance, and civic engagement.

People are never likely to be content with isolation. Hence, the detachment from core institutions sent people searching for new kinds of connections and new sources of meaning and order better attuned to an individualist age. But these would take some time to emerge, and they generally failed to run as deep as the relational commitments they sought to replace. "As people were liberated from their traditional ties to spouses, families, neighborhoods, workplaces, or churches," Francis Fukuyama has written regarding this period, "they thought they could have social connectedness at the same time, this time the connections being those they chose for themselves. But they began to realize that such elective affinities, which they could slide in and out of at will, left them feeling lonely and disoriented, longing for deeper and more permanent relationships with other people."[18]

With this emerging isolation—which would grow increasingly prominent in the subsequent decades—America had in some ways come full circle. The consolidation of midcentury generated an overriding fear of conformity. The age of individualism produced its opposite: a deep and anxious loneliness.

Although these troubling trends persisted, Americans certainly were beginning to find their new circumstances less disorienting than they had in the 1970s. They were enjoying the upside of liberalization while seeking for ways to mitigate the downside. The sense of sheer chaos and breakdown of the 1970s had subsided somewhat, and with it the pessimism and defeatism of the time. Ronald Reagan's assertion, in his 1984 campaign, that it was "morning in America" again after a long, dark night was in tune with the improving mood of the public (which reelected Reagan that year with the biggest landslide electoral-college victory since George Washington's presidency).

That Republican victory was also a function of the fact that the American Right had learned the lessons of the 1970s faster than the Left. Republicans had emerged from the 1970s with something of a response to the diffusion of American life: they called for accelerating the liberalization of the economy to improve prosperity, on the one hand, while, on the other, reestablishing some of the order society needed, but without reimposing the old constrictions. Competition and personal responsibility would take the place of the regulation and solidarity of the old order.

The Left at first resisted this formula, and for much of the 1980s, the face the Democrats put before the public retained the unkempt, pessimistic intensity of the 1970s—to the Democrats' detriment. As the decade went on, however, more moderate voices that came to be known as the "New Democrats" began to sketch out a left-of-center version of the basic Reaganite platform: openness to deregulation, free trade, and competitive markets; a relatively tough line on crime and welfare that emphasized individual responsibility; and a fairly assertive foreign policy.

The New Democrats were still on the Left, to be sure: they wanted higher taxes, if nowhere near as high as they had been before Reagan's reforms. They were friendlier to some of the cultural liberation of the late 1960s and 1970s, and perhaps, above all, to the extreme and utterly unrestrained abortion regime established by the Supreme Court's *Roe v. Wade* decision. They had far greater faith than Republicans did in the potential of government planning and administration to address great public problems, and they clung to the social-democratic dreams that had long energized the Left. But in some important economic and cultural respects they embodied a liberal version of Reagan's kind of response to America's continuing diffusion and fracturing.

And in 1992, the most prominent elected official among these New Democrats, Arkansas governor Bill Clinton, was elected president. His agenda largely embodied the New Democrats' insights, and (especially under the pressure of Republican Congresses starting in 1995) therefore made the 1990s largely an extension of the 1980s. The two decades together constitute what has been termed the "late century boom."

The top marginal personal-income tax rate did increase some in the 1990s: as noted earlier, after rising from 28 percent to 31 percent under President George H.W. Bush, it rose further, to a top rate of nearly 40 percent, under Clinton, but it was still nowhere near the 70 percent rate that preceded Reagan's reforms. And, pressured by the Republican Congress, Clinton also signed reductions in some taxes on business and investment and accepted a Republican proposal for new tax relief for parents. Meanwhile, he allowed continuing deregulation in key sectors to take place (especially telecommunications), signed a Republican-championed reform of a key welfare program to give it a greater emphasis on employment, and continued Reagan's and Bush's efforts to combat violent crime and drug abuse.

Interrupted only by a brief recession in 1990–1991, the nearly two-decade expansion of that era was reasonably broad and robust. As economist Robert Shapiro put it in 2015, "through the 1980s and 1990s households of virtually every type experienced large, steady income gains, whether they were headed by men or women, by blacks, whites or Hispanics, or by people with high school diplomas or college degrees."[19] The resulting growth (amid higher tax rates, and propelled at the end of the 1990s by a boom in Internet-related technology businesses) even increased federal revenues to the point of making two balanced budgets possible, in 1998 and 1999.

But as in the 1980s, so in the 1990s this economic progress involved greater income inequality. More important, it occurred as many Americans were becoming even more detached from the core social institutions of family, work, faith, and community. This was a genuinely prosperous time, yet it was also in many respects a period of declining social capital—the common stock of rules and norms that enable people to live and work together. The great renorming slowed that process, but it did not reverse it.

Declines in social capital tend to be self-intensifying: as people come to have less in common with their fellow citizens, they find it more difficult to cooperate and identify with one another, which brings a further weakening of remaining social bonds. The breakdown of family norms clearly played a central part in this process in the last decades of the twentieth century. But beginning especially in the 1990s, that breakdown began to take a peculiar shape: as diversity and deconsolidation intensified, they tended to create sharp bifurcations in one area of American life after another—with people at the top moving higher and higher, and those at the bottom lower and lower, while the middle hollowed out (mostly moving upward). Family trends were no exception: they divided sharply in two, so that aggregate national statistics could no longer tell any clear story.

In the aggregate, for instance, divorce rates basically plateaued in the 1990s, after several decades of sharp rises. But more careful analysis shows that divorce rates continued to rise for people with lower levels of education and income, but declined for the educated and well-to-do. Marriage rates followed a similar pattern. Out-of-wedlock births did as well (though in this case rates had always been quite low for women with college degrees and higher incomes). So while some Americans continued to experience a significant recovery of social order and norms in the 1990s, others saw their estrangement from America's core institutions intensify.

Attachment to work fared somewhat better in the strong economy of the 1990s. A transformative reform of a key welfare program helped millions of poor Americans, most of them women, become better integrated into the workforce. But a basic pattern of declining workforce attachment among men with modest educations had by then taken hold, and it persisted through the decade. This pattern also contributed to declining marriage rates, further driving men to become detached from essential sources of stability and order.[20]

The language of loosening attachment aptly describes the state of our other key institutions as well. As many Americans moved from a strong affiliation with clearly defined, institutional structures to less stable, more dynamic, but more casual arrangements—economic, familial, social, and religious—people's connections to what had been the defining institutions of American life weakened and became more casual throughout the 1980s and 1990s, continuing the pattern that had begun in postwar America. When asked about religious belief, for instance, more and more Americans described themselves as "unaffiliated," which did not necessarily mean they did not believe in God, or even that they did not attend a church occasionally, but that they did not see themselves as connected to the large, established institutions of American Christianity.

The same could be said about attachments to community and participation in civil society. In his 2000 book *Bowling Alone*, Robert Putnam traced this phenomenon, describing how Americans were abandoning formerly robust institutions of civil society (from the PTA to the Lions Club to organized bowling leagues) and becoming isolated in their own communities. Putnam's thesis came under criticism from a variety of analysts who argued that the decline of the institutions that had been strongest in midcentury did not mean Americans were becoming isolated, but that they were joining new and different kinds of institutions, which were often smaller and less demanding. People do not live in isolation, these critics suggested; they adjust and build new patterns of social interaction. This is surely right. But these different patterns, adapted as they are to new circumstances, reflect important changes in American life—and especially a loosening of attachments.[21]

Francis Fukuyama described this same process—the process of replacing attachments to large, established institutions with attachments to smaller, more flexible, but less established networks—as a "narrowing of the radius of trust" and a "miniaturization of community." The same pattern, and the larger deconsolidation of American life that drove it, also contributed to what journalist Bill Bishop has called "the big sort." Using demographic data, Bishop showed that in the final decades of the twentieth century, Americans increasingly sorted themselves into homogeneous communities—both real, geographic communities and, with the rise of a profusion of media options and the Internet, social and virtual communities—in which they were able to interact mostly with like-minded people with similar assumptions and experiences. In a sense, the dissolution of our core institutions and the country's increasing diversity drove people from large institutions to small ones, and from large communities to micro-networks, in search of homogeneity, commonality, and trust.[22]

That search was also driven by the growing diversity of American society, thanks in large part to the explosion of immigration—legal and illegal—that America experienced in the final decades of the century. In 1970, just 4.7 percent of the residents of the United States had been born abroad. By 1990, the figure was 8 percent, and in 2000 it was 11 percent. The sheer number of foreign-born residents more than tripled in that time, from 9.6 million to 31.1 million. By the end of the twentieth century, immigration levels were near where they had been at the beginning of the century. But that early twentieth-century wave was received by a consolidating America, which, for all its hostility to outsiders, was far better suited to *assimilate* immigrants than later generations would be. This second, late twentieth-century wave hit a deconsolidating nation that was in no position to press new immigrants to adopt a cohesive American identity.

The melting pot was not working nearly as well in late twentieth-century America as it had a century earlier. Therefore, the largest immigrant groups in this wave of newcomers—especially those from Latin America, which was by far the foremost source of immigration during this period—seemed to remain relatively distinct and unified, rather than becoming melded into the American whole. Ironically, the individualism of late-century America, by weakening that instinct to digest and integrate new immigrants into a self-confident whole, created more coherent subgroups, and therefore less assimilation into a culture of individualism.

The identity politics of the 1990s evinced a similar pattern. With the decline of the idea of a strong and coherent national identity, many Americans—especially those belonging to ethnic minority groups—naturally sought to emphasize subnational identities. So while individualism might have been the driving force behind the nation's cultural deconsolidation, it resulted in the emergence of a politics of group rights and multiculturalism. This, too, was an instance of the emergence of new norms in place of declining old ones. Culture abhors a vacuum, and human beings will always rush in to establish new cultural patterns and arrangements when existing ones decline and fade. But the century-long assault on America's mediating institutions—first by hyper-consolidation and then by hyper-individualism—meant that American civil society was not well positioned to turn subnational *identities* into interpersonal *communities*, and multiculturalism ultimately tended to reinforce rather than counteract our individualism.

THE ERA OF THE LATE-CENTURY boom was thus a mixed bag. On the one hand, the economy grew meaningfully stronger and the country saw a partial renorming in some key social and cultural indicators. In some crucial respects, Americans found a way to make the most of the centrifugal forces pulling them apart, and to recover a bit from the disorienting frenzy of the 1970s. On the other hand, as that deconsolidation persisted, its effects increasingly involved a detachment of many Americans from the nation's core institutions, and therefore also an increasing bifurcation of the top and the bottom along with (especially at the bottom) a growing sense of isolation.

This is how the nation approached the new century: having traveled a great distance from the midcentury golden age, clearly still struggling to find some balance amid change, but having at least managed to recover from the worst disorientation and disillusionment of the 1970s. We were by then a thoroughly individualist society, and that was not about to change. But whether breakdown or recovery, disillusion or renorming, would shape the next chapter of our story seemed a genuinely open question at the turn of the millennium.

4

THE AGE OF ANXIETY

PERHAPS THE MOST BASIC QUESTION facing America as the twenty-first century began was whether the strong economy and the partial renorming of the 1980s and 1990s would afford us some room for confidence, or our persistent deconsolidation would yield yet more disorientation and unease. So far, after a decade and a half, the answer certainly seems closer to the latter.

The early twenty-first century has, for one thing, been a period of relative stagnation for the US economy. The century began with a recession, which seemed to be driven in large part by the bursting of an economic bubble, which in turn was inflated by the emergence of the Internet in the late 1990s. And the recovery following that downturn was significantly weaker than those that followed most previous recessions, leaving observers of the economy waiting for growth to snap back to late twentieth-century levels—which never quite happened.[1]

Then came the economic cataclysm of 2007–2009, which followed yet another bubble—a mark perhaps of the frenzied and unstable nature of our postmodern prosperity. The culprit this time was a housing bubble that burst, unleashing a massive crisis in the financial sector. The resulting so-called Great Recession was easily the most severe economic slowdown in America since the Great Depression. Between December 2007 and June 2009, the labor market lost 8.4 million jobs, with the unemployment rate reaching 10 percent at the peak of the crisis—nearly a postwar record.

Almost every economic indicator fell sharply in the recession, and most have not recovered their pre-crisis levels even half a decade after the downturn officially ended. Indeed, in some cases, "recovery" may simply not be the right word to use. The recession accelerated some of the more pernicious trends we have been tracing over the past five decades, so that we should not be surprised that not all of its consequences could be quickly reversed. The sharp decline in the labor-force participation rate, for instance, was a hastening of a long-running process, and it is unlikely to be undone anytime soon. Employment in some key industrial sectors also looks unlikely to recover fully, as the recession sped up a preexisting trend toward automation. Federal spending, too, jumped sharply in response to the recession, but because of demographic pressures driving up entitlement costs, it is not projected to return to prerecession levels in the foreseeable future.

Not all the troubling trends that emerged in the recession have proven to be durable, thankfully. Unemployment (as distinct from labor-force participation) had significantly declined by mid-2015, and some of the distressing socioeconomic patterns that presented themselves in the wake of the recession (from adult millennials living with their parents at unusually high rates to a slowdown in suburban construction) had abated. But as with the century's milder first recession, the Great Recession was not followed by the kind of galloping recovery that has historically been known to trail sharp downturns. Even in years of recovery and growth, America's economic engine has been sluggish. Since 2001, the economy has yet to see a single year of 4 percent growth or better (there were four such years in the 1990s, four in the 1980s, five in the 1970s, six in the 1960s, and six in the 1950s).[2]

Perhaps even more distressing, this overall slowdown appears to be rooted in some structural factors—particularly demographic ones—that will not be easy to counteract. Economic growth is in essence a function of two elements: workforce expansion and productivity improvements. The healthy growth of the second half of the twentieth century involved both in roughly equal measure. As the population grew in the wake of the baby boom, immigration increased significantly, and women entered the workforce en masse, the American labor force saw robust expansion, accounting for just under half the total economic growth in that period. Productivity gains accounted for the rest, as new technologies and business-model innovations emerged in fierce succession.

It is already perfectly clear that this balance of factors cannot be sustained in the twenty-first century. As the baby boomers retire and the proportion of women in the workforce plateaus, the growth of the labor force contributes less and less to the growth of the economy. No amount of immigration is likely to make up the difference—especially given the mismatch between the demand for labor and the skill-sets of contemporary immigrants. In the first decade of this century, productivity gains accounted for approximately 80 percent of total economic growth, up from 53 percent in the 1990s and 47 percent in the 1980s.[3]

As a result, economic growth in the coming decades will depend decisively on productivity growth. If we are to experience anything like the prosperity of the postwar era, our economy will need to be more productive than ever. Efficiency must be a watchword of our economic life, which means that our economic policies may well have to push even further in the direction of diffusion and deconsolidation (or diversification and specialization), rather than pushing back against them.

But man cannot live by efficiency alone. Some of the other challenges we have confronted in this century have been exacerbated by the push for a more efficient economy and by the broader diffusion of American life of which that push has been one facet. These challenges have posed serious obstacles to any growth agenda—and more importantly, to the ultimate goal of a flourishing society. And many of them have been functions of the persistence and extension of three key patterns we have been following: the weakening of our established institutions, a growing detachment from the traditional sources of order and structure in American life, and an intensifying bifurcation of ways of living.

Weakening institutions have certainly been a prominent feature of the past fifteen years. One crucial source of the intense unease that has shaped our twenty-first-century politics is the widespread sense that major American institutions just don't work very well anymore. This view has not always been justified—on the whole, our indescribably complex society functions remarkably well. But it is often justified when it comes to the established public and private institutions that managed much of our national life at midcentury.

We have been following the decline of many such *private* institutions through the course of the previous two chapters. The large, bureaucratic, near-monopolistic corporations that commanded the key sectors of America's economy after World War II, thanks to an arrangement with big labor and big government, began to give way in the 1970s to more nimble competitors, and in the subsequent decades, amid deregulation and more intense competition, they either evolved or died.[4]

In a few important sectors that are especially dominated by government (particularly education and health care), some older, bureaucratic, noncompetitive institutions continue to dominate. But in most of the private economy, they have long since lost their sway, and those that have kept something of their original forms (like the big three automakers) have frequently been models of sclerosis.[5]

But the truest models of sclerosis in our time are the *public* institutions that hail from the era of consolidation. These are the centralized, bureaucratized programs and agencies at all levels of government (from Medicare to state welfare agencies to large school districts, among many others) that persist in the model of midcentury technocracy. They have been able to resist evolutionary pressures to change because they truly do possess some monopolistic powers in their domains, and because the continuing hold of midcentury ideas on our political imagination has sustained them.[6]

This century, however, has so far been marked by the continuing breakdown of these consolidated public institutions: the entitlement system built for the demographics of midcentury America, the civil-service system that is now among the only midcentury-style employers left, the regulatory architecture meant to manage a highly consolidated society from the center, and the technocratic instincts of modern government that incline to one-size-fits-all solutions. These are all very poorly suited to our diffuse and decentralizing society, and they are all in varying states of dysfunction.

These institutions have not kept pace with our changing society, but because our political debates are themselves deeply nostalgic, we tend to argue about whether such institutions should be kept as they are or government should be rolled back to what it was before they existed—neither of which looks very plausible. Conservatives, in particular, have too rarely seen that moving forward from the liberal welfare state (toward a set of leaner, decentralized, market-oriented safety net programs better suited to our deconsolidated society) could well advance our causes better than moving backward from it, even if such a reversal were possible.

As a result, the public's trust in many different types of institutions has continued to decline in this century. Trust in the federal government has been falling rapidly, under presidents and Congresses of both parties. Trust in the traditional professions (for example, the medical and legal professions) and in almost all large institutions (major corporations, the mainstream media, the academy, hospitals, banks, and many others) has continued to fall as well.[7]

As this decline in trust has persisted, so has a second major trend we have been following: detachment from some core sources of social order and meaning. The most damaging form of this estrangement involves its own kind of institutional breakdown—in this case of the family, our foremost social institution. Although rates of teen pregnancy, abortion, and drug abuse have declined since the 1990s, out-of-wedlock birth rates have remained extremely high, and family breakdown, especially among lower-income Americans, has persisted and in some respects intensified. On the whole, the American family has continued to grow weaker in this century.[8]

Meanwhile, attachment to the labor force, especially among men, has been falling further and faster. Men's overall labor-force participation rate was 74.3 percent in January 2000 and 68.8 percent in January 2015. (The rate for women declined as well, if somewhat less precipitously.) The place and promise of work in the lives of many Americans, especially those lacking higher education, has faded.[9]

Traditional attachments to local communities, to the extent they are measurable, and religious affiliation and practice have also continued their downward trajectories. The percentage of Americans reporting they were religiously unaffiliated, for instance, has been rising over the past decade and a half, reaching 23 percent by the middle of 2015, according to the Pew Research Center.[10]

In all of these ways, the twenty-first century has been an extension of the twentieth. The increasing detachment of Americans from core social institutions has exacerbated isolation and all of its attendant challenges.

There have also been some vitally important countervailing forces in this century. Declining teen pregnancy and abortion rates are hardly insignificant. American religion has diversified and deconsolidated, but this means it has also kept up with changes in the culture. Although its forms are changing, it remains a powerful and constructive social force. And while traditional community attachments may have frayed, new technologies—empowered especially by the Internet—have created entirely new kinds of communities, linking people across vast distances and establishing new social norms and practices, with the usual human mix of edification and wretchedness.

The Internet has also created new economic opportunities and empowered people in ways unthinkable just two decades ago. It is particularly well suited to our individualist, deconsolidated way of life. In some respects, the Internet embodies the kind of society we are in the process of becoming: it is decentralized, personalized, and individualized. It possesses few large centers of authority and few strong mediating institutions, but many distinct, narrow circles of trust. It is well suited to chosen engagement and the creation of broad but shallow social networks, but poorly suited to reinforcing unchosen obligations and deep relational ties. Indeed, it would be easy to imagine that the Internet has *created* the forces pushing in this direction in our time, because they are now so often most powerfully in evidence in our online lives. But as we have seen, these are forces that have been building for decades. They have merely found a natural home in the new virtual world of the Internet.

As it always does, then, life in our country has been becoming both better and worse in this century. But the sum of these changes has tended to leave Americans anxious and uneasy. The good, so far, has not seemed capable of outweighing the bad. And it all seems to be the direct result—a kind of logical conclusion—of the process of diffusion that we have been following. The estrangement of growing numbers of Americans from the social institutions that long anchored American life has led to the emergence of sharp bifurcations (of poverty and wealth, power and powerlessness, order and disorder) between the top and bottom of our society.

After the decline of the public's trust in institutions and the general detachment from sources of social order, this pattern of bifurcation is the third of the major postwar trends persisting and intensifying in this century. It is the dark side of the flowering of diversity, the profusion of lifestyle choices, and the explosion of opportunities for personalization and customization that have also defined twenty-first-century America. The powerful forces pushing each American to become more like himself or herself tend particularly to hollow out the middle of our society and therefore to create greater distances between the ends. So while our society is much less consolidated on the whole, it is still (and in some respects more than ever) subject to the ill effects of concentrations of power. American life is still highly concentrated—just not in the middle (in ways that might pull us together), but instead at both ends (in ways that pull us apart).

This observation points to a distinction worth highlighting between *centralization* and *concentration*. In economic, cultural, and social terms, American society has clearly grown less centralized in the past half-century and more. The large, established institutions of the economy are less significant; the elite cultural mainstream is less powerful and has far less of a monopoly over its domain; and the two large political parties are no longer bound together in a broad consensus, and each has grown less powerful itself. But this has meant that although the nation as a whole has grown more diverse and fractured, the differences that have emerged among Americans have themselves bunched together in a telltale pattern of what I would call not just bifurcation, but *bifurcated concentration.*

Thus, centralization has diminished, but concentration has not gone away. Obviously, centralization can and does lead to concentrations of power, wealth, and opinion, as well as to particularly harmful, confining, and insidious constraints on freedom and progress. But diffusion and individualism, if allowed to work themselves out, reintroduce some of the dangers of concentration combined with new and challenging features.

So, for instance, while economic power is less centralized than it used to be, our economy now evinces both more concentrated wealth and more concentrated poverty. This set of trends is often (if crudely) grouped under the rubric of *inequality*. And economic bifurcation has expressed itself in more than just income disparities. Throughout the economy, centralization and concentration have become very different and distinct forces. Thus, for example, while in some respects we have a greater profusion of economic actors than we used to, the biggest companies in America are actually the fastest-growing companies in our time.[11]

Owing to the nature of decentralization in our culture and economy, dependent as it has been on the Internet and related information technologies, the companies that provide our technology infrastructure—Google, Apple, and others—have grown particularly large and dominant. They command vast stores of personalized information, and their access to that data gives them concentrated power that prior generations of economic giants could hardly have dreamt of, even as the information economy continues to decentralize.

The same pattern is evident well beyond the technology sector. Decentralization has not toppled the giants in our economy. Far from it. Walmart and other big-box retailers have continued to put mom-and-pop stores out of business. This century has so far been much better for America's largest companies than for its small businesses. But it has been particularly challenging for those in the middle. We have witnessed the simultaneous growth of the giants and the dwarves—large companies and tiny small businesses. (In time we might also see a tendency toward independent contract work over traditional employee arrangements.)[12]

We can see similar trends in the political world. The institutional strength of the political parties has greatly diminished, but the ideological (and also demographic and even geographic) differences between them have grown greater, yielding a set of trends often grouped under the rubric of *polarization*. The ends of our political continuum have grown more concentrated and intense, while the middle has tended to empty out.

Growing concentration and diminishing centralization are therefore not opposite forces, but increasingly complementary patterns in our time—both embodied in the bifurcation of American life. This peculiar combination is closely related to the tendency (which turned up several times in the historical overview of the previous two chapters) toward a greater centralization of power in the federal government to accompany greater individualism in the culture and economy. Increasingly, society consists of individuals and a national state, while the mediating institutions—family, community, church, unions, and others—fade and falter. Again, we find concentration at the ends and a growing vacuum in the middle.

Such bifurcated concentration also involves a kind of constriction of movement or change—a sense in which everyone is always in the process of becoming more like what they already are. This phenomenon presents itself as more constrained mobility in our economy, as a growing rigidity in politics, and as a narrowing of the radius of trust in the larger society.

The Internet has facilitated a similar set of trends in our social lives—hollowing out the middle while concentrating the ends. It allows us to stay in constant contact with our family and closest friends, and also to build loose networks with people around the nation and the world who might share a single interest or hobby, but at the expense of the more middling relationships we might otherwise have had with some of the people who constitute our actual real-world *communities*.

Political scientist Marc Dunkelman has chronicled this pattern. "Why hang out with the random assortment that frequents the neighborhood pub," he writes, "when you can join a discussion group comprised exclusively of people who share your love of crochet? . . . Why endure the mixed membership of the local Kiwanis club when you can fundraise and kibitz online with activists who share precisely your vision of political change?" Thus, for perfectly sensible reasons, our approach to socialization and friendship takes on the form of bifurcated concentrations rather than a capacious middle space, limiting our exposure to different points of view while intensifying our commitments to our own points of view.[13]

This pattern is evident in the broader culture, too, and in ways that are closely related to economic and social bifurcation. While our mainstream cultural institutions matter less than they used to, that stream has been dividing into tributaries in which intense subcultures exert great power over subsets of the larger society. Americans tend to have fewer truly mass cultural experiences in common but to inhabit more intense and distinct subcultures.[14]

Different socioeconomic classes of Americans are also leading increasingly disparate lives. When you break down American society into those who have a college education and those who do not, for instance, you find some astonishing and often growing distinctions. These are the kinds of differences and distances that some of the diagnosticians of our current dilemmas (most notably, in recent years, Charles Murray and Robert Putnam) tend to highlight in contrasting American life today with decades past. And the pattern, again, is one of bifurcated concentrations: increasingly distinct ends and a thinner middle.[15]

Attachment to work is, perhaps most predictably, closely linked to educational attainment. In June 2015, well into the economic recovery, 74.1 percent of college graduates over the age of twenty-five were in the workforce, compared to just 56.9 percent of those in that age group with only a high school diploma.[16]

But the same is true of social indicators, which are not nearly so closely tied to the direct benefits of educational attainment. Marriage rates are now significantly higher among college-educated Americans than among those without a college degree, for instance. And increasingly, Americans are self-sorting according to education and income—so that, for example, US Census Bureau data show that 71 percent of college graduates who got married in 2011 married another college graduate.[17]

Divorce rates evince the same pattern. Couples without college degrees who were married in the early 2000s had divorce rates roughly 50 percent higher by 2014 than their counterparts with college degrees. And similar trends are evident in family formation statistics more broadly. The most notable example may be out-of-wedlock childbearing: between 2006 and 2010, 68 percent of women without a high school degree who gave birth were not married, 41 percent of women with a high school degree but no college degree who gave birth were unmarried, while only *6 percent* of women with college degrees who gave birth were unmarried.[18]

Measures of religious attendance tell much the same story. Perhaps surprisingly, more educated Americans are significantly more attached to traditional religious institutions. University of Virginia sociologist W. Bradford Wilcox has found that church attendance has declined twice as fast among Americans with no more than a high school diploma as among those with a college degree in recent decades. University of Nebraska sociologist Philip Schwadel, examining data from the General Social Survey, found that with each additional year of education, the likelihood of attending religious services increased by 15 percent.[19]

These figures are not best understood as a case for increasing college attendance (though the case for doing that is surely strong). Rather, educational attainment in these numbers stands in for social class and economic status. These figures show that Americans at the top are living far more stable lives, and are much more firmly attached to our core social institutions, than Americans at the bottom today, and that these differences are growing. The basic experience of American life looks remarkably different at these different ends of our society. And there is less and less of a middle between them.

In this realm and in general, such bifurcation is without question a defining feature of twenty-first-century America. And it looks to be massively overdetermined—driven further and harder by almost every one of the many implications of America's diffusion and fracture. Growing income inequality, which has been a function in part of otherwise highly beneficial economic liberalization, has certainly meant growing differences in lifestyle and opportunity at the top and bottom. The great sorting, which has continued apace in our time and for rational and understandable reasons, has put the wealthy and the poor at greater distance, both literally and figuratively. An enormous influx of immigration, which has increased diversity and done some real economic good for our country, has also thinned our common social capital and increased the burdens on our safety net and social policy—further exacerbating differences and distances.

The liberalization of cultural mores, which has allowed many Americans to live as they choose without sanction or stigma, has also driven a polarization in family-formation patterns and their attendant benefits and burdens. The long-term breakdown of our broad political consensus and the sharpening ideological identities of the two major parties have allowed for a more ideal-driven politics that better represents our most intensely engaged citizens, but they have also meant greater political polarization that has turned already heated debates into veritable war zones. And the growing specialization of our economy has increasingly left us with high-end and low-end jobs but fewer opportunities for middle-skill, middle-pay, middle-class employment. Again and again, we find this hollowing out of the middle and greater concentrations at both ends—the characteristic pattern of the twenty-first-century American experience.[20]

Our republic has become deeply fractured, and our politicians have struggled to pin the blame for this phenomenon somewhere without fully acknowledging its character. The Left sees economic inequality as the root of all other forms of social fracturing, and argues therefore that a policy of more aggressive redistribution would not only help ease income inequality but also mitigate the political power of the wealthy, strengthen poor communities and families, and create more opportunities for all. An emphasis on cultural problems like family breakdown, many liberals suggest, is a distraction from these real causes—if not an attempt to blame the victims and opportunistically advance an oppressive cultural agenda that can only further burden the most disadvantaged.

The Right sees cultural disintegration and polarization—marked by dysfunction at the bottom and reinforced by a loss of cultural self-confidence at the top—as the source of the persistence of entrenched poverty in America. Conservatives therefore argue that social policy must focus on family and community, and worry that the Left's misguided, if not opportunistic, efforts to address entrenched poverty through greater economic redistribution can only make things worse by hampering the economy, distorting the personal choices of the disadvantaged with perverse incentives, and exacerbating dependency.

In an effort to avoid the (rather obvious) conclusion that cultural and economic factors are inseparable, liberals and conservatives tend to exaggerate the implications of their favored explanation. They predict that either growing inequality or increasing family and cultural breakdown, respectively, will turn out to be unsustainable, and so lead to a cataclysm, or a rip in the social fabric that will force a great reckoning.

But things are likely both better and worse than that: Both growing inequality and increasing social breakdown may well be sustainable, but may not be compatible with human flourishing. We are not headed for a cataclysm, but we are stuck in a rut, and getting out of it will require understanding it. No moment of change will be forced upon us, so if we are to revive the fortunes of the least among us, we will need to act.

Our debates about whether culture or economics ultimately matters most keep us from seeing what kind of action might be plausible. These debates often implicitly revolve around the question of whether we should attempt a reversal of the profound diffusion and decentralization of the past half-century and more in the economic sphere (as the Left would prefer) or the social sphere (as the Right would like), when the fact is that we stand little chance of any wholesale reversal in either realm. This leaves us with a politics of dual denial: in any given policy debate, one party (be it Republicans on cultural matters or Democrats in economics) denies the fact that the diffusion of our society is a dominant and essentially irreversible fact about contemporary America, while the other party denies that this fact entails some very significant problems.

This pattern suggests a broad and deep failure of self-understanding—and perhaps, above all, a failure to grasp precisely the social, cultural, economic, and political dynamics of America's postwar evolution. It is a failure that has much to do with the blinding nostalgia with which we began, and that has shaped and sharpened the unease and disorientation of twenty-first-century America. This is where a half-century and more of fragmentation and fracture, or liberalization and diffusion, has left us.

THIS CHAPTER AND THE TWO before it have of course offered only a brief and partial telling of our recent history, focused as they are on a few key trends. The intent has not been to be comprehensive, but to trace some particular threads and patterns that are too easily obscured by our nostalgia for the 1950s and 1960s, in order to better understand our own time.

Pulling tight those threads that emerge from this overview leaves us with four key lessons to consider above all.

First, across a wide range of different facets of our national life, the past century has seen a pattern of *drawing together and then pulling apart.* American society became intensely consolidated and cohesive as it modernized through the middle of the twentieth century, and then more diverse and diffuse.

We might illustrate this pattern in many different ways, but perhaps three distinct representations will suffice to help us see its broad outlines. In the social arena, we would want some measure of the diversity of our society as it has changed over time. The percentage of Americans born abroad is one plausible metric on that front, and as tracked by the US Census Bureau over the past century or so it reveals a pattern of dramatic change (see Figure 4.1).

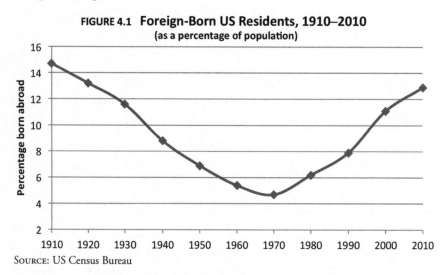

FIGURE 4.1 Foreign-Born US Residents, 1910–2010
(as a percentage of population)

SOURCE: US Census Bureau

In the political arena, there is probably no similarly convenient metric, but a measure of polarization will provide one gauge of unity and disparity in our democracy. Examining party loyalty in congressional roll-call votes over more than a century, political scientists Nolan McCarty, Keith T. Poole, and Howard Rosenthal crafted an ingenious index that quantifies party polarization in Congress, and the picture it provides gestures toward a similar pattern (see Figure 4.2).

FIGURE 4.2 **Party Polarization in Congress, 1910–2010**

SOURCE: Nolan McCarty, Keith T. Poole, and Howard Rosenthal, *Polarized America: The Dance of Ideology and Unequal Riches* (Cambridge, MA: MIT Press, 2006). Figures updated by the authors in 2010.

In the economic arena, the most commonly used measure of polarization and cohesion is income inequality. Debates have long raged about exactly what figures best represent the relevant facts about inequality, but a measure of the proportion of all income earned by the top 1 percent of earners has been commonly used to stand in for overall trends. Economists Thomas Piketty and Emmanuel Saez have used income-tax data to track that percentage over the past century (see Figure 4.3).

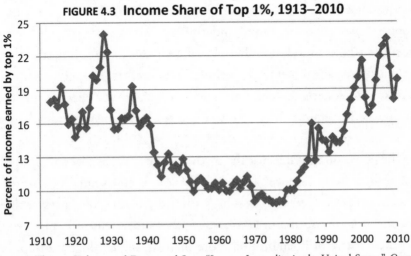

FIGURE 4.3 **Income Share of Top 1%, 1913–2010**

SOURCE: Thomas Piketty and Emmanuel Saez, "Income Inequality in the United States," *Quarterly Journal of Economics* 118, no. 1 (2003). Figures updated by the authors in 2013.

In all three cases, and many others that have followed a similar trajectory, what we see are very significant changes, not slight ups and downs. They tell a tale of intense consolidation followed by intense diffusion.[21]

To describe the broad pattern in these terms is not to render judgment on it. As we have seen, drawing together meant greater solidarity and order but also stricter boundaries of exclusion and intense pressures to conform—more unity but less dynamism and freedom. Pulling apart has meant sharper differences, but also more diversity, variety, and choice—more individual liberty but less cohesion, structure, and common purpose.

Second, this pattern shows us that midcentury America straddled two broad trends, which surely contributed to its exceptional character. It experienced the liberalization of a consolidated society. Many Americans in that time could therefore take for granted some of the benefits of consolidation (such as relatively stable families and communities, confidence in institutions, a sense of national purpose, modest inequality, a broad moral consensus, and robust cultural cohesion) while actively combatting some of its least attractive downsides (like institutional racism, sexism, overbearing cultural conformity, and a dearth of economic freedom). Combined with America's unique global economic position following World War II, this made for a period of unprecedented prosperity and confidence.

But it was an inherently unstable and unsustainable combination of circumstances. The liberalization that was so important to the character of postwar America was bound to undermine—indeed, was intended to undermine—the consolidation that played a no less important part in forming that unusual moment. Over time, therefore, the change became the context, and Americans could no longer take stability, cohesion, and self-confidence for granted as a counterforce to their growing individualism and dynamism.

The powerful nostalgia for the 1950s and early 1960s that so dominates our politics is, in essence, a longing for a safe and stable backdrop for various forms of liberalization—be it toward a culture of expressive individualism or toward market economics. But Americans have plainly valued these forms of liberalization more than we valued the backdrop, and it is folly now to wish we could recapture the very circumstances that

America has been systematically demolishing for six decades and more just so we could more comfortably engage in the very same demolition.

Midcentury America has a lot to teach us about what we ought to value: we should want to enjoy the best of both stability and dynamism, diversity and cohesion, opportunity and prosperity—even knowing that these goods will always be in tension and that any balance we achieve among them will always be precarious. But midcentury America does not tell us very much about *how* to best achieve such a balance now, given the kind of society that decades of liberalization have made us.

Third, that kind of society is a diffuse and still diffusing democracy, and this fact must help shape our understanding of both the problems we confront and any plausible solutions. This diffusion is, to borrow Alexis de Tocqueville's description of equality in early nineteenth-century America, a "generative fact" of our particular time. It can be channeled and directed, perhaps mitigated at the margins, but it cannot be meaningfully reversed, at least in the foreseeable future. Any policy that relies on significantly counteracting it is likely to prove foolhardy. No one can claim to see the future, of course, but the available signs all suggest we are not at the end of the age of diffusion.

Grasping that our societal diffusion cannot simply be undone means we must also understand that the most serious problems we face are not just obstacles to our pursuit of our society's highest hopes, but also consequences of that pursuit. They are the price of progress. In liberating many individuals from oppressive social constraints, we have also estranged many from their families and unmoored them from their communities, work, and faith. In accepting a profusion of options in every part of our lives to meet our particular needs and wants, we have also unraveled the established institutions of an earlier era, and with it the public's broader faith in institutions of all kinds. In loosening the reins of cultural conformity and national identity and opening ourselves to an immense diversity of cultures, we have weakened the roots of mutual trust. In unleashing markets to meet the needs and wants of consumers, we have freed them also to treat workers as dispensable and interchangeable. In pursuing meritocracy, we have magnified inequality. In looking for a more personalized, representative politics, we have propelled polarization. In seeking to treat every person equally and individually rather than forcing all to conform, we have accentuated and concentrated the differences between the top and bottom in our society, and hollowed out the middle.

In all of these ways and more, as patterns of diffusion evolve into patterns of bifurcated concentration, we have done more than change the structures of institutions and relationships. We have altered the shapes of lives and souls. We have set loose a scourge of loneliness and isolation that we are still afraid to acknowledge as the distinct social dysfunction of our age of individualism, just as a crushing conformity was the characteristic scourge of an era of cohesion and national unity.

And yet, for all that, this is not an indictment of our time. We could surely make the case that the benefits of all of this in personal freedom, wealth, justice, and happiness have been worth the costs. But that does not release us from the obligation to confront the costs, and to do what we can to address them. And that obligation, in turn, does not negate the obstinate, insurmountable reality of our era—our commitment to individualism and to deconsolidation.

All of this means, to paraphrase James Madison, that we must seek diffusing, individualist remedies for the diseases most incident to a diffuse, individualist society. And this is why midcentury nostalgia will not do as a guide for action in our time. To be effective, attractive, and durable in twenty-first-century America, the political, cultural, and economic solutions we pursue need to be indigenous to twenty-first-century America.[22]

Our constitutional system, built to be resilient, flexible, and realistic about human limitations, allows for a variety of dispositions and approaches to public policy in changing times. But our welfare state is not similarly adaptable. Largely constructed between the mid-1930s and the mid-1960s, and drawing on a political outlook that arose in response to the consolidating pressures of modernization, it is a relic of an earlier America with a different attitude, different problems, and a different set of expectations than our own. Using it as a template for policy now is a recipe for gross inefficiency, unpopularity, dysfunction, and failure.[23]

The corporatism of that earlier America is also not well suited to our time. The idea that big government, big labor, and big business working together will responsibly meet the nation's needs simply defies belief in an individualistic, decentralized, dynamic, networked America. Just as an earlier era required a politics of consolidation to match an economically and culturally consolidating society, our time requires a politics of decentralization and customization to address the challenges of a diffusing society in that society's own terms.

Younger Americans are growing up amid a profusion of options in every realm of life, with far more choice but far less predictability and security. Dynamism is increasingly driven not by economies of scale but by competitively driven marginal improvements. Our culture is becoming a sea of subcultures. Sources of information, entertainment, and education are proliferating. Practical solutions to the problems this dynamic society faces will need to conform to this broader ecosystem of American life—just as the big, centralized, one-size-fits-all industrial model of the welfare state did in its time.

Fourth and finally, key to understanding what this modernized approach to our problems might look like is grasping the further point that the diffusion and polarization of our national life have involved the hollowing out of the middle layers of American society and the American experience. The solutions we seek will often involve a recovery and reinforcement of those middle layers, advanced by means that are friendly to diffusion, diversity, and decentralization. This will mean pushing back against both individualism and statism. Rather than conceiving of our politics as a war between those two extremes, we should see it as an effort to open up the space between them—the space where a free society can genuinely thrive.

Individualism involves the corrosion of people's sense of themselves as defined by a variety of strong affiliations and unchosen bonds and its replacement by a sense that all connections are matters of individual choice and preference. It breaks up clusters of people into more isolated individuals held together by more casual affinities and more utilitarian relationships—each best understood in relation to the needs and wants of the

. Politically, such individualism tends to weaken mediating _nters_ that stand between the individual and the nation as a w... from families to local communities (including local governments), religious institutions, fraternal bodies, civil-society organizations, labor groups, and the small and medium-sized businesses that make up much of the private economy. In their place, it strengthens individuals, on the one hand, and a central government, on the other, since such a government is most able to treat individuals equally by treating them all impersonally. For this reason, a hyper-individualist culture is likely to be governed by a hyper-centralized government, and each is likely to exacerbate the worst inclinations of the other.

It is vital to see, too, that the middle layers of society had already been weakened by the modernizing, consolidating forces of the early twentieth century, even before our age of individualism began to tear at them. Both in an era of national consolidation and in an age of individualist diffusion, the mediating institutions of family, community, and civil society have been under heavy stress—first pulled from above, as it were, and then pulled from below. A vision of society that consists of isolated individuals and a national state undermines these middle layers in both respects. But the damage has become most evident only as the age of diffusion has worked itself out—as the increasing breakdown of national institutions has left many people without even local, interpersonal institutions to fall back on, since these have now been enervated for a century.[24]

Some of the most distinctive problems of our era—the detachment from family, work, faith, and community, and the persistent patterns of bifurcated concentration throughout the American experience—are in important respects functions of a view of society as consisting only of individuals and a state, and it is particularly difficult for a nation that understands itself in that way to address them. That view of society, after all, itself advances precisely a form of bifurcated concentration, seeking to empower the individual and the central government and disempower everything in between.

The problems we confront therefore call for solutions that involve decentralization (since reconsolidation is not a real option in our time) and yet avoid this pattern of bifurcated concentration. That means they call out for a reinvigoration of the middle layers of society and a resuscitation of our mediating institutions. Those institutions may be the ones most capable of addressing the characteristic problems of our diffusing society—and the isolation and loneliness that are such prominent symptoms of so many of those problems—without requiring the kind of wholesale national reconsolidation and recentralization that simply are no longer plausible. They offer diversity without atomism, profusion without isolation, and a great variety of ways of life without estrangement from the sources of human flourishing.

The need to reinforce these institutions makes *subsidiarity*—the entrusting of power and authority to the lowest and least centralized institutions capable of using them well—a key to addressing the particular problems of our age of individualism. The empowerment of a diverse array of mediating institutions, as opposed to a single, central national authority, was always one important way of dealing with the multiplicity and diffusion of American life before the intense consolidation of the early twentieth century, and modernized forms of that approach to social life must now come to serve that purpose again.

Subsidiarity can allow for a pluralism of communities, and so avoid the worst excesses of both conformism and individualism. It can liberate people to pursue the good as they understand it together with others who share their understanding. But precisely by enabling people to be ensconced in a dense web of community, rather than being alone in the great mass of the public, it can also afford them the opportunity to benefit from moral order and structure and from the aid and love and support that can only be extended at the level of the person.

The century of history we have reviewed witnessed a dual rejection of and assault on this approach to American life (from national consolidation and then from individualism) and has left us with a dual problem: a loss of order in the lives of many individuals, and a loss of diversity in the means by which we govern ourselves. We have hollowed out the institutions that might stand some chance of better enabling us to balance order and diversity, or freedom and stability.

The distinctly modern (or perhaps postmodern) challenges America now confronts are thus the challenges of a hollow polity. An effective and appropriate response that does not surrender more than we have to of what we have gained, yet still goes some distance toward healing what is broken and recovering what is lost, will involve drawing people back into the middle layers, and doing so in a twenty-first-century way: by offering choices and options there. This is what it would mean to move forward from our troubles and unease, rather than yearning in vain to go back.

THESE FOUR CONCLUSIONS ABOUT OUR past and present point toward an agenda for renewal. But as we will see, it will not be easy for anyone in our politics to pursue that agenda. Our politics of competing nostalgias often translates into a fight between individualism and statism that neglects the middle layers of society: the Right wants unmitigated economic individualism but a return to common moral norms. The Left wants unrestrained moral individualism but economic consolidation. Both will need to come to terms with some uncomfortable realities of twenty-first-century America.

The Left will need to come to terms with the fact that the modern US economy is a deconsolidated economy, in which union power is diminished, high inequality is a reality, centrifugal cultural and economic pressures interact to keep mobility low, and large, centralized federal programs (the last, vestigial remnants of the old consolidated American order) are a very poor fit for how people live.

That means liberals must think about the role that government might play in providing greater economic security and fairness in terms of offering more options to a society that will brook no fewer. It means they must see that cultural liberation has real costs, especially for the most vulnerable. And it means they must look at our mediating institutions not as threats or as relics of prejudice and backwardness, but as partners and as constructive means of change.

For the Right, taking these lessons seriously and defining an agenda for the future would be a little easier. Modern conservatism has frequently (though far from always) emphasized the mediating institutions of society and resisted both radical individualism and wholesale centralization, and so will have more to offer in the coming years. But the Right, too, will have a great deal of adjusting and learning to do.

Conservatives will need to better come to terms, for instance, with the fact that modern American society is highly diverse, individualistic, dynamic, and deconsolidated, and that a significant degree of cultural fracturing, family breakdown, and estrangement from tradition and religion—not unrelated to our economic dynamism—is a fact of life. This means conservatives should think about preserving the preconditions for moral living in terms of building cohesive, attractive, moral *subcultures* in those mediating layers of society, rather than just struggling for control of the old institutions of a once-consolidated "mainstream" culture. It means focusing inward and close to home. And it means the Right must take note of the ways in which the distinct problems of our age are as much challenges of dissolution as of concentration, and therefore that the conservative struggle against the scourge of statism should more frequently employ a vocabulary of middling communitarianism rather than of radical individualism.

It also means recognizing that capitalism depends upon some very demanding cultural preconditions and yet frequently undermines those very preconditions, so that its very preservation demands some limits on its freedom to shape our society in its image. And it means seeing that gigantism in the economy is not much less pernicious than gigantism in government—so that a conservatism of the mediating institutions will need to combat the ways in which big corporations (sometimes working together with big government) consolidate their power over workers and consumers and restrict the very competition and dynamism to which friends of the market ought to be devoted.

These sets of pressures on liberals and conservatives, respectively, are closely related, since the nostalgia-driven blindness of the Left and the Right are close kin, too. No one in our politics will find the coming years very easy. America is more divided and diverse than we are used to imagining. Our national government is over-institutionalized, heavily indebted, and frequently dysfunctional. Too many Americans are detached from some core sources and channels of human flourishing—family, work, faith, and community. The challenges of governing are great. But they are made even greater than they have to be by our inability to grasp our circumstances as they are.

And yet, although we have grown less cohesive and unified, not everything has changed about America. We are, as Americans always have been, living in the midst of change. But we are also, as we always have been, blessed with a great political and cultural inheritance, with enormous strengths, and with a history of adjusting to great change. America is still America. Most of what we have always known about ourselves remains as relevant as ever and should continue to inform us. And high among the timeless facets of the American character that will serve us well in the coming years is our inveterate inventiveness in ways of living. Americans adjust to pressure, and are clearly already adjusting to the pressures of the present age.

We are uneasy. And unease leads men and women to seek change, to innovate, to build on the best that they have and to uproot the worst. The economy, the culture, and the politics of a free society are built to respond to unease with experimentation at the margins that ultimately leads to action and to change. Our keen sense of our own unease does not mean that we are stuck, therefore. It means that we are already moving. But where, and how?

PART II

THE NEXT AMERICA

5

THE UNBUNDLED MARKET

ADAM SMITH'S *THE WEALTH OF NATIONS*, the first guidebook to capitalism, opens with this simple observation:

> The greatest improvements in the productive powers of labour, and the greater part of the skill, dexterity, or judgment with which it is any-where directed or applied, seem to have been the effects of the division of labour.[1]

The very first thing to notice about the market economy, Smith told his late eighteenth-century readers, was that *specialization* lay at its core. Observers of America's early twenty-first-century economy could hardly do better than to begin from this insight.

Specialization is in a sense the economic equivalent of the trends we have been tracking: the historic shift toward diffusion, diversity, fracturing, and individualism and away from consolidation, conformity, cohesion, and solidarity. Specialization replaces the generally able worker with the narrowly skilled expert, the integrated firm with the dedicated contractor, and the ethic of self-sufficiency with the logic of comparative advantage.

A great many of the changes, good and bad, that our economy is undergoing in this century are functions of intensifying specialization. And many of the economic and social policy reforms we now require will therefore need to be forms of specialization too. One-size-fits-all universal programs suited to a consolidating society should give way to more narrowly tailored, leaner, local and personal, bottom-up systems of protections and supports suited to a dynamic and diverse society.

We must use specialization to fight the negative effects of specialization. Thinking through how this might work is a crucial task for our politics in the coming years. It is a task that could sharpen and strengthen both the Left and the Right in different ways. But as things now stand, neither is particularly well placed to understand our economic challenges as functions of a largely irreversible fragmentation or specialization, and therefore to offer plausible responses. Each remains, in its own way, mired in the past.

BECAUSE BOTH DEMOCRATS AND REPUBLICANS now tend to see the world through a veil of nostalgia, they both characterize the contemporary American economy in terms of falling away from a glorious past, or at least straying from a successful path.

Each has its own version of that story, of course. On the Left, it is the story of an America that was on its way toward becoming a thoroughgoing social democracy but was pushed off that course by a misguided gang of free-market fanatics. In January 2015, the Center for American Progress, a liberal think tank in Washington, DC, assigned a commission of academics and former public officials from the Left (led by former Harvard president and Obama and Clinton administration economic adviser Lawrence Summers) to produce an economic agenda that might inform what Democrats offer the country in the 2016 election. The commission's report opens with a kind of narrative economic history that hews to a general form we can well recognize by now:

In the decades following World War II, the advanced industrial economies experienced rapid growth and brought an increasing share of households into prosperity. With these changes came a revolution in living standards. Hundreds of millions of people across developed countries were able to work and gain economic security through higher salaries and a series of benefits provided either directly through employers or through government social security systems. Most households came to believe that hard work and careful planning would deliver heightened levels of security for themselves and opportunity for their children, year after year. It was possible for ordinary families to enjoy better housing, and health care, and a secure retirement, and to provide their children with higher education and the prospect of economic opportunity as incomes rose broadly as the economy grew.

By the end of the 1970s, inflation and unemployment seemed out of control. In the 1980s, conservative leaders such as Ronald Reagan and Margaret Thatcher came to power with an anti-government agenda of market fundamentalism and individualism. Measures of inequality, which had been stable or declining, began to increase.[2]

I have not removed any transitional paragraph or other text from this quoted passage—the report's opening narrative history does not pause over just what happened between the emergence of the exemplary postwar economy and the rise of inflation and unemployment. It seeks only to make it clear that our problems began in the 1970s and have persisted. While it later strives mightily to give President Bill Clinton some credit for pursuing a different path, the report ultimately describes our economy as having followed a long downward trajectory since the midcentury golden age.

This is the dominant economic narrative of today's progressives: that our economy has been failing most Americans for forty years, leaving wages stagnant and working families falling behind. In February 2015, Jason Furman, chairman of President Obama's Council of Economic Advisers, argued that the key priority of policymakers should be "to address a long-standing challenge for the US economy—the 40-year stagnation in incomes for the middle class and those working to get into the middle class." In a 2015 report for the progressive Roosevelt Institute, economist

Joseph Stiglitz similarly argued that "for the promise of innovation to be realized, we must first solve the legacy of problems left to us by 35 years of supply-side thinking and the corresponding set of rules that has reshaped all aspects of our economy and society."[3]

Their proposed solution, needless to say, is in essence to reinstate the economic arrangements of the postwar decades. In order to present the Left's long-standing agenda as the cure for what ails us, progressives need to describe the entirety of the period since that agenda was last dominant as a disastrous failure for America.

But that description is simply wrong in crucial respects, and leaves the Left painting a preposterously gloomy picture of America's relatively recent past. The 1980s and 1990s saw a significant economic boom in America, which meaningfully raised the living standards not only of the wealthy but also of the middle class and the poor. Inflation was reined in, incomes rose—albeit not as swiftly as they had in the 1950s and 1960s—and economic mobility was largely unchanged from the postwar boom years. Some of the basic elements of the Left's economic story—that growth in compensation lagged significantly behind growth in productivity for decades, that labor's share of income declined, that incomes fell or stagnated over that period, that mobility declined and the middle class was crushed— simply do not hold up.[4]

The twenty-first century has seen a significantly weaker economy, of course, but even in these years some of the problems progressives often point to (from a retirement-security crisis to rising economic uncertainty) have been wildly exaggerated. And over the span of the past four decades as a whole, middle-class incomes have risen by about 40 percent, and it would be difficult to argue that we have simply lived through a failed experiment. Even if it were possible to return to the midcentury economy, which it is not, it's not altogether clear that we would want to.[5]

This talking down of the past four decades of economic performance has some serious implications for progressive economic policy beyond its hearkening to midcentury America. It causes progressives to think that the American middle class is in far worse shape than it is, and at the same time it leaves them utterly dismissive of the potential of the modern economy to offer the poor reliable employment. Consequently, the left champions major expansions in the reach of public-assistance programs and rejects out of hand reforms of the welfare system that emphasize work or require some reciprocal obligations in return for benefits.[6]

Examples that argue against the Left's insistence on the economy's inability to provide work for lower-income Americans, such as the welfare reform of the 1990s or the recent experience of states that have limited the duration of unemployment benefits, are dismissed as aberrations from the norm of a fundamentally failed modern economy. Only the recovery of a set of far more strictly consolidated economic arrangements—the resurgence of powerful labor unions, stringent reregulation of the labor market, and government intrusion deep into the internal decisionmaking of firms, among other changes—is held out to offer much chance of relief. Liberals want the golden age to return, so they too often turn their backs on the resources the contemporary economy might offer us for addressing the real problems we confront.

But the standard conservative economic narrative is not much more plausible or complete. That story, too, is a tale of success interrupted. For the Right, the very period that the Left describes as the fall from grace is cast as an age of glory that we should now seek to emulate. And indeed, the 1980s and 1990s (though conservatives tend not to emphasize the latter decade) were a time of meaningful and fairly broadly shared prosperity and growth. But the lesson some Republicans draw from that history is that we should therefore replay the policy agenda of those decades to achieve the same result. They imply that it has all been undone, and we are back in the late 1970s. "One of the nice things about being very old," conservative economist Arthur Laffer told an interviewer in 2015, "is you can actually remember old time events. This is 1979 exactly."[7]

But the twenty-first century has not seen a return to the economic policies, tax rates, or regulatory regimes of the 1970s or earlier. In Washington, the elected branches have gone through nearly all the possible permutations of party control in the past fifteen years, so neither Left nor Right has really held the wheel for long. Tax rates declined modestly in 2001 and 2003 and then returned roughly to their 1990s levels in 2013.

Regulatory policy eased some in the Bush years and then grew far more constricted in the Obama years, when the government's control of the massive health sector and the scope of its energy and environmental regulation have also increased greatly. But the past decade and a half has not seen a reversal of the Reagan Revolution or of Bill Clinton's entrenchment of its essential elements.

The insistence by some conservatives that a return to the precise tax rates of the Reagan years is what would bring the roaring growth of those years back mistakes means for ends and elides vast differences in circumstances. It risks taking what were solutions to specific discrete problems of the late 1970s and treating them like abstract principles instead of concrete applications of principle to particular situations. The Reagan tax reforms were adapted to a moment when extremely high federal personal-income tax rates were plainly a primary obstacle to productivity and growth, and those reforms were part of a broader agenda, with other elements adapted to other particular challenges of that time (most notably hyperinflation).[8]

In our different time, even tax reform, let alone a broader economic agenda, would have to be different from Reagan's in order to advance the same principles and goals. Business taxes are now relatively greater barriers to growth than they were then, for instance, and payroll taxes represent a far greater portion of most people's tax burdens than they did in the 1980s. But even more important, tax policy in general is likely a relatively less significant obstacle to broadly shared growth than it was in an era of 70 percent tax rates, while other obstacles—including the aging of our population, pernicious overregulation, and the inefficiency of health-care and higher education financing—have emerged or grown relatively larger.

The urge to define today's problems as simply a reversal of Reagan-era achievements leaves many conservatives speaking to the public far too abstractly about economic policy. They paint in broad strokes an economy that could grow with gusto if only some straightforward, misguided restraints were removed. In casting this tale, Republicans fail to address what many people rightly experience as the real faults of today's economy—stagnant wages, rising health-care and education costs, insecure employment, and more—as well as much of what seems in fact to be holding back prosperity.

The competing nostalgias of the Left and Right lead to a kind of unreality in many debates about the economy. The Left distorts and exaggerates America's economic problems and the Right discounts or ignores them. So what are they missing? What are those problems?

The trends summarized in chapters 2 through 4 cannot reveal everything about our economic challenges, needless to say. But they can clarify a crucial point: the core of what our bipartisan nostalgia obscures has to do with the effects of persistent diffusion and diversification—which in this case involves especially the effects of an intensifying specialization in our economic life. The story of the modern US economy is not really a story of success interrupted, or of advance and reversal, but of this everescalating tendency in our national life. As long as both liberals and conservatives fail to grasp this process and its implications, they will remain incapable of speaking effectively to some of the public's most basic economic concerns.

ONE OF THE MOST EXTRAORDINARY features of America's midcentury economy was its simultaneous expansion of the high-skill, mid-skill, and low-skill segments of the labor market. In the decades after World War II, the United States was the world's foremost manufacturing powerhouse, its principal agricultural producer, the leading edge of the emerging service economy, and home to the most advanced scientific and technological breakthroughs in almost every subfield of science, engineering, medicine, and computing.

This dominance was as much a function of the relative weakness of America's economic competitors in the wake of the war as of America's own exceptional postwar character, but both were important. We had an all-purpose economy (large parts of which were dominated by some enormous, vertically integrated, multipurpose firms) and an extraordinarily broad labor market.

Those days are over. The scope of our strength, and the extent of our labor market, have narrowed for a series of reasons that we tend to regard as individual structural transformations but that can also be understood as different facets of increasing specialization. Simply put, much about America's all-purpose economy, for all its strengths, was actually a function of inefficiency resulting from the constrained character of the global economy and the consolidated nature of American life in those decades. As that balance has changed, America's all-purpose economy has come to concentrate more on its strengths—to the benefit of some but not others in our society.

Four kinds of structural transformations in the economy are particularly relevant in this regard: globalization, automation, immigration, and consumerization. These four variables do not by any means account for everything that is happening to our economy, but they can shed light on the effects, in particular, of specialization, and therefore on the economic implications of our society's diffusion. And all four point to ways in which the consolidated order of midcentury America has broken down.

The *first* structural transformation that has shaped the modern economy is perhaps the most familiar: globalization, which we generally perceive as increasing international competition for manufacturing and other jobs that workers in other countries can perform more cheaply than Americans. Globalization is, among other things, a classic instance of increasing specialization. Here Adam Smith can again be our guide. "As it is the power of exchanging that gives occasion to the division of labour," he wrote in *The Wealth of Nations*, "so the extent of this division must always be limited by the extent of that power, or, in other words, by the extent of the market."[9]

Work grows more specialized the larger the market in which its products can be sold becomes. And since many markets have become truly global, specialization has intensified dramatically. With specialization, every nation can play to its comparative advantage, which reduces the overall cost of production for the benefit of consumers worldwide.

Globalization has increasingly meant that rather than our *national* economy offering fairly plentiful low-skill, medium-skill, and high-skill jobs (and therefore opportunities for people with a wide range of aptitudes and in a wide variety of circumstances), it is the *global* economy as a whole that features those same three categories of work. And the United States, as the world's wealthiest nation, has increasingly specialized in higher-skill work, while countries with lower costs of living and labor have specialized in lower-skill work. Such specialization is good for the global economy, and therefore also for the consumers of its products, but it is not so good if you are a low-skilled worker in a nation increasingly specializing in higher-skill work.

That doesn't mean that there are no low-skill and medium-skill jobs in our economy, of course. Some jobs simply can't be outsourced. A new building still has to be built by human beings present on the construction site. Some kinds of service and sales work cannot be done remotely. A plumber in China can't unclog your drain in the United States—or at least not yet. But it does mean that there are fewer such jobs than there once were, and that those that can be outsourced often are.

Various ways of restraining this process have been attempted—from the implementation of protectionist policies and tariffs to the establishment of special benefits for domestic manufacturers or for products made in America. Such strategies will always have a significant political constituency, but as a practical matter they are largely futile. The economic advantages of global specialization and trade are just too great.

The less economically developed regions of the world are increasingly entering the global marketplace and developing their economies, to the great benefit of vast swaths of humanity. We should welcome such improvements even as we recognize that advances in other nations may well diminish our own outsized economic advantages in some areas. We are not likely to find ways to manufacture finished goods or to produce agricultural goods more cheaply than nations with far lower costs of living for workers. As a result, lower-skilled workers in our country will not often have a comparative advantage in producing goods that can be traded. That is not something we can change. We can, however, change the skill level of our population, and we can also try to channel unskilled labor from manufacturing and production toward services that cannot be so readily outsourced.

This kind of globalization has been going on for decades, but it has intensified (at least until recently) as more of the world's developing economies have entered the global marketplace. Some of the most populous nations in the world are steadily modernizing their economies, and their workers are now entering the global labor force at a rapid clip. Their participation in the global economy makes consumer goods cheaper, but it also makes low-skill employment harder to find in America. In other words, it means that our economy is growing more specialized in ways that require us to rethink our expectations, to reconceive some of our approaches to equipping Americans for employment, and to transform the sorts of protections we afford vulnerable workers.[10]

The automation (and computerization) of work is a *second* structural force that contributes to our increasingly specialized economy. Like globalization, it tends to leave fewer opportunities for workers with middling or unspecialized skills. Of course, fears that automation would decimate employment have been with us since the birth of modern capitalism, yet have always proven exaggerated in the long run. Machines have not made human workers dispensable, and they aren't going to. But in our time, machines (and not just brute-force industrial automation, but also, in many sectors of the economy, smart machines) *are* changing the nature of work in ways that exacerbate the pattern of bifurcated concentration that already increasingly characterizes our economy and society.

A large body of academic work (ably summarized in 2014 by economist David Autor of the Massachusetts Institute of Technology) suggests that such bifurcation, or, in Autor's terms, "job polarization," has been a result of the trend toward the computerization of work in recent decades. Machines, he noted, are particularly good at accomplishing routinized tasks, and often do so more reliably and cheaply than workers. Work involving nonroutine tasks will be more likely to survive the increasing computerization and automation of the economy, and such tasks fall into two broad categories: abstract tasks and interactive manual tasks.

Abstract tasks constitute the kind of "knowledge work" that many highly educated professionals engage in, which requires a mastery of language, symbols, or arguments and some amount of managerial work or technical expertise. Interactive manual tasks, Autor said, require "adaptability, visual and language recognition, and in-person interactions." Cooks, barbers, janitors, security guards, home health aides, and the like belong to this category. Their efforts might require only modest formal training, but their work is far from mechanical or repetitive and cannot be done remotely.[11]

Between these two kinds of work are many middle-skill and middle-pay jobs (from accountants to factory workers) that can be far more easily automated, outsourced, or both. In this way, automation and computerization can tend to alter the patterns of coordinated specialization that compose the modern economy, hollowing out the middle of the labor market, and so leaving that market increasingly bifurcated—with high-skill abstract work and low-skill service (but not production) work. The effect of automation is thus very similar to that of globalization, and indeed to that of the broader trends toward diffusion we traced earlier: all tend to create bifurcated concentrations in our society.

Again, the emergence of this pattern surely does not mean that middle-skill work disappears, but that it grows less plentiful and its character changes. It tends to make access to skills and the distribution of lower-skill work increasingly important to employment and productivity in our economy, and to the economic prospects of Americans.

This hollowing out of the middle is often a bigger problem for those at the bottom of our skill and income distributions (who are denied a next rung of the ladder to climb) than for those actually now in the middle (who are driven to pursue greater education and skills, or to have their children do so). For most of the past half-century, the middle class has shrunk more by moving up than down; the bigger problem is that those at the bottom are unable to rise.[12]

A *third* important structural influence on the labor market is immigration. Here, as we have seen, there has been some dramatic change in recent decades—and the tendency of elites in both of our political parties to ignore and deny the implications of that change can be particularly destructive.

As an influence on the labor market, immigration is almost inherently a bifurcating force. Immigrants tend to match one of two profiles: they are either lower-skilled individuals from poor nations looking for greater opportunity through low-wage work that pays them more than they could earn at home, or they are high-skilled individuals from more advanced nations looking to benefit from the exceptional opportunities at the higher reaches of the American economy. Those with skills somewhere in the middle, and in the middle class in their own countries, are less likely to undergo the rigors of emigrating for what would often be a lateral move. For this reason, immigration tends inherently to increase the specialization of our economy and to reinforce its bifurcation.

But the effects of immigration on the upper and lower tiers of our economy are quite distinct. Immigration as a whole is generally held to be an economic good for the United States, and the evidence for that proposition is quite strong. It is also almost certainly a significant net benefit, in particular, to people in the upper reaches of the economy, since it tends to make the goods and (especially) the services they purchase cheaper, thereby making them effectively wealthier.

But in the lower reaches of the labor force, the effects of immigration are far more mixed—and particularly so for lower-skilled immigrants who are already here (and who make up well over a tenth of the US labor force). New low-skilled immigration tends not to improve the wages and prospects of low-skilled workers who are already here, but instead to undermine them, and so to further complicate the bifurcation of our society.[13]

The enormous, largely unplanned, and poorly understood explosion in America's immigration levels since the 1970s has exacerbated the polarization of our society in other ways as well. It has, for one thing, left the country with a large population of unauthorized immigrants, who are in many cases now deeply rooted in American life, but living in a legal limbo that undermines both their prospects and the rule of law. This situation is not only harmful and dangerous for the immigrants involved, but also bad for Americans and legal immigrants who are on the lower end of the skill and income distributions, who must now compete with a massive gray market in the labor force—semi-legal workers performing semi-legal work outside the bounds of the usual rules.

Trends in both legal and illegal immigration have also swelled the ranks of people with lower literacy and numeracy in America—the same people who face other obstacles to mobility in our society owing to globalization. These problems complicate and counteract our efforts to fight poverty and promote economic mobility. Decades of large-scale immigration under these circumstances, moreover, have given rise to concentrated ethnic poverty, which has tended to undermine assimilation. In addition, our large federal welfare apparatus—which was mostly created during an unprecedented trough in immigration to America, when the foreign-born portion of our population was about half its current level—is poorly suited to our society's increasing diversity.

None of this means that immigration is not good for America. But it does mean that our current immigration policies have had some detrimental effects that are especially challenging for our diffusing society. These challenges have been apparent for a generation, but our political system has striven mightily to ignore them. The immigration debates that have roiled our politics over the past decade have tended to be defined by a broad cosmopolitan coalition of different groups that seek to further increase immigration for a variety of reasons. These groups have worked together to force the rest of the country into a blunt yes or no decision on a comprehensive immigration-reform package, rather than allowing for some modulation of existing policies to bring immigration into better accord with the nation's circumstances and priorities. This counterproductive formulation of the immigration question has not only made it more difficult to face up to the ongoing diffusion of our society, but also only further polarized an inherently contentious public debate, and thereby further fractured our politics more generally. Thus the familiar media spectacle of fearful xenophobia squaring off against self-loathing post-Americanism—even though very few Americans of any political persuasion answer to either description. This Manichean approach to immigration, too, has tended to empty out the middle range of our options and leave us stuck with two extremes.

Fourth, we are witnessing a subtler set of changes in employment arrangements that is leaving many workers feeling insecure. These changes, too, are deeply rooted in the diffusion we have been tracing. And they are raising some complex challenges that policymakers have yet to confront.

Simply put, workers in many of the fields that have benefited the most from the generous employment terms that were made possible by the consolidated character of the postwar economy are now seeing those benefits fade away. Protections for tenured academic faculty, defined-benefit pensions for public (and some private) employees, generous benefit packages for unionized workers in manufacturing, average salaries in some elite professions (like medicine and law), and even starting salaries for college graduates in many fields are ebbing. Many of these protections and benefits have been coming under threat for some decades now, but they are even more endangered in this century. As a result, many observers of the economy now have a sense that worker security is under siege.

This diminishing economic security for workers is yet another outgrowth of deconsolidation and specialization—driven in this case by a shift in the balance of power between workers and consumers. Simply put, nearly all of us in a market economy are both workers and consumers at the same time, yet our expectations of the economy in these two roles are often vastly different. As workers (at any level of the labor market), we want well-paying jobs with appealing terms of employment, flexibility, security, and satisfaction. As consumers, we want low-cost yet high-quality goods and services that are delivered on attractive terms. Obviously there is a tension between these sets of expectations. Better terms of employment for the people who make and sell what we want will increase the price of consumer goods; more competitive prices often come at the expense of attractive working conditions.

This conflict between our roles as consumers and our roles as workers is often mediated by the people who stand between the two sets of pressures, such as regulators or (most often) employers. Employers need to attract consumers in order to sell their products or services, and they need to attract workers in order to produce the products or perform the services—and so they must find a workable balance between the two. Regulators can push back against particular excesses to protect consumers or workers, but they cannot ultimately change the worker-consumer balance in ways that are out of line with the broad preferences of the larger society. And the nature of those preferences has changed.

In a highly consolidated society, such as midcentury America, the needs of workers will tend to predominate heavily over those of consumers. People are more likely to think of themselves first as workers under such circumstances, and as united with other workers in a common set of struggles and pressures. They are also more likely to think about the economy in terms of relational obligations rather than in terms of individual preferences. Moreover, organizations representing worker interests are far stronger in such a society (for example, the labor unions in the corporatist American economy at midcentury). Finally, as we have seen, competition among producers and providers is usually less intense in highly consolidated economies than in more diffuse economies, so that employers feel less consumer pressure even as they feel more worker pressure.

As our economy grew less consolidated and more fractured over the second half of the twentieth century, worker bargaining power came to be replaced increasingly by consumer bargaining power. Americans came to understand themselves first as individuals and consumers, and employers facing greater competition for customers grew more concerned with meeting consumers' demands than those of workers.

Over time, then, the economy has become better at meeting individual consumer needs, but worse at protecting workers as a class. And the workers who enjoyed the most far-reaching protections (such as unionized factory workers) have seen the greatest amount of change. There have been some exceptions, primarily in sectors of the economy that have not been subject to the same competitive pressures prevailing in the rest of the American landscape. Government work, for instance, usually does not face the kind of competition that many industries face. The sectors most heavily regulated and influenced by government, particularly health care and education, have also been shielded from some of those pressures, for similar reasons.

But in more recent years, as the relative inefficiency of these public and pseudo-public sectors has become increasingly controversial, they, too, have begun to feel these pressures. As the costs of higher education have increased, weighing down American families, for instance, professors have found their tenure weakened, their pay grow more slowly, and their research time constrained. As tensions arise between the commitments of governments at all levels to their citizens, on the one hand, and to their employees, on the other, public-sector workers are facing weaker protections and diminished benefits. The final remaining employment arrangements of the consolidated midcentury American economy have begun to fade away.

These changes do not affect everyone equally, even within industries and companies. In general, employers have tried to apply new rules to new employees but not existing ones: old professors keep their tenure, but new ones find it much harder to get it; older manufacturing workers keep their benefits, but new hires do not receive them; older public employees stay in the old pension systems, but new ones get something different. This way of dealing with the problem has added the quandaries of intergenerational fairness to the demands of a massive economic transition.[14]

It would be easy to blame avaricious employers and business owners for the increased insecurity of workers. But the story is not nearly so simple. The power of employers, like that of most intermediaries, has tended to decline rather than increase in our time. A number of the key functions of firms have come under threat of unbundling in our diffusing society. And the desires of consumers appear in any case to be far more significant drivers of the mediating trends. As the economic journalist Megan McArdle has put it, "the average American is at the heart of this story—as the victim and as the perpetrator. We suffer as employees because we exert influence as consumers."[15]

The greater consumer orientation of the US economy, and the greater consumerism of the public at large, are functions of the diffusion of American life that we have traced, and which at this point seems essentially irreversible. Its consequences for workers cannot be ignored (though they also should not be exaggerated, as they often are now). But solutions that involve undoing its causes—through a return to midcentury economic arrangements, such as large-scale reunionization of the labor market or wholesale reregulation of the private economy—are worse than implausible. Real solutions will need to be indigenous to our diffuse, twenty-first-century society.

These four forces—globalization, automation, immigration, and consumerization—are by no means the only factors relevant to American economic life in this century. But they are among the challenges we most often tend to overlook in our politics of dueling nostalgias. And they are driven and united by the continuing fracture and deconsolidation of our society, even as they further intensify that very deconsolidation.

The economic diagnoses and prescriptions of the Left and the Right are far from entirely wrong, of course. Each side is right about a lot. But because both liberals and conservatives often miss or ignore the consequences of growing deconsolidation, they often fail to offer plausible solutions. Such solutions would need to take into account the nature of the problems we confront as well as the changing character of the society that will confront them. And they will need especially to address the challenges the deconsolidating economy poses for the most vulnerable Americans, in particular—those living in poverty, or lacking the skills for the work our economy increasingly requires.

Indeed, when it comes to our economic debates, the story of diffusion in America adds up to a case for emphasizing economic *mobility* above all. Low-income Americans' potential for mobility is often impaired by family breakdown, cultural dysfunction, and the polarization of norms we noted in the previous chapters, and then further depressed by the economic pressures we have been considering here. The concerns of vulnerable workers and the poor, and their particular susceptibility to the ill effects of the diffusing forces operating in our society and economy, therefore need to be front and center in our economic thinking.

This means prioritizing efforts to combat immobility, and it means, perhaps above all, modernizing and fundamentally reconfiguring the safety net. Let us briefly consider each in turn.

INCREASED INCOME INEQUALITY IS ONE of the consequences of the diffusion of our national life, and a classic example of bifurcated concentration. There is reason to worry about its implications for social cohesion and for our civic health. But it is important not to mistake it for the primary *cause* of the social and economic forces of which it is primarily an *effect*.

Wealth is not a social problem, but poverty is. And at least in our society, the wealth of some does not appear to cause the poverty of others. The fracturing of our society has certainly exacerbated inequality: both the social and the economic consequences of our growing diffusion have hit the poorest Americans as punishments and the wealthiest as rewards. But that does not mean that addressing the effects of our economic and cultural diffusion on the poorest Americans would be a matter of closing the distance between the top and the bottom by any means possible. The means matter, because the end is not combatting inequality as such, but combatting *immobility*, and counteracting the isolation and estrangement of some Americans from the core institutions and relationships essential to building thriving lives.

Our political debates, with their overemphasis on income inequality (and especially a bizarre obsession with the super-rich), have done a great deal to obscure the obstacles to mobility for lower-income Americans. The notion that income inequality per se causes immobility, or, for that matter, causes other significant economic problems, is simply not well supported by evidence.[16]

And the public generally has not prioritized inequality concerns in the way that progressives have in recent years. Mobility offers a better way to think about what is threatened in our time. An emphasis on inequality can be divisive, moreover, whereas an emphasis on mobility for those at the bottom could be a broadly unifying goal for our economic policy. At a time when unity is in short supply, it could make for a rare consensus.

What, then, is the state of mobility in America? We can approach that complex question by breaking it down into two key components: *relative mobility* and *absolute mobility*. Relative mobility refers to a person's economic status in relation to the nation as a whole. Economists often describe it in terms of moving up the income quintiles; the rest of us tend to think of it in the form of rags-to-riches stories. Absolute mobility involves changes in a person's living standards not relative to society as a whole, but relative to one's own past or the prior generation. It is a measure of whether you are better off than you used to be—or better off than your parents were at your age—but not of where you stand compared to everyone else.

Although you would not know it from some of our political debates, the data suggest that relative mobility has been remarkably stable—and remarkably low—for at least the past five decades in the United States. A child born to parents living in poverty at any point since the 1960s has had only about a 30 percent chance of ever making it into the middle class, and about a 5 percent chance of ending up in the highest fifth of income earners. Rags-to-riches stories, and even rags-to-comfort stories, are awfully rare. And this has not changed much in living memory.[17]

This is the first and most important piece of the mobility puzzle: it is far too difficult to rise out of poverty in America, and it was so even throughout most of what we have thought of as America's postwar economic golden age. This problem has not gotten markedly worse (or better) as inequality has grown, and it has not improved or worsened with rising or falling growth, tax rates, or spending levels. Neither party's economic prescriptions seem likely to change it much. It will require some new thinking.

But immobility is nonetheless more of a problem than it used to be, in part because of the state of absolute mobility. Absolute mobility is still high: data from the Pew Economic Mobility Project show that the vast majority of Americans, about 84 percent, do now have higher incomes than their parents did at their ages—adjusted for both inflation and family size. Such intergenerational absolute mobility is actually highest among the poor: fully 93 percent of Americans in the lowest fifth of earners have higher incomes and greater purchasing power than their parents did at their ages, compared to 70 percent of Americans in the top fifth. Overall, American living standards have certainly risen over time, and this improvement has lifted essentially everyone's living standards somewhat, even if it has not done much to change people's relative positions in society.[18]

But absolute mobility appears to have slowed over the past two decades, so that while most Americans are doing better than their parents did at the same age, they are often not doing as well as similarly situated families (and maybe even their own families) were doing ten or fifteen years ago. Americans are feeling the sting of immobility as more stagnant wages create the sense that they're running in place.

Yet even apart from any slowing of absolute mobility, our long-standing weakness in relative mobility is more of a problem than it used to be precisely because of the diffusion and fracturing of American life. The emergence of patterns of bifurcated concentration means that being in the bottom income quintile now means something different, and in some important ways something worse, than it meant at midcentury.

The poor are more isolated—economically, culturally, and socially—than they used to be in America. This is not a function of the top 1 percent of income earners, who so fascinate those who emphasize inequality in our economic debates, somehow hoarding resources. It is a function of entrenched, intergenerational poverty that isolates too many lower-income Americans from even middle-class economic, cultural, and social opportunities and norms. The problem surely does have to do in part with economic polarization, among other forms of polarization. But that does not mean that the solution should focus on the closing of income disparities at the very top, or on a (largely impossible) reversal of the economic diffusion of the past several decades.

It means, rather, that we should emphasize increasing opportunity and mobility for Americans at the bottom (and to some extent in the middle as well). We must revitalize the institutions that will enable vulnerable Americans to thrive.

Focusing on the right problem does not mean we have adequate solutions, of course. Clearly, we have not figured out how to address entrenched poverty in our country. But it is possible to sketch at least the broad outlines of a mobility agenda that could take better account of the diffusion of our society and of the value and importance of America's middle layers and mediating institutions, and work from there. That agenda would involve changing both how we remove burdens and obstacles to immobility and how we provide concrete assistance and protection to Americans in need.

Any such agenda must begin with growth, which is a necessary, if not sufficient, condition for economic mobility. The preconditions for growth—such as an efficient tax code and regulatory environment, a health-care system geared to enabling real competition and cost containment, restrained public spending and deficits, monetary stability and predictability, and more—are preconditions for prosperity, and so for mobility. But while a mobility agenda must begin with growth, it cannot end there, as it too often does—especially for Republicans.

Such an agenda would also, for instance, need to make a lower cost of living a primary goal of economic policy. Reform efforts would therefore need to be focused where costs have grown most aggressively in recent decades (largely as a result of public policy), perhaps especially in health care, higher education, and the costs involved in raising children.[19]

A twenty-first-century mobility agenda would also have to take on cronyism—the tendency of public policy to favor entrenched, well-connected, wealthy interests at the expense of the general public and therefore effectively to redistribute resources upward. Rules and rents that protect entrenched incumbents generally do so precisely by restricting mobility: by closing off access to economic and professional opportunities through special-interest-driven licensing requirements, regulations that burden newcomers, subsidies and protections for favored players, and other barriers to entry and innovation. Cronyism is a decidedly bipartisan problem—and it contributes both to inequality (to a far greater degree than liberals tend to acknowledge) and to the growth of government (far more than conservatives usually admit). It was actually much more rampant in the corporatist age of consolidation, but it creates some uniquely pernicious problems in our era of diffusion. For example, it threatens to exacerbate the disillusionment and mistrust that already undermine our political life.

Both rising living costs and the perverse effects of cronyism obstruct the upward path for many Americans in a particular way that policymakers would be wise to notice: they create bottlenecks to prosperity. A bottleneck narrows people's options. In some important respects, the path into and through the middle class has become narrower in America in recent decades; the goal must be to broaden it. A mobility agenda in our increasingly fractured society therefore needs to lift burdens off of those struggling to rise by affording them a greater profusion of *options*.

Here our higher-education system offers a clear example. A college degree has become an increasingly essential ticket into middle-class life. And yet in recent years higher education has become vastly more expensive than in the past while providing fewer guarantees of future success. Tuition costs have tripled over the past three decades, so that an average year of college now costs about half the annual income of the average American family. For many families, sending a child to college means going deeply into debt—and often it is the college student who is burdened with that debt as he or she graduates and enters the workforce. And while a college degree continues to provide an important economic advantage, growth in the earnings of graduates has been slowing for over a decade, and many in recent years have failed to find work in their fields. Higher costs, lower value, and growing debt make for a bad deal, and families know that, but they are short on other options for upward mobility. Rather than a path to prosperity, college itself is something of a bottleneck.[20]

Plausible solutions would not involve simply pushing more people through the higher-education system—especially by having government bear more of the ever-rising costs. Shoving more people through is no way to address a bottleneck. To solve the problem, we need to widen the aperture and open up more paths to the same destination. We must create competition and give families more choices.

Policymakers should, for instance, allow the states to experiment with new approaches to accreditation that look beyond the model of the standard campus. They should allow credit hours to be unbundled and so pursued one by one, at different paces and in a variety of venues—from the college campus to the union hall to the church basement to the Internet. They should clear the way for more professional certificates, apprenticeships, and other ways of gaining the skills for well-paid employment that do not require a college degree. And they should enable parents and students to access information about career paths and earnings for graduates of different programs (information the federal government has, but is barred by law from making available). This strategy would enable families and students to better understand their choices and make smarter decisions about their investments of time and money into education. For twenty-first-century solutions to work, they must empower families and provide them with options.[21]

The path to rewarding work and economic independence, like the path to higher education, is also often bottlenecked today. The oppressive array of licensing and professional-certification requirements in many states and regions obstructs the upward path of many lower-income Americans. Barbers, manicurists, interior designers, and countless other professional groups have successfully lobbied for stringent barriers to entry into their professions in order to minimize competition. Such rules essentially install incumbents as gatekeepers. They are holdovers from a more consolidated American labor market and now generally serve merely as tools for well-established interests to keep out new competitors. Lifting and loosening the requirements would create new avenues of mobility for millions of people interested in those fields.

It is not a coincidence that we repeatedly find education and access to work at the core of the mobility dilemma in America. Our review of the forces shaping the US economy today should lead us to see that education and skills training (which are not the same thing) are absolutely essential to the revival of mobility. The gradual transition in the economy from a full-spectrum labor market to an increasingly specialized one means that avenues for acquiring sophisticated skills and habits are more important than ever.

Conservatives, in particular, need to put greater emphasis on education and skills in their economic thinking, and liberals need to modernize their understanding of how education and skills are best attained, as well as the role government might play in making them more attainable. That means the Right should take early childhood education more seriously, for instance, and redouble its efforts to advance primary and secondary education reform, along with making higher-education reform a priority. And it means the Left must break free of its antiquated views about what reform of these institutions should involve. Rather than cheaper loans, more aid, and more government power over educational institutions, policymakers should focus on more flexibility and choice beyond the four-year college model. They should look for ways to make more options available to citizens who understand themselves to be consumers, not to create new centralized public programs and further consolidate the programs we already have.[22]

Indeed, the dire need for modernization points to a larger problem for the Left in particular. A mobility agenda, whether advanced by the Right or the Left, must start with growth and build to the lifting of burdens, the clearing of paths, and the revitalization of American education. But it will also need to involve a transformation of our approach to actively aiding the poor and the vulnerable—to bring it into line with changes in American life that have almost entirely failed to register in our welfare and public-assistance policies. If the Left is to help America modernize, and lift up those Americans made most vulnerable by the trends we have been following, it will need to free itself of the anachronism of social democracy. This may well be the greatest challenge posed to the Left by the diffusion of American life, because it will require progressives to alter their idea (and ideal) of the shape of the future.

AMERICAN PROGRESSIVISM WAS A PRODUCT of the age of consolidation, and its assumptions and ideals have therefore always implicitly involved administrative centralization. It has been motivated by a vision of *social democracy*. Rooted in European political thought of the nineteenth century and embodied in some European welfare states in the twentieth, the principles of social democracy have never been entirely at home in the American political system, but they have done much to transform that system.

The social democratic vision begins with the observation that capitalism, while capable of producing great prosperity, leaves many people profoundly insecure. This fact suggests to social democrats that the functioning of the market economy should be strictly controlled by a system of robust regulations, and that its effects should be softened by a system of robust social insurance. From birth to death, citizens should be ensconced in a series of protections and benefits: universal child care, universal health care, universal public schooling and higher education, welfare benefits for the poor, generous labor protections for workers, dexterous management of the levers of the economy to ease the cycles of boom and bust, skillful direction of public funds to spur private productivity and efficiency. Each would be overseen by a competent and rational bureaucracy, and the whole would make for a system that is not only beneficent but unifying and dignifying, and that enables the pursuit of common national goals while also liberating individuals from oppressive social strictures and from a crippling material dependence on family and community.

This general vision has implicitly shaped our politics for most of the past century. Much of it has been enacted (but by no means all), with decidedly mixed results. But the American Left has long acted on the premise that advocates of this view are, as liberals sometimes actually say, "on the right side of history," and that steps along the social-democratic trajectory constitute progress, while steps in any other direction amount to retrenchment.

Some liberals have been in the habit of thinking this way for so long that they have come to take the logic of the social-democratic vision for granted, and so to defend the *means* and particular programs and structures of our welfare state as though they were identical to the broad *ends* and objectives they purport to advance. Policies that would employ any tools other than the national state are taken to be unserious about their own goals. When many liberals listen to conservative proposals—for example, in the health-care debate of the past few years—they don't even hear alternatives to their own ideas; they just hear a "no" to the social-democratic vision and react accordingly.

This implicit identification of means with ends, and the understanding of social democracy as the wave of the future, has left some liberals unwilling to consider the faults and failures of the particular welfare-state institutions we have. Those institutions, largely designed and built at midcentury, embody an ideal of centralized administration that is increasingly out of step with American life: it assumes immense competence on the part of the federal bureaucracy; requires public spending at levels that are increasingly unaffordable; undermines (and deeply mistrusts) the mediating institutions of society; and demands a degree of public confidence in our national institutions that we have not seen in half a century.

Indeed, this outdated model for solving problems is what now stands out most about the social-democratic vision that implicitly guides the American Left: although it offers itself up as a vision of the future, it is an anachronism. It is how the past used to think about the future.

It is anachronistic in three ways above all. First, the social-democratic vision takes a degree of social cohesion for granted that is no longer realistic. Our chief welfare-state institutions were in large part built at two high points of American cultural and political consolidation, the 1930s and the 1960s. They therefore assume a level of stability and social order that we can no longer assume. That means they don't work to create such order, and in fact that they frequently undermine it—especially by creating incentives against family formation and work. In our time, society's concern for those who have been displaced in modern life must not take forms that further alienate those very Americans from the broader society. Today's welfare state too often does just that. We need alternatives that actively encourage the integration of needy and vulnerable Americans into the mediating institutions of family, community, and work. Such alternatives will function *through* such institutions rather than *around* them whenever possible. Viable solutions will also recognize that estrangement from these mediating structures has been at the heart of the crisis of entrenched poverty and contributed to the hollowness of our social order.

Second, our welfare state also looks and functions like the institutions of a bygone age. It often still embodies the modernizing assumption that more advanced institutions will be larger and more consolidated, rather than the postmodernizing assumption that more advanced institutions will be nimbler and more responsive, customizable, and adaptable. Progressive public institutions took the shapes they did in response to the shape that the larger society and its economic, social, and cultural institutions were taking. As those other institutions are transformed, our public institutions will need to start taking new shapes, too.

Finally, the social-democratic vision points back to a fundamentally anachronistic epistemology, or theory of knowledge. At the core of the original progressive vision was the idea that in order for government to be effective, political and administrative functions (the "what" and the "how" of American government) would have to be separated. Politics would continue to answer to the fundamentally competitive electoral logic of our democracy, while administration would answer to a separate and fundamentally technocratic managerial logic. In this view, the most effective way to regulate and manage a complex modern society was for the legitimately elected government to empower social scientists to employ their centralized expert knowledge. Effective private institutions were run by these principles, and effective public institutions should be run that way as well.

Some distinction between politics and administration makes sense, of course. But the progressives' top-down theory of technical knowledge is no longer our reigning epistemology. Throughout our culture and economy today, the top-down theory has given way to a kind of bottom-up theory of distributed knowledge suggesting that the expertise needed to make complex decisions is not concentrated in the hands of a small band of experts, but dispersed among all, and best aggregated through the medium of individual choice in a diverse society. This is the logic of economic competition and cultural diversity—the consumer market and individualism. And it will increasingly need to be applied to public administration. We should look to our competitive democracy to set public ends and, where we can, should look to something like the model of competitive markets to achieve those ends.

Looking to market mechanisms doesn't have to mean prioritizing profits, or putting money at the center of the policy arena. Markets are systems for solving problems by a distributed process of experimentation, evaluation, and evolution. In the private economy, this approach means that different providers of goods and services offer consumers a wide range of options, consumers choose those they find most appealing, and those that are not chosen fall away. This effectively allows the people who need or want a particular product or service to help providers evolve toward offering them just what they require. In public policy, market-oriented solutions would mean that, instead of trying to address complex problems with uniform programs imposed in a centralized way, we would allow an assortment of potential problem-solvers (public and private, local, regional, and national) to propose or attempt various solutions in different circumstances. People in need of help or support would be empowered to choose from among different options, and their choices would matter: the options that prove popular and effective would be retained and emphasized, and those that weren't chosen would fade away.

Some conservatives in recent years have begun coalescing around a reform agenda of this sort. This group (of which I have been part) has proposed various ways of replacing the institutions of the liberal welfare state with more market-oriented mechanisms, many of which would function through society's mediating institutions. The emphasis is on finding solutions to public problems by learning from the bottom up, and empowering citizens who are accustomed to think like consumers in other parts of their lives to apply the same logic to their interactions with public services and benefits.[23]

This principle underlies, for instance, the idea of school choice as a substitute for some large public-school systems that have been failing their students. It empowers families rather than centralized bureaucracies. Some of us on the Right would like to bring about similar reforms in higher education: if we could remove barriers to new kinds of competitors in that arena, instead of just funneling more dollars into the existing, rigid system, we could give students and parents more power and new choices. Some conservatives have proposed to transform the health-care system using the same approach: instead of centralized decisionmaking and a narrow range of options for insurance coverage, this new approach could free providers and insurers to experiment widely with different business models and forms of insurance, empowering consumers to make choices among them and thereby increasing the efficiency and improving the quality of American health care. Some Republicans have proposed to take on the welfare system in the same way: we could use the resources now funneled through the one-size-fits-all benefit programs that have undermined families and communities to instead revitalize the institutions of civil society by empowering them to play a meaningful part in offering options to the poor. The idea in each case is to channel power and resources to the mediating institutions of society and allow for bottom-up problem solving that takes a variety of specialized, adapted forms.

Progressives tend to see proposals like these as embodiments of some kind of fetish to privatize. But in fact, they are expressions of humility. Experimentation is what you do when you do not know the answer, and when it comes to many of our biggest public problems today, we are lacking answers.

For example, we do not know how to address the scourge of entrenched poverty in America. The challenge facing welfare reformers is daunting: they have to find ways to help people who lack not only money but often also stable families, functional communities, and decent schools. They have to encourage work and responsibility while offering aid, and they often have to help people break bad habits or confront addiction or abuse while also respecting their dignity and independence.

All of this cannot be done by a government check alone or with a rigid set of rules. Both financial help and rules do have a role to play, and a modernized approach to providing direct monetary aid would need to be part of any serious mobility agenda (especially if it encouraged and supported work, as with an expanded Earned Income Tax Credit, or wage subsidies). But welfare often works best when it is accompanied by advice, by obligations, and by compassion at a personal level. Using public resources to let various kinds of institutions—from state social agencies to local civic groups to churches, schools, and nonprofits—try different ways of meeting this daunting challenge in different circumstances is not market idolatry; it is what you do when you haven't found the right solution, and when it isn't clear that any one solution will suffice over time.

The same is true in education, in health care, and across the range of public services provided to vulnerable Americans. These other areas may not require experimentation with hands-on assistance in the way that welfare does. But they do call for experimentation with different models, practices, and products in search of ways to provide better access to private goods and to higher-quality public services at lower costs. Here, too, civic groups, labor unions, schools, churches, and charitable groups could play far greater roles, as could the existing professional providers of services who are now often compelled to function as public utilities. An adaptive approach, by embodying the logic of twenty-first-century life much more closely than the social-democratic vision generally does, would offer ways to overcome the administrative dysfunction and the glaring anachronism of the liberal welfare state.

Some progressives are keenly aware of the failures of contemporary government, of course. But so far they have largely sought to deal with these failures by making a case for a renewed consolidation of the structure and power of the federal bureaucracy. Public-administration scholars John DiIulio of the University of Pennsylvania and Steven Teles of Johns Hopkins University, for example, contend that the dysfunction of the federal bureaucracy is the result of its complexity, especially its intricate mix of federal employees, private contractors, grants to states and localities, regulation of private actors, and a host of incentives, subsidies, benefits, and penalties.

That administrative complexity, they argue, is in turn a function of the public's contradictory expectations: voters want to reduce the role of government while continuing to benefit from government, which makes it extremely difficult to design rational public programs, and even to discern the successes and diagnose the failures of government action. Programs and policies take the form of what Teles terms "kludges": clumsy patchwork mechanisms that lack coherence and uniformity and make government needlessly difficult to manage and direct. The solution, Teles and DiIulio argue, is to radically simplify public administration by assigning it to centralized federal agencies with clear mandates and adequate resources. The answer to the disorderly hodgepodge of proxies that now passes for government is to declutter and bring order.[24]

But this prescription merely doubles down on the fundamental progressive assumption that characterized public administration in the age of consolidation—the assumption that large, centralized institutions are the types of entities best suited to reining in and handling complexity. That view was always dubious, and it is now a particularly poor fit for our liberalizing society. The problems we expect government to handle are themselves highly complex, and internalizing complexity in a centralized bureaucracy does not make it go away; it merely assigns it to an institution likely to be uniquely ill-suited to handling it.

We would do better to assign such complex challenges to a widely dispersed network of local, on-the-ground problem-solvers who, given the right kinds of rules and incentives, will be more likely to possess the needed knowledge and the capacity to seek out solutions in a flexible way. That doesn't mean just contracting out the execution of bureaucratic mandates (which is what the system DiIulio and Teles criticize does); it means permitting a genuine diversity of attempted solutions. This won't be simple and neat. It will be almost as complex as the problems we seek to address. That is what evolved, adapted systems look like. Doubling down on the model of public policy as industrial engineering, as opposed to adaptive evolution, seems unlikely to serve the Left well in our era of diffusion.

Instead, the next progressivism might well require a gradual move from an ideal of public *programs* in a social democracy to an ideal of public *options* in a decentralized society. The Left's response to the conservative case for providing assistance to the needy and vulnerable in the form of subsidized entry into competitive private markets (through vouchers and the like) may ultimately be some form of a progressive case for disciplining those markets by compelling private providers of services to compete with public ones.

Direct competition between public and private options rarely happens now. There are arenas, like K-12 education, where private providers compete with a large, dominant, and essentially default public provider, but the logic of these arrangements is generally the opposite of the one that would animate a public-options progressivism: the private institutions are held out as ways to compel the public system to become more effective and responsive by offering people otherwise trapped in that system an exit ramp.

There are also arenas, most notably health care, where powerful public systems (like the fee-for-service Medicare system) exist alongside partially private but heavily regulated "markets" of providers (like the Medicare

Advantage system and the Obamacare exchanges) as well as more competitive private markets (like the employer-provided insurance market). But there is rarely direct competition among these, since consumers can't readily move between them. The same is true, for instance, of Social Security and private retirement savings options. And there are arenas, like the bulk of our welfare programs, where state agencies provide benefits by contracting with private operators. But these contracting relationships are not competitive—private providers essentially just administer monopolistic public programs.

A public-options progressivism, as envisioned by a small band of theorists and activists on the Left at this point, would include elements of all of these, but would function by introducing public providers into competitive markets alongside a conservative effort to introduce private competitors to public monopolies. As the Roosevelt Institute's Mike Konczal, one of the innovators in this area, has argued, "a public option amplifies private options. It provides cost-control in cases where firms have monopolistic price-setting powers. It helps reduce informational problems, by creating a long-term, stable baseline for private providers to innovate and expand against."[25]

Such an approach might try to address market failure not by effectively replacing the market in question (through regulation or monopolistic preemption), but by filling gaps and correcting distortions in the functioning of that market from within. The economist J. W. Mason, another advocate of a public-options progressivism, has noted that in the provision of certain benefits, public subsidies for the purchase of a private good or service (grants and loans for college, for example) will just increase its price, while a public option competing with the private ones (thanks to some level of implicit subsidy combined with diminished pressure for profitability) will tend to drive all the prices in the market down, achieving essentially the same intended effect with fewer negative unintended ones.[26]

Another champion of such an approach, policy consultant and journalist Eric Schnurer, sees it above all as a way to improve the effectiveness of service provision in key areas, writing, "There's no good reason why the private sector shouldn't be allowed to compete to provide many, if not most, government services—but there's no good reason why government shouldn't, and can't successfully, compete back."[27]

This kind of approach would involve some degree of privatization of public services, as conservatives have sought for decades, while leaving in place public providers that would compete on equal terms. But it might also involve the introduction of some public options in currently private markets—like offering checking and savings accounts at post offices, public options for long-term care insurance or (as many Democrats wanted to include in Obamacare) health insurance—while leaving private providers to compete for the same business on the same terms. And these arrangements would accompany what some of the same activists and theorists refer to as a "rewriting of the rules" of relationships among consumers, providers, and workers—in place of the social-democratic ambition to wrest control of those relationships through government monopolies.

This isn't an altogether new idea. But for the Left to see such arrangements as the *goal*, or as the ideal way to reshape market systems, would be something quite new. It is happening in some tiny corners of progressivism now, but the hold of the anachronistic social-democratic model is very strong, and loosening it will require a great deal of intellectual work.

Even if the Left did move in this direction or something like it, our political controversies would hardly die down. The Right would not be friendly to a public-options progressivism, for instance, since, after all, it would partake of some assumptions about the proper role of government and the nature of markets that conservatives (myself included) consider badly misguided—and likely to undermine the fairness and effectiveness of the private economy and hurt the very people it is meant to help.[28]

Indeed, today's decentralizing "reform conservatism" is, if anything, well to the right of the nostalgic Republican agenda it seeks to replace, and a public-options progressivism (or any other plausible path the Left could take to accommodate the realities of our diffusing society) may in fact be further to the left than most of today's corporatist Democrats. The basic Left-Right argument would persist, and perhaps even intensify, if both sides were to modernize, and appropriately so—it is a debate about some deep and important differences.

But such a modernization of our core domestic policy debates would nonetheless mean that our political controversies would be directed toward addressing today's challenges, instead of being stuck in the past, and could speak to the public's contemporary concerns in the language of twenty-first-century America. The Left and the Right would begin to focus their best thinking on our actual problems, led by an informed appreciation of the costs and benefits of our liberalized, diffuse way of life. For better or worse, the diffusion of our national life will likely mean that the nation's economic and social policy debates in the coming decades will be more firmly rooted in the assumptions of a market society, and will increasingly address Americans as consumers of diverse protections from risk, not as passive recipients of uniform public benefits.[29]

As we have seen, however, those debates will also need to address Americans as workers. While we are now certainly more inclined to understand ourselves as consumers than we once were, some of the challenges and risks posed by today's economy have to do with the disintegration of some of the institutional structures of work in our economy. The (so far very gradual) decline of the traditional definitions of the job, the firm, and the employee, and the growing pressures facing more isolated workers in a global economy, require new thinking.

Some on the Left who are concerned about workers' rights have made efforts to revive organized labor and spur unionization. There may be room for this approach in some corners of the private economy—labor unions have certainly played a pivotal role in American civil society—but reunionization on any significant scale seems highly unlikely to succeed as a general solution for workers today. Instead, worker protections in the coming decades will need to take the form of portable, individualized benefits and rights that are not attached to workplaces in ways that assume long-term employment relationships. They will need to help make a diffuse labor market more secure, rather than trying to reverse its diffusion. Here, too, a modernization of the Left's understanding of American life would go a long way toward advancing a rational debate.[30]

But the Right has much work to do, too. The personalization of worker benefits (through personal retirement-savings accounts, consumer-driven health care, and the like) can be of real help, but making worker protections more portable and meaningful in a diffusing economy will require some more fundamental policy innovations, and it is not yet evident just what those will be.[31]

Generally speaking, however, and for all of its troubles, the Right may well be closer to a twenty-first-century governing vision than the Left is at this point, in part because its basic epistemology—its view that knowledge is inherently dispersed and can usually only be channeled by decentralized mechanisms (and traditional institutions) for the sake of marginal improvements—is an increasingly good fit for the structure of our national life. This view points toward a modernizing approach to governing that makes use of the mediating institutions of society and the federalist structure of our system of government to experiment with local solutions to great national problems. Such an approach could serve the country well, not just as a way of testing ideas that could then be "scaled up" and nationalized, but as a way of addressing problems in tailored, specialized ways on an ongoing basis.

In many of our key domestic policy debates, therefore, conservatives should be working for a greater market orientation in the provision of services while actively resisting the tendency of market thinking to atomize social institutions. They should not take the liberal welfare state as the epitome of modern government, and fight merely to make it smaller or roll it back (and so, in essence, engage in an inevitably reactionary struggle). Rather, they should see that by taking the programs we have, and replacing their centralized administrative forms with decentralized mechanisms of knowledge discovery at the margins, we could both dramatically reduce the scope of government and better meet the public's needs and expectations, especially by empowering our mediating institutions. A modernized Left could advocate for public provision as an option in the resulting competitive markets to restrain the excesses of market provision and serve the unmet needs of the vulnerable.[32]

This approach does not offer simple, straightforward solutions to all of the difficult problems of the modern economy. Rather, it is a way of organizing public policy so as to continuously seek and refine solutions and learn from experience. It begins from the premise that we do not already have all the answers—a premise that should be increasingly obvious to anyone following our policy debates in recent years.

A DECENTRALIZED APPROACH TO SOCIAL and economic policy would not only recognize the limits of our knowledge but also speak to the particular problems we now confront. It embodies not just an epistemic humility but also a commitment to subsidiarity—to empowering institutions at different levels of our society to address those problems for which they are best suited.

The weakening and hollowing out of some of those mediating institutions is an important part of the challenge we face, and a notable consequence of a half-century and more of deconsolidation. By giving such institutions a role in public policy, by channeling resources through them and allowing them to offer various ways of helping to meet needs and solve problems, we can draw people into them. We can offer those institutions renewed purpose and an opportunity to construct social capital around them, and to bring into being vibrant subcultures of mutual commitment with real moral content. And by giving them a role in the work of addressing material problems, we can strengthen their ability to deal with some more-than-material problems and to pull people into the space we have too frequently been rushing out of for a century now—the space between the individual and the state.

What happens in that space generally happens face to face, at a personal, human level. It therefore answers to immediately felt needs, and is tailored to the characters and sentiments of the people involved. This is both good and bad, to be sure. It means that what happens in that space can be moved by resentments and prejudices, by old hostilities, and by greed and vanity. Concern about these possibilities, and perhaps especially about racial and class animosities, is at the heart of what worries many progressives about subsidiarity.[33]

But what happens in that space also can be, and often is, moved by warmer sentiments—by the love that binds families; by fraternity, friendship, and loyalty; by compassion for the poor and the weak; by a passion to see wrongs righted; by ambition and a drive to excel and to be seen as excellent; by a desire to give our children more opportunities; by commitment to the places we are from and the mutual support of neighbors; and by love of country. These sentiments, not systems of material provision, are what makes society tick and holds it together. Centralized administration never could adequately replace them, and it certainly cannot do so now. We must be alert to the dark side of our mediating institutions, but we must also understand that their vitality is essential to our health as a nation.

Moreover, in our era of dismally low trust in large institutions, these kinds of human-scale middling structures can act as mediators between our increasingly ideological political parties and a public wary of their ambitions. By empowering mediating institutions, rather than only using the levers of federal power directly in the lives of individuals, both conservatives and liberals can temper their own (and one another's) aspirations and help make their agendas more palatable to the American public.

The mediating institutions also offer us a means of counterbalancing the market without unduly undermining its potential to improve our society's wealth and freedom. By enabling experimentation and evaluation to happen through institutions (schools, churches, local civic groups, nonprofits, and the like) that are not themselves fundamentally dominated by the moral logic of the market, we can create a constructive tension that can help us to make the most of democratic capitalism. Markets are rooted in some deep truths about the human condition, but so are families, communities, charities, religious congregations, fraternal groups, unions, and countless other institutions. Precisely if we are going to give market mechanisms an even greater role in the life of our society, as we should, we must also recognize their limits and their risks, and empower other free institutions that will incline to balance their excesses. Putting our trust in a centralized government to strike that balance is not only imprudent but also misguided, because, as we have seen again and again, a powerful central state will tend to pose many of the same dangers as unbounded markets, and will tend to drive our society toward the same peculiar combination of individualism and excessive concentrations of power. A better balance could be found in the fertile space between the two.

Finally, empowering the mediating institutions is also a way to deal with the sheer diversity and profusion of our society. The fact is that Americans now have very different ways of living, cultural mores, and assumptions and expectations. We are much more diverse than we were half a century ago, in a moment of unusual conformity. And in looking for ways to mitigate the ill effects of this diversity (and to enjoy its benefits, too), we can look to the example of some earlier generations of Americans who contended with the multiplicity of our society by restricting the power of the central government. American life did not then require an impossible homogeneity, but instead made room for some differences while also holding all of us together. Federalism has at times served us well in that regard.

The age of consolidation was rooted in the premise that genuine federalism and localism were no longer tenable, and perhaps they weren't for a time. But now subsidiarity is again becoming essential, and we should use the exceptional advantages it offers us in addressing our modern dilemmas. That is to say, we should allow different economic and social models to operate simultaneously in different places and to serve the many needs of a diverse nation in accordance with a wide variety of priorities and preferences.

If we do turn over more responsibility to the institutions of our civil society and local government, we will need to do so with the recognition that these institutions have been weakened in recent decades, for all the reasons we have seen. It would be a mistake to imagine that they stand waiting, ready and strong, just beneath our liberal welfare state, so that we need only roll back that state and they will step up. That assumption would, for one thing, partake of a misleading fantasy of volunteerism that paints a partially distorted picture of America's past—as if all the things now done by our programs of public assistance were once done by churches and fraternal organizations. And it would also ignore the erosion of families, communities, and civil society in our time. The mediating institutions do not just need to be unleashed—they need to be revived, reinforced, and empowered. This, too, is an important reason to give them roles to play in the modernization of our approach to mobility and welfare.[34]

Of course, this can only be a very partial set of solutions, at best. Indeed, the term "solutions" is much too strong. What a humble, subsidiarity-based approach to social policy in the age of diffusion can offer is a way to push back against the pressures of hyper-individualism without attempting an impossible return—or, to put the point more cheerfully, to retain the greatest benefits of diversity and dynamism while mitigating some of their greatest costs. It is a way to live in tension, not to resolve the tension.

And it is not an approach we can or should pursue in every instance. Sometimes, we will need to press for reconsolidation at the margins, and resist forthrightly the inclination toward diffusion and fracturing. Sometimes, we will need to reject the ethic of the consumer and insist on the ethic of the citizen. And sometimes, we will need to resist the implicit premise of so much of modern politics—that improved living standards are the equivalent of an improving society—and will need instead to reach for other, deeper visions of the good by recovering some sliver of the ethic of a prior, precapitalist age, both through liberal education and through unabashed allegiances to sacred, premodern truths.

We must do these things knowing that they are essential counterbalances to the tendencies of our time, but knowing also that none of us can live a purely countercultural existence, and that our society cannot thrive at war with itself. Even as we resist the excesses of our age, we should nonetheless find the best in its predilections. We should seek for ways to run with the grain and to make diffusion and diversity work in favor of the human good, as for now we can hardly hope to reverse them, and most of us would hardly want to.

When it comes to economic questions, we should therefore find the best in the age of the specialist and use it to address the worst. We can do this by putting an intense emphasis on mobility in our policy debates, and by empowering our mediating institutions as a means of discovering solutions and offering aid. And we can do it by seeing the difference between material comfort and genuine flourishing.

But ultimately, we can really only achieve these goals by recognizing that economic debates are not the only ones worth having, and are usually not the ones that run the deepest or that do the most to shape our society. Economic arguments are inseparable from cultural ones, and the arrow of causality runs in both directions. Our culture shapes our economic goals and is shaped by our economic relations; our economy reflects our cultural priorities and is reflected in our cultural trends and patterns.

And the relentless drive toward diffusion and specialization evident in America's contemporary economic life is also plainly apparent in our fracturing culture—which has been losing its mainstream, but gaining a near infinity of tributaries.

6

SUBCULTURE WARS

THE ECONOMIC TRANSFORMATIONS OF OUR age of fracture have been intense and challenging. But the cultural transformations have run much deeper. The postwar diffusion of American life began in the culture and has proceeded furthest there, and the accompanying economic and political changes have in many cases been responses to vast changes in mores, norms, beliefs, social expectations, and mental habits.

In the culture, as in the economy, these changes have frequently involved a kind of greater specialization, or rather lesser generalization. In the first half of the twentieth century, America's culture drew the nation together as the rise of mass media and mass public and private institutions, along with a series of national mobilizations, homogenized the public's experiences and drove Americans to prioritize solidarity and unity. But over the past half-century and more, our culture has been moved by an increasingly individualistic ideal, and so by a drive for greater distinction, more customization, and the elevation of personal choice and identity.

Capitalism has always been characterized by patterns of specialization, so the diffusion of our economic life represents an intensification, but not a fundamental transformation, of the character of the US economy. But in the culture, the nation has witnessed an extraordinary turn from self-effacing solidarity to self-acclaiming individualism—a dramatic transformation that has remade the character of our common life in a great many ways, both for good and for ill.

The ethic of our age has been aptly called *expressive individualism*. That term suggests not only a desire to pursue one's own path but also a yearning for fulfillment through the definition and articulation of one's own identity. It is a drive both to be more like whatever you already are and also to live in society by fully asserting who you are. The capacity of individuals to define the terms of their own existence by defining their personal identities is increasingly equated with liberty and with the meaning of some of our basic rights, and it is given pride of place in our self-understanding.[1]

The reigning spirit of this era of expressive individualism has been a spirit of liberation—a breaking of constraints, enabling people who might previously have felt compelled to repress some feature of their character or facet of their cultural, personal, or sexual identity to now openly express it without fear of condemnation or social sanction. This spirit has made our society more welcoming, accepting, and accommodating, and so in many ways has made it vastly better. Much of the power of the social transformation we have experienced has been drawn from the moral appeal of this kind of liberation—a softening of our society's hard edges and a warming of its cold places.

That appeal also motivates some of our nostalgia for midcentury, since Americans in that period could revel in the unquestionable satisfactions of the same kind of liberation without yet really having to endure, or even acknowledge, its costs. Those costs have emerged slowly as the logic of liberation has driven further and further toward the core of our culture. Inevitably, the loosening of social strictures and the blurring of moral boundaries unleashes not only gentle toleration but also harsh chaos. Liberation is meant not to sow disorder, but to free from oppression and conformity. But the moral consensus it breaks—with the best of intentions—was itself well-intentioned. It aimed not to deny freedom to the individual but to provide the order and structure often essential for thriving, and indeed for freedom. This paradox of liberation, a tragedy of good intentions, plagues all modern societies.

Beyond the abject thrill of liberation and the moral fulfillment of offering acceptance in place of exclusion, the rise of expressive individualism has also driven a surge in the sheer variety of American life, even as it has necessarily involved the fracturing and division of our common culture. We now have a profusion of narrow grooves of cultural experience where before there had been fewer but far broader channels. Vastly more options for communicating, for obtaining information, for finding entertainment, for pursuing high and low culture, for reaching targeted audiences, and for finding personalized "content" have meant that, over the past several decades, people have been increasingly able to tailor their experiences and their connections with others as they chose. There are now fewer mass common cultural occasions and more narrow but intense engagements as a result.

This trend has unavoidably left us with less in common at every level of our culture. The highest-rated television program of the 1950s, *I Love Lucy*, earned a 67.3 Nielsen rating at its height in 1953. This meant that roughly 67 percent of active television sets in the country were tuned to the program during its highest-rated episode that year. By contrast, the highest-rated program of the current decade, *Sunday Night Football*, maxed out at a 14.8 rating in 2014. Midcentury America saw the rise of mass-circulation, general-interest magazines, with readership and reach (relative to the size of the reading population) that would now be unimaginable. The idea that the publication of a new novel by a leading author, or the latest production by a noted playwright, would be huge cultural moments, as they might have been even a few decades ago, now seems impossibly quaint. Such moments matter to the subcultures in which they emerge, but there is barely a mainstream culture at all to receive them. On the other hand, though, there are many more options and opportunities to reach audiences of meaningful (if not immense) size, far lower barriers to prominence within each of these subcultures, and many more avenues for edification, if edification is what you're after.

What you're after, what the individual wants, has increasingly been the key to what our culture offers each of us, and there has been less and less directed at us that we did not seek or might not have imagined. Our cultural experiences thus come to be specialized around our individual preferences. Purveyors of cultural goods certainly try to shape our preferences and manufacture our wants, but they generally do so in the mode of giving us what we seek rather than really forming our tastes.

Ironically, this profusion of personalized options has therefore in some ways slowed rather than hastened cultural change. As journalist Kurt Andersen has argued, American culture in the second half of the twentieth century saw a seemingly unending procession of innovations, so that from film to fashion to books, music, design, and art the public's basic cultural environment and experiences changed quite a bit over the decades. But today, an extraordinary number of our most prominent cultural creations are homages to the experience of the past two generations. Hollywood producers remake the movies of their youth, clothing fashions offer a parade of throwbacks, the worlds of art and design seem stuck. If you were shown photos of Americans on a city street in 1955, 1975, and 1995, you would have no trouble telling which was which. But distinguishing 1995 from 2015 by looking at clothing, art, music, or design would not be easy at all. "Even as technological and scientific leaps have continued to revolutionize life, popular style has been stuck on repeat, consuming the past instead of creating the new," Andersen wrote.[2]

The solipsism inherent in our expressive individualism propels this culture of nostalgia: if everything is set up to give us what we want, it will all tend to give us what we already know, since our desires often just aren't very imaginative. Our culture as a whole will, like each of us, tend to become more like what it already is. Ironically, less uniformity and fewer common experiences mean that the power of innovators to introduce new strands into the fabric of society may be diminished.

But even if a diversity of subcultures does not necessarily mean a greater intensity of overall cultural innovation, it does almost inevitably involve a decline in the power of large, mainstream institutions of all sorts. These institutions—in publishing, media, culture, politics, and beyond—aren't disappearing, they're just becoming much less authoritative in relative terms, so that control of them is worth less than it used to be. They face far more competition for our attention than they once did, and a society much less inclined to put its trust in their authority.[3]

What is more, the substantive cultural messages that even these still-relevant elite institutions communicate mostly consist of the gospel of individualism—especially on the cultural and moral fronts. Large corporations are constantly telling us to be ourselves and have things our own way (which they are, of course, pleased to provide). The elite organs of the mass media, from the *New York Times* to the three legacy television networks, are prominent megaphones for the culture of diversity and the appeal of the small. They preach diffusion even as it undermines them—because they believe in it, and because resisting it would be even more disastrous for them than championing it.

As centralized authoritative institutions decline in relative stature and power, a variety of looser, self-selected networks are arising—from narrowcast cable television channels and streaming services that let you watch what you want, whenever you choose, to an infinity of online options for entertainment, information, and, perhaps most important, direct communication and engagement. Online social networks serve as fonts of aggregated experience and knowledge—providing advice, pointing to new sources of information or entertainment, channeling social pressure, and serving as venues for the development of common opinions and views. These are almost inherently narrow and personalized networks, and they build up subcultures rather than a mass culture.

The Internet has been developing in our time in ways perfectly suited to advance this process of fragmentation. The Web is almost endlessly malleable, tailorable, and individual. It supports the emergence of chosen channels of experience and information, and it requires no centralized management, and few mediating structures. It is a kind of embodiment of the ethic of expressive individualism—it lets all of us put ourselves out there, but it generally gives us only what we want and seek out. This combination of features makes it personalized but not spontaneous, responsive but not prone to yielding unexpected opportunities.

Critics of how the Internet is changing our social lives have focused on the ways it can undermine common experience and social trust, but it is also

in which we build up trust and construct new forms of social capital that are uniquely suited to our decentralizing society. Our twenty-first-
century social grids offer us the means to take and give crucial cues and to
learn from one another in ways that help us form practical judgments. They
enable us to make the most of the narrowing circles of cohesion and reliance
that we now tend to inhabit—not by constructing massive, centralized
stores of authority, but by building smaller, decentralized networks of trust.[4]

And just as the centralizing cultural forces of the era of consolidation
bled unavoidably into economic relations, so the emerging networked
social architecture of our time has increasingly shaped a so-called "sharing
economy." Economic relationships in this emerging realm make use of
social networks and technological tools in ways that skirt some traditional
definitions of consumers and providers of goods and services. The actual
"sharing" component of these exchanges can easily be overstated: Uber,
Airbnb, and the countless other brands now emerging in the sharing economy generally involve straightforward economic relationships built on
new technological infrastructure, and the idea of sharing is something of
a marketing tool used to increase their appeal. But as economic relationships, these new options are often nonetheless promising models that afford a greater variety of opportunities for both buyers and sellers and
increase constructive competition in the economy in ways that can lower
costs for all involved.[5]

THESE CHANGES IN HOW WE communicate, express ourselves, form and
share opinions, seek news, find entertainment, and buy and sell often
come up first when we consider the cultural facets of our society's
still-growing diffusion. They are important, and filled with peril and
promise. But they revolve around an understanding of culture that takes
the freely and rationally choosing human person for granted and assumes
that culture is about identity, expression, and experience. That understanding is surely grossly incomplete, and some of the most profound
cultural questions are actually those that arise when we note its inade-
quacy. Culture encompasses not just how people interact and the experiences they are exposed to, after all. Culture also *forms* us.

This is what the very word "culture" refers to: Drawing on an analogy to agriculture, it connotes the environment in which we arise and thrive. Our culture involves not only institutions of artistic and intellectual expression, but also—and perhaps above all—those familial, religious, civic, communal, and educational institutions essential to moral formation, particularly of the young. These two sets of institutions are not always distinct, and their purposes are often intertwined. But the state of our cultural institutions of moral formation deserves special attention in our time. The aims these institutions serve are (as ever) essential, and the particular dynamics of our diffusing society present some special challenges for them.

The solipsism of our age of individualism is uniquely dangerous to the institutions of moral formation. Because much of the good they do is a function of their ability to shape and structure our desires rather than serve them, to form our habits rather than reflect them, and to direct our longings rather than simply satisfy them, these institutions stand in particular tension with the ethic of our time. This tension is not a function of the Internet or other technological developments, and it is not primarily a function of economic changes sweeping over our society. It is a function, and ultimately perhaps the most significant social consequence, of modern individualism itself.

As each of us is encouraged by our culture, economy, and politics to be more like our individual selves, we are naturally inclined to recoil from any demands that we conform to the requirements of some external moral standard—a set of rules that keeps "me" from being "the real me," "true to myself," "living my truth." We are, of course, still powerfully influenced, if not downright coerced, by peer pressure and the weight of public sentiment on important questions, and indeed, our very individualism itself draws much of its power from its being so widely accepted and heralded. But we often flinch at explicit claims to moral authority over us and chafe against institutions that demand our full commitment and so restrict our range of choices.[6]

Our institutions of cultural traditionalism, which in the age of consolidation could reinforce cultural inclinations to restraint and conformity, have therefore in our time increasingly had to become countercultural

resistance. They pose a direct challenge to the culture of expressive individualism, so they have become controversial by default—combatants in a struggle for the very soul of our society.

That multilayered struggle has been evident first and foremost in some
extraordinary changes in the *practice* of family life in America over the past
half-century and more. But as our heated debates about that practice have
evolved, they have also revealed some real divisions about the *ideal* of
family life, and with it many of the other norms, mores, and cultural assumptions that give society its shape. It is on these fronts that the diffusion
of American beliefs and ways of living has likely had the most direct and
concrete consequences of all. And it is on these fronts that the struggle for
the future of our culture is really being waged.

THE FACT THAT FAMILY LIFE has changed, and that this change has sometimes taken the form of a fracturing of norms in practice, is perhaps best
illustrated by the trajectory of out-of-wedlock birth rates since midcentury. In 1955, at the heart of the postwar golden age and the baby boom,
roughly 4.5 percent of children born in the United States were born to
unmarried mothers, according to the National Center for Health Statistics. By 1965, that figure had risen to 7.7 percent; by 1975, it was 14.3
percent; in 1985, it was 22 percent; in 1995, it was 32 percent; in 2005, it
was 37 percent; and in 2015, according to preliminary census figures, it
looks to have been just over 41 percent of births.[7]

These figures describe an immense transformation of the basic structure
of American society, often with dire implications for the people involved.
They take the shape of a diffusion that has become a set of bifurcated concentrations, like so many of the trends we have been tracing, as the breakdown of a nearly universal norm gradually morphed into two distinct and
distant norms at the top and bottom of the income distribution charts.
They are especially important because they trace a change taking place at
the juncture of the generations, right at the core of what makes us a society
at all. And to cultural traditionalists (like me) these figures suggest a failure
on a massive scale by our society to provide the next generation with some
of the basic prerequisites for a truly thriving life.

Some of the consequences of this transformation are material and practical. The share of families headed by a single parent in a community is the single best predictor of social mobility in that community, according to recent work by Stanford economist Raj Chetty and colleagues. According to US Census Bureau reports, nearly half of children raised by single mothers now live in poverty, while roughly a tenth of children raised by their married parents are poor. Children who grow up in single-parent families are also significantly more likely than their peers to exhibit behavioral problems, drop out of school, experience mental-health problems, attempt suicide, and fail to enter the workforce as young adults. The breakdown of traditional family formation is therefore closely linked, as both cause and effect, to the bifurcated concentrations evident in many of the other cultural, economic, and even political trends of recent decades.[8]

None of this is to diminish the extraordinary and often heroic efforts of countless single mothers to help their children avert such consequences. On the contrary, it helps us see just how daunting the challenges faced by mothers raising children alone can be. Single mothers frequently have few alternatives, and few models to look to. They are themselves caught up in the crisis of family formation that is so deeply intertwined with poverty in America.

But describing the crisis of the family in terms of poverty and mobility may itself be a way of avoiding the deeper problem of which these are but symptoms. The family is the core character-forming institution of every human society. It the primary source of the most basic order, structure, discipline, support, and loving guidance that every human being requires. It is simply essential to human flourishing, and its weakening puts at risk the very possibility of a society worthy of the name.

And, of course, the rise in out-of-wedlock births is only one part of a broader trend toward the breakdown of traditional familial and cultural norms. A similar general pattern, if less stark and dramatic, can be discerned in a broad range of other social statistics, as we have seen in prior chapters. Our age has been witness to immense transformations in social arrangements, especially involving family life and sexuality. The sheer pace of these cultural changes, and of the accompanying changes in attitudes and norms, has further endangered our traditional institutions of moral formation and social order and made them controversial. Moral norms involving premarital sex, abortion, adultery, divorce, pornography, and more that had been in place in one form or another for many centuries have dissolved in the span of decades—liberating many people who would otherwise have felt repressed, but also eliminating boundaries that had given shape and order to the complex web of passions, desires, and power relations that undergird our social life.

This wave of liberation has been driven by the ethic of expressive individualism and the desire for greater personal choice and control. Its benefits are easy to see and experience, and they are very real. But social traditionalists have argued that its costs are evident precisely in the estrangement, isolation, and social breakdown that have also characterized the past half-century, and that they ultimately pose grave risks to our society. Debates about whether that is true or to what extent have shaped some of our starkest cultural conflicts. And they have frequently revolved, at least implicitly, around the question of whether dramatic changes in our cultural practices have been the result of our failure to live up to a shared moral ideal, or a loss of consensus about the value of that ideal itself.

As it has become increasingly apparent that the latter is closer to the truth—that our society is no longer united by a general agreement about the virtues and benefits of the traditional family and of traditional sexual mores—the significance of the diffusion of key social trends has come into sharper focus. If the problem we have is not that we are increasingly failing to live up to our own moral standards, but that we increasingly do not have such standards in common, then wholesale solutions become ever more difficult to imagine, and the role and purpose of moral traditionalism and social conservatism in our common life will itself need to change.

Social conservatives have been gradually coming to this conclusion the hard way. For much of the past half-century, they could plausibly believe that their views about the ideal forms and norms of society were in fact very widely shared—while also recognizing that many Americans (including many social conservatives) were not living up to those ideals. Human vice and imperfection were nothing new, and took nothing away from the value of shared standards held high by society as measures of virtue and criteria of moral improvement. Social conservatives could therefore understand themselves as part of a broad "moral majority," overtly opposed only by a small if influential sliver of radical cultural elites. They felt justified in expecting the political system ultimately to reflect their own views and priorities.

That confidence has largely been lost in these early years of the twenty-first century. Social conservatives have had to confront the deep diffusion of our society, which has transformed not only practice but also belief and expectation, and undermined norms we might once have thought were nearly universal. The public's commitment to these norms has changed in an instructive way: driven by the general diffusion of our society, this trend has generally not been a function of great erosion in the ranks of social conservatives themselves; rather, we have witnessed a change in the dispositions of Americans who had long been more loosely connected with traditionalist aims and ideas. These Americans were attached to a vague cultural conservatism mostly because of the seemingly broad consensus around it, rather than by deep personal commitment. As that consensus, like most forms of consensus in our national life, has frayed, their attachment has weakened.

TRENDS IN RELIGIOUS OBSERVANCE AMONG American Christians can help us trace this process, provided we understand the relation of such trends to the trajectory of traditionalism or social conservatism in American culture more broadly. "Social conservatism" is a broad term, yet in practice it can also be a relatively narrow one. It does not refer only to religious Christians of various denominations, to be sure. There are many social conservatives who aren't religious, or who are adherents of religions other than Christianity (like me). And, of course, there are many Christian believers of various sects who are not social conservatives. And yet, because the very great bulk of social conservatives in America are practicing Catholic, Protestant, or Orthodox Christians, and because their social conservatism—their attachment to traditional views about morality—is often an inseparable extension of their religious convictions and commitments, it is reasonable to tie a discussion of the state of American social conservatism to a discussion of the state of traditionalist American Christianity. The discussion that follows takes note of many important exceptions to this rule, and so speaks largely of "traditionalists" or "social conservatives." But it also takes note of the rule itself, and so of the unavoidable link between American social conservatism and American Christian traditionalism.[9]

Thus, public-opinion surveys that inquire about people's religious affiliations and beliefs can help us better understand how the place of cultural traditionalism in our society has been changing. The basic trajectory of such surveys in this century has displayed what appears at first glance to be a decline in American religiosity. The Pew Research Center has found that the share of Americans who call themselves Christians fell by 8 percentage points between 2007 and 2014, continuing a steady decline that began in the 1990s. This change has been widely (and plausibly) read to suggest a collapse of religious traditionalism in American culture. But in fact, the data actually suggest something else—not a collapse of religious traditionalism, but a change in attitudes among people who were not particularly traditionalist to begin with but have grown more comfortable saying so.[10]

Ed Stetzer, executive director of LifeWay Research, an evangelical Christian group, has spent years carefully studying mountains of data on American religious practice and belief. He divides the population into three broad groups: *convictional believers*, people who orient their lives by their religious faith and are cultural traditionalists; *nominal religious* Americans, who identify with some religious community but rarely attend religious services and do not orient their lives by their faith; and *unaffiliated* Americans, who do not identify with an organized religion or faith community. Those in the third group are not necessarily atheists, but they are generally social liberals.

The ranks of convictional believers, Stetzer notes, have not declined much at all in recent decades. Over the seven-year period in which Pew saw a decline in the number of Americans who call themselves Christians, for instance, the same Pew data show a slight increase in the portion of Americans who identify as evangelicals (from 34 to 35 percent). And the religious practice of Americans in this group has not declined either. In fact, according to the University of Chicago's General Social Survey, the percentage of evangelicals who attended church every week in 2014 (55 percent) was the highest in four decades.[11]

Nor has there been a dramatic decline in self-reported committed religious practice beyond the evangelical world. In 2013, Gallup reviewed its research findings about church attendance starting in the 1940s, noting that figures of self-reported weekly attendance had varied only within a relatively narrow range over that long stretch. "Americans' self-reported church attendance since 2008 has averaged 39%, down only slightly from the overall average of 42% since 1939," the Gallup researchers concluded.[12]

What explains the apparent decline in American religiosity in the past few years, then? The change has come among the "nominal" religious, who have generally composed nearly half the population. "In short," Stetzer argues, "nominals—people whose religious affiliation is in name only—are becoming nones—people who check 'none of the above' on a survey."[13]

The Pew survey supports this theory, noting that the ranks of the "nones" have grown significantly in recent years—from 16 to 23 percent of the public between 2007 and 2014. The rise has come largely at the expense of the numbers of Americans who identify themselves as Catholics or mainline Protestants. But within those denominations, the numbers identifying as most observant—those who attend church weekly, or nearly so—have not changed all that much. It is the nominally religious who are increasingly declaring themselves to be nonreligious.

So the ranks of religiously observant Americans and serious cultural traditionalists appear not to be thinning dramatically. But the attitudes of other Americans toward them are changing: many have ceased to view religious traditionalism as an ideal with which to nominally identify and have come instead to see it as an option to reject. This is not a minor shift. It is in fact a kind of revolution in the structure of American religiosity: formerly loosely affiliated members of the traditional streams of Christianity are drifting away and a broader array of softer and thinner religious and spiritual views is emerging. It has also, without doubt, involved more Americans becoming hostile to religion to varying degrees.

This trend has certainly been driven in part by the very diffusion we have been tracing. With the declining power of consolidated, authoritative institutions and the weakening of nearly every national consensus, there has been less social pressure on loosely committed or uncommitted Americans even to pay lip service to traditional views or communities and a greater sense of freedom to express more lax views, or no views at all, on key moral questions.

The greater deference that religious conservatives might once have been given to shape publicly accepted moral ideals could easily have left them with the impression that they spoke for a far greater portion of the country than they ever truly represented. It also gave them more actual authority over laws, mores, practices, and norms than they can expect to exercise in the coming decades. That deference, and with it that impression and authority, have been badly degraded. But it is nonetheless crucial to see that this change has resulted in the main not from a great deterioration in the commitment of the people who make up the core of American social conservatism, but from a diffusion of the barely committed periphery.

In a sense, this means that Americans are now more honest about their religious and moral views. There is less pretense of piety and a deeper commitment among those who identify themselves as Christians and/or moral traditionalists. As in other arenas, people feel freer to be themselves. Some religious conservatives welcome this change. It is only casual Christianity that is declining, they argue, so that people who were loosely affiliated are drifting away. But what remains is a very large body of believers growing more orthodox in a variety of ways, and therefore better able to live out their faith and model it for others.

Russell Moore, president of the Ethics and Religious Liberty Commission of the Southern Baptist Convention and an intellectual leader of contemporary evangelicalism, put it this way in 2015:

For much of the twentieth century, especially in the South and parts of the Midwest, one had to at least claim to be a Christian to be "normal." . . . It took courage to be an atheist, because explicit unbelief meant social marginalization. Rising rates of secularization, along with individualism, means that those days are over—and good riddance to them. . . . We do not have more atheists in America. We have more honest atheists in America. Again, that's good news. The gospel comes to sinners, not to the righteous. It is easier to speak a gospel to the lost than it is to speak a gospel to the kind-of-saved. And what those honest atheists grapple with is what every sinner grapples with, what all of us grapple with, burdened consciences that point to judgment. Our calling is to bear witness.[14]

More honest self-identification across the board in America can actually free convictional believers from the burden of defining the norm, Moore suggested, and can allow them to stand more forthrightly for their faith and their vision. "Christianity isn't normal anymore, and that's good news," he wrote. "The Book of Acts, like the Gospels before it, shows us that Christianity thrives when it is, as Kierkegaard put it, a sign of contradiction. Only a strange gospel can differentiate itself from the worlds we construct."[15]

But that power to define the norm was not just a burden; it was also a source of great strength and stability. It held up as a standard a generally traditional, broadly Christian (or Jewish and Christian) moral outlook that contributed enormously to the cohesion and success of American society. And that standard, although it clearly was not always rooted in deep belief, was nonetheless embodied in practical norms—lived out by individuals and enforced implicitly by their communities—that helped to shape the lives of the vast majority of Americans until the past half-century or so. These were the norms against which a liberalizing society could rebel—so that they gave some structure and order even to that rebellion. As these norms have waned, even liberalization has lost its focus in American society; it has been loosed from its moorings while struggling to become the new norm.[16]

But social and religious conservatives have lost even more than that: they have lost their place of honor in the moral life of our society, and they have lost the ability to speak for a set of norms and ideals that, even if many Americans chafed against them and found them burdensome and judgmental, were taken to be proper aspirations. They can no longer set the standard, and have instead increasingly found themselves locked into conflict with social liberals who present themselves as rejecting all moral judgmentalism, but who in fact, unavoidably, end up trying to judge society by a new standard instead.

EVEN UNDER THE BEST OF circumstances, this transformation puts social conservatives into a challenging position. Rather than working to enforce a set of norms that large majorities of Americans at least claimed to accept, they now find themselves needing to make the basic case for their ideals and moral premises. And they are out of practice, and do not always do that as effectively as they might.

Having long been accustomed to speaking from the point of view of commonly shared goals, social conservatives often incline not to speak in ways that seek to appeal, but rather in ways that seek to lament. They have been much clearer about what they are saying no to than what they are saying yes to, and therefore emphasize the options they would close off rather than the options they would offer. They have operated implicitly as the guardians of a broadly shared consensus working to enforce it rather than as the champions of a poorly known ideal working to draw converts.

They therefore speak of what is lost more often and more forcefully than of what might be gained. And in pointing to losses, they incline to prophesize doom where their neighbors often see harmless change or welcome liberation. This tendency has a lot to do with the basic *subject* of most of our moral debates. The warnings and worries expressed by social conservatives most often involve the consequences of lightning-fast changes in some very long-standing moral strictures, especially surrounding sexuality. Because the problems these changes may create often arise at the juncture of the generations, they often take many years to present themselves, while the benefits can be instant and obvious. So social conservatives now often find themselves deeply alarmed about the future in ways that leave many other Americans scratching their heads.

Such worries have certainly been proven accurate in some important respects. As the out-of-wedlock birth statistics considered above would suggest, basic patterns of family formation have degraded dramatically over the past half-century, just as social conservatives warned they would throughout that period. And when it comes to the *implications* of various transformations and breakdowns of our social order, cultural conservatives have at times been able to see over the horizon. Whether regarding the effects of fully legalizing abortion on out-of-wedlock births, or the consequences of no-fault divorce for marriage in America, or the implications of in vitro fertilization technologies for the commodification of life, their predictive record has been nothing to sneer at.[17]

Of course, conservatives have also been proven wrong in some dire predictions. In recent decades, for instance, violent crime has declined in America, teen pregnancy and drug abuse have fallen, and the abuse of women and children has decreased. Some recent data suggest that marriage patterns among younger Americans are stabilizing as millennials grope for new patterns of family life. And many other social indicators have been relatively steady amid rapid social change.[18]

Indeed, even the statistics regarding out-of-wedlock births considered above can be read in two rather different ways. If you had told an American in 1955 that the rate of out-of-wedlock births in our country would rise from 4 percent to more than 40 percent over the subsequent six decades and asked him to describe the resulting America, he probably have painted a nightmarish spectacle that would bear little resemblance to our relatively thriving society. This is an inherent problem with arguments by jeremiad: they tend to assume that alarming trends will prove unsustainable and lead to cataclysms. When those outcomes do not materialize, the Jeremiahs look unreasonable, and their arguments for an uplifting moral order come to be seen as thinly veiled justifications for repression.

Liberals and conservatives both incline to such alarmist arguments in different realms in our time: The Left tends to talk about economic trends, and especially inequality, in ways that suggest the sky could fall on our society any minute. The Right surveys the culture and finds the seeds of moral apocalypse. But human beings are resilient and adaptable; we adjust to difficulties and grow accustomed to problems. Projections that suggest we won't are rarely plausible.

This may sound like good news, but it isn't. It suggests that no action-forcing cataclysm will compel us to turn things around. The breakdown of the family among lower-income Americans and estrangement from community, religion, work, and other edifying attachments may not bring our culture crashing to the ground, but they nonetheless can prevent large numbers of Americans from building flourishing lives. Our enormous investment in antipoverty efforts over the past half-century has done much to reduce material poverty, but not to reduce this spiritual poverty—which may well be sustainable but should not be acceptable, and which, as we have seen, also stands in the way of opportunity.

Prophesying total meltdown is not the way to draw people's attention to this failure to flourish. The problem we face is not the risk of cataclysm, but the acceptance of widespread despair and disorder in the lives of millions of our fellow citizens. We risk getting used to living in a society that denies a great many of its most vulnerable people the opportunity to thrive. Making the case against such acquiescence in the torpor and misery of so many would mean calling people's attention to just what it is these Americans are being denied—to the possibility of flourishing, and to its appeal.

Social conservatives must therefore make a positive case, not just a negative one. Rather than decrying the collapse of moral order, we must draw people's eyes and hearts to the alternative: to the vast and beautiful "yes" for the sake of which an occasional narrow but insistent "no" is required. We can do this with arguments up to a point, but ultimately, the case for an alternative that might alleviate the loneliness and brokenness evident in our culture requires attractive examples of that alternative in practice, in the form of living communities that provide people with better opportunities to thrive. Especially when we are in no position to enforce or enact our ideals as national norms, social conservatives need to emphasize and prioritize such modeling of alternatives—illustrating the possibility of a more appealing form of modern life by living it.

But the need for such an approach to our neighbors can be difficult to see, particularly for those accustomed to thinking in the terms of a consolidated America in which social conservatives could understand themselves as the keepers of a broad consensus and entitled to set the tone. The evident loss of that position has, rather naturally, persuaded some traditionalists that they have lost their place to their adversaries in the culture wars—that the tables have turned, and that now social liberals with radical views are taking over our society's institutions and turning them against the traditional family, religion, and the cultural inheritance of Western civilization. Some social liberals seem to think that's what is happening, too, and are setting out to banish religion from the public square.

But both sides are ignoring the diffusion of American life that has helped bring about the changes we are seeing: we are certainly witnessing something of a long-term hostile takeover of the dominant mainstream institutions of our society, but we are also living through the collapsing power and influence of those very institutions, which may turn out to be far more important. All sides in our culture wars would be wise to focus less attention than they have been on dominating our core cultural institutions, and more on building thriving subcultures. For social conservatives mourning the loss of their dominant position in some of those core institutions, it is particularly important (and particularly difficult) to keep this imperative in mind.

IN THE LAST FEW DECADES of the twentieth century, social conservatives tended to vastly exaggerate their dominance over the culture, dependent as that dominance was on the silent assent of large numbers of casual, nominal Christians (and other nominal but uncommitted traditionalists). Now, some particularly radical liberals who would aggressively suppress religious and moral traditionalism in the public square are making the same mistake. Both errors involve an over-reading of the politics of some culture-war battles.

The last time cultural conservatives really saw themselves as politically ascendant was probably in 2004. Immediately after that year's presidential election, many analysts on both the Right and the Left claimed that George W. Bush's reelection signaled a rising tide of "values voters" who would yield an enduring nationwide advantage for Republicans on social issues. In a postelection *New York Times* op-ed piece subtly entitled "The Day the Enlightenment Went Out," author Garry Wills said the American people were giving up on modernity. On CNN the day after the election, conservative commentator Tucker Carlson said "it is clear that it was not the war on terror, but the issue of what we're calling moral values that drove President Bush and other Republicans to victory."[19]

Many social conservatives now look wistfully upon that moment and see in the years that followed what traditionalists are apt to see in the world in general: a sorry decline. Both politics and the culture now seem increasingly hostile to social conservatism, and religious believers in the public square are often fighting for even minimal tolerance. The same kinds of analysts who saw a traditionalist ascendancy then now observe only social liberalism as far as the eye can see. Some social conservatives have internalized the notion that history is on the side of the Left, and are preparing for the catacombs.

But the false dawn of 2004 should actually temper today's dire mood on the Right, precisely because it was false. Some of the political dynamics around the 2004 election (like same-sex marriage referenda in several conservative states timed to coincide with a presidential race), along with a poorly worded question on an exit poll (which combined vast swaths of issues under the rubric of "values"), created a misimpression about the electorate's priorities. The closest watchers of the public mood in that campaign, more thorough subsequent polling, and academic analyses of public opinion all argue that social issues were not actually crucial to the outcome, and that the electorate was not unusually concerned with them on Election Day.[20]

That rethinking of the 2004 election suggests that social conservatives were not ascendant in the middle of the past decade, but it also suggests that their situation has not grown so dramatically worse since. That doesn't mean social conservatives are imagining their troubles these days. But it might mean they're blurring the distinction between politics and the larger culture a bit more than they should. The experience of both the Bush years and the Obama years suggests that whichever side of our culture wars commands the White House has a great deal of control over the form and character of the battles we fight in those wars. Such control can make it seem like history is on the side of the president's party.

Many of the most heated public battles about moral and cultural issues in the Obama years were carefully, if not cynically, orchestrated by the White House to frighten key Democratic constituencies and cast their opponents in the worst possible light. One of the most prominent battles over religious liberty in that period, which involved the administration's decision to enforce the Affordable Care Act in a way that required employers who provide insurance coverage to their employees to cover access to contraceptive and abortive drugs, was simply a culture war of choice initiated by the president.[21]

The tone and intensity of the same-sex marriage debate evinced a related pattern, with social liberals capitalizing on a change in public attitudes about homosexuality and on the liberal leanings of key federal courts to threaten religious liberty and freedom of association in ways the public is much less likely to endorse. Around 2013, same-sex marriage advocates chose to move their efforts from the legislatures to the courts, based in part on an assessment of the relative political leanings of the two sets of venues. That decision ultimately led to the Supreme Court's 2015 decision universalizing a right to same-sex marriage nationwide, but it also meant an unavoidable increase in the temperature and intensity of the same-sex marriage debate. A legislative effort tends to drive advocates to put forward the most broadly appealing face of their agenda and to compromise in order to win votes, and so might well have opened a path to more accommodations of religious liberty alongside new marriage laws. But a court battle requires advocates to paint their opponents as irrational, and to deny that their concerns have merit. The marriage debate certainly drew upon (and fanned) a dramatic change in public attitudes. But the tenor of the debate, and its implications for the rights and freedoms of conscientious objectors to the new dispensation, was at least in part also a function of a tactical judgment by one side to the argument—a judgment that may prove to have overreached in the long run.[22]

And in all these cases, there has been on the Left something of a mirror-image of the Right's exaggerated view of its own dominance in decades past: the public has moved some to the Left, but not nearly as much as the most vocal advocates of social liberalism seek to imply. While Americans have become more open to a wider range of social practices, a narrow elite of aggressive cultural liberals standing well to the left of the public at large has been intent on pressing its advantage and taking authoritative control of the mainstream culture and its institutions. These liberal activists are champions of a particularly radical and unbounded form of the very expressive individualism that has come to characterize our culture, so they can easily feel like they have the wind at their backs, and cultural conservatives can easily feel like these adversaries speak for the larger culture and so pose a grave threat.

In some ways, they surely do pose a threat. Within days of the Supreme Court's 2015 same-sex marriage decision, for instance, prominent voices on the Left raised the possibility of eliminating the tax-exempt status of churches and other religious institutions, or targeting employment-discrimination suits at religious nonprofits operating in the public square. Efforts at the state level (in Indiana, Arkansas, and elsewhere) to protect the liberty of private citizens and institutions who objected to same-sex marriage were met with elite and media outrage and threats of boycotts by large corporations. The American Civil Liberties Union even announced, in the wake of the decision, that it would withdraw its support from religious-liberty measures it had backed for decades. It is not hard to see why cultural conservatives have felt besieged, and have made religious liberty—America's first freedom—a foremost priority.[23]

But the evolution of American life that we have been tracing in these pages should offer those concerned for their liberty some solace. The arrogant minority of liberals clamoring to consolidate its victories and crush dissent in our cultural battles is plainly exaggerating its power and ignoring the very trends—the diffusion and fracture of our older moral consensus—that have made its recent successes possible. It is working to weaponize our culture's expressive individualism into a bludgeon to be used for enforcing conformity and repressing dissent. But the spirit it seeks to turn to its benefit may not be so easily turned.

The relationship of cultural conservatives and liberals has gone through a kind of multi-decade role reversal. At the height of the era of consolidation, in midcentury America, anti-traditionalists and moral liberationists were a countercultural force—outcasts, rebels, and dissenters fighting the forces of a conformist consensus and elite convention. Over time, as liberalization and deconsolidation became the dominant ethic of American life, the consensus broke down and cultural liberalism came to be at least implicitly the ideology of the American elite. It has become so in a decisive way in this century, and almost inevitably this has manifested itself in efforts to enforce that ideology as a new conformist consensus—to impose it over public institutions, to require it of private actors, and to actively root out dissent from its strictures. It is cultural traditionalists who are now in the role of outcasts, rebels, and dissenters. That is a role to which most conservatives are unaccustomed, yet also one in which our traditions have frequently thrived in the past. But finding ways to thrive in this role now will require recognizing the advantages it offers, especially in our diverse and still diffusing society.

As social conservatives survey the changing landscape and recognize that, rather than just fighting for control of dying mainstream institutions, they would be wise to also make themselves an attractive minority in a nation of minorities, they will also come to see that their adversaries in the culture wars are not as strong as they might seem. Conservative journalists Benjamin Domenech and Robert Tracinski aptly put the point this way in 2015: "History teaches us two clear lessons about the ebb and flow of the Culture Wars: first, that whichever side believes it is winning will tend to overreach, pushing too far, too fast, and in the process alienating the public. The second is that the American people tend to oppose whoever they see as the aggressor in the Culture Wars—whoever they see as trying to intrusively impose their values on other people and bullying everyone who disagrees." If cultural liberals imagine that they are now in decisive command of our mainstream culture and its institutions, they will be making the same mistake some cultural conservatives made in recent decades—ignoring the fact of our diffusing society and undermining their own capacity to appeal to a broad public outside their narrow circle of the converted.

For the moment, at least, a significant portion of the cultural Left appears to be making just this mistake.[24]

In response, cultural conservatives have been pushed in the general direction they actually would be wise to pursue in our culture. The sight of orthodox Christians and Jews "crowdsourcing" funds to help business owners whose religious liberty is threatened, or rising up for common sense at school board meetings, should fill traditionalist hearts with hope. But the cultural Right has so far been largely walking backward into this new role. Simply by defending traditional understandings of the family, for instance, religious conservatives have become countercultural, and they are only slowly warming to the upside of this rather unfamiliar role.

Their first experience of it has been fundamentally defensive—the experience of losing ground and seeing their institutions threatened. And it has driven social conservatives to turn to religious liberty for shelter. In recent years, under attack in some important instances by the Obama administration and feeling besieged in the same-sex marriage debates and their aftermath, social conservatives have elevated religious liberty to the very top of their public agenda, making it their chief rallying cry.

Religious liberty, guaranteed by the First Amendment to the Constitution, is without question an essential prerequisite to the endurance of our free society, and at this time it is an especially crucial shield for social conservatives. But although it is necessary, it is far from sufficient for the defense and advancement of traditional moral and cultural norms in America. And failing to see its limits, and the risks posed by an intense reliance on it, could turn out to be quite perilous.

First, the argument from religious liberty inherently involves an almost exclusively defensive posture. When social conservatives put religious liberty at the top of their list of priorities, they approach the larger public in the guise of a fundamentally plaintive and inward-looking minority asking to protect what it has and in essence to be left alone. But what social conservatives "have" is a vision of the good life and a deep conviction that it would be good for everyone—and therefore ought to be shared and made available as widely as possible. Approaching the larger society defensively is hardly the way to make the truths and advantages of social conservatism apparent to our fellow citizens.

What is more, the specific nature of the defensive posture of contemporary social conservatism—because it tends to focus so intently on sexual morality—risks further distorting the larger public's understanding of what is at stake in the culture wars. The flashpoints in our recent cultural battles have frequently involved questions of sexuality, with the social Left working to impose liberationist sexual mores on our public institutions of education, welfare, and health while conservatives resist. An essentially defensive posture in these struggles would involve religious conservatives in a constant struggle over narrow questions of sexuality—distorting the message they would seek to offer the larger society and reinforcing an impression already popular among their detractors that religious conservatives are obsessed with sex.

That impression is, of course, terribly unfair. Religious conservatives today can seem obsessed with sex for the same reason that someone just poked in the eye can't seem to change the subject: they are being attacked on a particular front and are struggling to defend themselves. They are not the ones who made sexuality the center of the culture wars. Social liberals have for the most part picked these fights because orthodox views about sexual morality (which insist on fundamental limits to the scope of personal choice) strike them as uniquely oppressive and backward, and they cannot abide their persistence. Indeed, many liberal combatants in our contemporary culture wars probably aren't otherwise troubled by religion much at all. This is why they are baffled to find themselves labeled enemies of Christianity. They believe sexual freedom is essential to the project of modern liberation but need not be essential to the project of Christian godliness.

Many social conservatives cannot be so nonchalant about sexuality when pressed about it. It matters a great deal to their understanding of virtue, flourishing, and moral order and their sense of their religious obligations. When they approach these matters purely defensively, however, they allow themselves to be dragged into a public posture that overemphasizes what is ultimately just one element of what they have to offer the country.

But perhaps most important, the defensive posture encouraged by the prioritization of religious liberty gives social liberals far too much credit and leaves social conservatives far too despairing. By taking as their starting point the presumption that a particularly radical social liberalism is now pervasive throughout American society, social conservatives grant their adversaries in the culture wars an unearned advantage. The fact is that the social Left is a minority, too, and it is a minority aspiring to dominate our institutions at a time when those institutions are particularly weak and diffuse. Social conservatives exaggerated their own dominance over the mainstream culture in decades past, and now they exaggerate the Left's dominance.

None of this means the struggle for religious liberty is unimportant. It is utterly crucial, but it is crucial as a means of restraining an overconfident and at times downright authoritarian social liberalism—tolerated by Americans well beyond its own partisans, but abusing that toleration to extend its reach and power. Conservatives should engage in the struggle for religious liberty to help highlight for that larger public one key way in which the Left is overreaching and to call on Americans' instinctive distaste for bullying and intimidation. But this defensive struggle cannot be the main event in our culture wars. It is a precondition for the essential work of social conservatism. Its goal is to keep open the space in which cultural conservatives might appeal to the larger society—but it must not substitute for that appeal.

That appeal, in turn, must come to be deeply informed by an understanding of the changes our society has been undergoing: it must be geared to addressing a diffuse and decentralizing America—a body of citizens accustomed to personal choice in every realm yet also often painfully conscious of the longings left unaddressed by expressive individualism and of the needs left unmet in the naked public square.

EXPRESSIVE INDIVIDUALISM, IF TAKEN ALL the way to its logical conclusions, points toward moral chaos, and moral traditionalists are therefore its natural critics and opponents. The work they do to restrain its reach and counteract its excesses is essential to the future of our society. But social conservatives have long been accustomed to thinking that what most threatens their ability to engage in this work is the breakdown of our consolidated, generally traditionalist moral order. They are therefore inclined to believe that they must also be defenders of consolidation—that they can only thrive as masters and possessors of a broad mainstream.

This surely is no longer true. In our time, the greatest threats facing social conservatives come not from the profusion of moral practices and views in American life, but from the efforts of some on the radical Left to use liberal-dominated institutions (from the federal bureaucracy to universities, the mainstream media, and much of the popular culture) to suppress and exclude traditionalist practices and views. The breakdown of dominant, centralized cultural institutions is therefore not necessarily a path to moral anarchy. Rather, moral anarchy has actually become something like the explicit goal of some of our most influential institutions. The weakening of those institutions, for all its perils, is hardly the end of the world for those concerned with the moral order of our society.

The fragmenting of the mainstream into numerous cultural tributaries could therefore actually enable some renorming of our culture if we let it. Any effective twenty-first-century solution to some of the most significant challenges we face would involve not less, but more diffusion and diversity, if it can be guided by the need to counteract the isolation and estrangement that now pervade our culture.

What might this mean for cultural conservatives? No longer able to imagine that they dominate the common culture, pressed into becoming a subculture whether they like it or not, and finding it necessary to offer the public something more than defensive pleading, cultural conservatives should assert themselves by offering living models of their alternative to the moral culture of our hyper-individualist age.

Not surprisingly, and not coincidentally, pursuing this path would again require a resort to the mediating institutions of our society—a reinvigoration of community life in ways that embody at a local, personal level the vision of the good that moral traditionalists want to offer. The Judeo-Christian moral vision is not, at its deepest and most fundamental level, a political vision, so its enactment does not require (and in some ways is surely even undermined by) control of the commanding heights of society. It generally looks to the forming of souls before the forming of nations. For this reason, it often functions best at the kind of personal level achievable only in a genuine community, situated between the singular individual and the mass state. It is a vision that requires mediating institutions for its enactment in the world, and that thrives by constructing such institutions around itself.

The predicament of social conservatives in our time is driving them toward just such a constructive subcultural traditionalism. Because the larger culture has drifted away from the traditional norms of family life, for instance, mere persistence in those norms is becoming a countercultural statement—and a community consciously built around them becomes, almost by default, a subculture with a moral life of its own, provided it is given the freedom to try.

Whether they intend to or not, practitioners of orthodoxy thus launch models of alternatives that, if they are successful, can appeal to outsiders seeking the path to flourishing that they might provide. They stand as living answers to the unrequited longings, and at times the destructive disorder, that emerge in the quarters of our society most deeply shaped by expressive individualism and its corollaries.

The problem and the solution are thus both before us already—what we lack too often is the ability to see them, because we are looking for something else. We are looking for a new norm, a new ethic to define the common culture. But the common culture is much less important than it used to be. That doesn't mean we can abandon it, or can stop struggling for its character and soul. But it does mean that we can probably help it most by living out what we propose to our neighbors as the good life. This is both more possible and more necessary in our fractured America than it used to be in the consolidated America of midcentury. And it offers a way forward—a way to hold on to those institutions and ideals that must remain important to our culture.

Subcultural traditionalism can be embodied in interpersonal institutions of various forms: in civic groups that channel their energies into making neighborhoods safe and attractive, or into helping the poor, or protecting the vulnerable, or assimilating immigrants, or helping fight addiction; in schools that build character and inculcate the values parents think are most important; in religious congregations that mold themselves into living communities of like-minded families, and that turn their faith into works to improve the lives of others; in the work of teachers and students who are committed to liberal learning and engagement with the deepest questions.[25]

The efforts and character of institutions like these can grow into a way of life when the people involved in them put them at the center of their cultural existence and identity and, as it were, fall into orbit around their rich moral core. That might take the form of a total, life-changing commitment, as when a group of families commits to building a new church community together, or devotes itself to the thriving of a charter school. But it might also involve a subtler shift in emphasis and focus—a withdrawal of some attention from the frantic commotion of national controversies and its reinvestment in mindful, practical engagement with local challenges of a more human scale.

Such communities often involve both at once, as when a minister who plants a new church at the heart of a broken community, and devotes himself to the hard work of healing, is backed by the time and resources of benefactors or parishioners where they are able. Institutions like these build living communities around them from the bottom up, and bring order to the lives of those communities and their members. America is full of examples of this approach in action, and it always has been, but it is time to see them less as rare exceptions and more as models for a new countercultural engagement with the broken, hurting places in our culture.[26]

Such communities can work together and reinforce one another, or they can separately pursue their similar ends. What unites them and defines them is a commitment to work at the personal level—at the level of individual human beings—and so to adapt to the multiplicity of circumstances that compose our country and to speak to human longings and human problems in their own terms. Rather than abstract from their moral vision and address everyone at once, or always search for ways to "scale up," such communities can make their vision more concrete by addressing the particular people around them in their particular place and time.

The importance of keeping things at the human scale implies that such a subcultural approach to addressing our country's weaknesses would be easier than it might seem. It does not have to require some great act of social founding. It often requires merely the living out of the virtues of community and family that orthodox traditionalists believe are required of all of us. They may not need to do something new, but they might need to understand what they are already doing in a new way—as at once a shelter and a model, a refuge and an act of edifying rebellion. And they need to see that most of the time, this can suffice, especially if they are willing to welcome into their circle outsiders who come in search of what they have to offer.

The idea of such a subcultural conservatism has been advanced by a small but growing band of visionary traditionalists in recent years. Their case for it has fallen into two broad modes: one more despairing, and the other more hopeful. The more despairing mode emphasizes the element of exile or escape in this subcultural approach, and inclines to overstate the power of a radical cultural liberalism in our society, and therefore to understate the potential redemptive and unifying power of community-centered alternatives. The more hopeful mode suggests that emphasizing the needs and well-being of one's near-at-hand community first and foremost can be, for social conservatives, not an alternative to fighting for the soul of the larger society, but a most effective means of doing so. The two are not entirely distinct—and the same individuals can sometimes be found voicing both—but the differences between them will be important in setting the tone of the next social conservatism.

A few cultural critics have been pointing in the first, darker, direction for decades. Especially notable among them has been the Scottish philosopher Alasdair MacIntyre. At the end of his groundbreaking 1981 book *After Virtue: A Study in Moral Theory*, MacIntyre drew some parallels between the contemporary West and the Roman world as it declined into the dark ages. "A crucial turning point in that earlier history," he wrote, "occurred when men and women of good will turned aside from the task of shoring up the Roman imperium and ceased to identify the continuation of civility and moral community with the maintenance of that imperium." Instead, they sought to build around themselves the kinds of human communities they believed essential to the survival of their way of life, and used those to escape a collapsing civilization.

Something of the same spirit is necessary for traditionalists to confront the challenges of our time, he argued. "This time however the barbarians are not waiting beyond the frontiers," McIntyre warned. "They have already been governing us for quite some time. And it is our lack of consciousness of this that constitutes part of our predicament. We are waiting not for a Godot, but for another—doubtless very different—St. Benedict." In the sixth century, St. Benedict of Nursia founded communities of monks intended to help safeguard Christian culture in a world that was quickly becoming unruly and dangerous—as MacIntyre clearly believed our own world is also becoming.[27]

MacIntyre's melancholy vision has inspired some contemporary champions of a turn to socially conservative subcultures, some of whom (led especially by the thoughtful conservative journalist Rod Dreher and the magazine for which he writes, *The American Conservative*) have been working to articulate such a vision under the banner of a "Benedict Option." Their work has sometimes gestured in the direction of despair and escape, and of rather simply equating the American project from its inception with a kind of hyper-individualism (if not Gnosticism) that dissolves the traditional moral architecture of society. But their work has also offered up deep and fertile reflection on the character and purpose of their Christian message and on the ways in which it might take shape in cohesive communities whose aim is not only defensive but also missionary.[28]

Dreher is careful to distance himself from a quietist or separatist interpretation of his project, and to argue that turning inward is essential if religious traditionalists are to keep alive the flame with which they are entrusted. As he put it in 2015: "What the Benedict Option asks you to think seriously about is the extent to which all of us need to withdraw strategically, in a limited fashion, into our own communities—churches, schools, and so forth—not to keep ourselves untainted by the world, but so we can deepen our knowledge, practice, and commitment to the faith, and our bonds with each other, precisely so we can be the salt and light that Christ commanded us to be." Other champions of the Benedict Option have been even more explicit about how an inward turn could strengthen the capacity of traditionalists to serve both their neighbors and their country.[29]

At their best, these thinkers offer something much more appealing than a refuge for miserable exiles. They point toward a more positive vision of a community-centered social conservatism, one which not only does not reject the larger society, but that ultimately works to repair, unify, and redeem it.

This more aspirational form of the quest for moral community seeks to turn inward from the national state not because some inevitable cataclysm is upon us, but because of precisely the trends we have been tracing. The center has not held in American life, so we must instead find our centers for ourselves as communities of like-minded citizens, and then build out the American ethic from there. A resurgence of orthodoxy in our time will not involve a recovery of the old mainline churches or a reclaiming of the mainstream, but an evolution of the paraphernalia of persuasion and conversion of our traditional religious and moral communities. Those seeking to reach Americans with an unfamiliar moral message must find them where they are, and increasingly, that means traditionalists must make their case not by planting themselves at the center of society, as large institutions, but by dispersing themselves to the peripheries as small outposts.

In this sense, focusing on your own near-at-hand community does not involve a withdrawal from contemporary America, but an increased attentiveness to it. It is the peculiar modern mix of individualism and centralization that amounts to a withdrawal from the world, or a willful blindness to the ways that it might be changing. It is a simple fact of contemporary American life—indeed, among its core generative facts—that our society is fracturing in ways that make the local and particular more significant. For social conservatives to turn more of their attention to the local and particular is not a surrender but an adaptation to current realities that will better enable them to approach their neighbors with meaningful help and understanding.

The notion that living models of practical orthodoxy could appeal to modern Americans may seem implausible. But observers of modern democracy at least since Alexis de Tocqueville have noted that in democratic times, and especially in eras dominated by individualism, it is precisely the moral and religious institutions that hold firm to orthodoxy that have proven most attractive—thanks in no small part to their countercultural character. In our time, no less than any other, traditionalists should live out their faiths and their ways in the world, confident that their instruction and example will make that world better and that people will be drawn to the spark. Without dominant institutions of mass conformity and uniformity, we are more than ever in need of institutions of interpersonal moral formation, and these will inevitably be institutions that address us at the level of an eye-to-eye community.[30]

It is an irony that should not escape our attention that, in turning toward this kind of subcultural approach to advancing their moral mission, social conservatives would be adapting some of the language and arguments of advocates of the kind of cultural diversity—if not multiculturalism—that the Right has frequently decried in recent decades. Indeed, as conservatives come to terms with an America whose diffusion we have too often willfully ignored in decades past, we may find some odd bedfellows. As the conservative journalist Michael Brendan Dougherty pointed out in 2015, conservatives in twenty-first-century America may come to look at some familiar subjects with new eyes:

> A social conservative might be predisposed to dislike union organizers, until he considers them as one of the last voices for voluntary social solidarity unaffiliated with the state. New Urbanists are not just allies in the fight for beauty, but against the dumbest features of municipal cronyism. Conservatives once loathed identity politics as an effacement of a common American culture they sought to protect, but it may turn out to be the last protection of conservative Christians if they become a minority movement.[31]

Dougherty's way of framing the point highlights just why there may be superficial similarities between the language of multiculturalism and the logic of a subcultural conservatism: in our diffusing society, the alternative to cohesive subnational communities is increasingly not a cohesive national spirit (which conservative critics of multiculturalism always sought to defend and to celebrate), but a thoroughgoing radical individualism. Given that alternative, the subculture is preferable even from the point of view of the champion of social cohesion. This is one reason why the pursuit of attractive moral subcultures should not be seen as a rejection of national unity, but as a means of drawing individuals out of themselves and toward the possibility of finding moral meaning in community—which might ultimately also prepare them for some common national aspirations and enterprises.

But this point also suggests that the analogy of subcultural conservatism to multiculturalism ultimately does not hold. Multiculturalism has generally worked to highlight what makes the members of different communities different: it has emphasized identity, and has often sought special benefits, special standing, and special recognition for members of groups it would set apart. But culturally conservative communities seek instead to embody ideals that their members take to be best for everyone, not just for themselves. A subcultural conservatism would seek not to highlight differences but to embody universal human truths that should shape the character of the larger society. Precisely by turning people's attention inward toward the moral lives of their own communities, it could also turn them outward toward the moral lives of their neighbors and fellow citizens. It would seek to build communities united not by something that would set their members apart from everyone else, but by something they believe they can offer everyone else.

This is why subsidiarity is not multiculturalism, or balkanization. And it is also why a subcultural conservatism would have to be embodied in actual, living *communities*—rather than in *identities*, which can be hung on individuals. Identity politics is the logical conclusion of the premises of our era of radical individualism. A subcultural communitarianism is a counterbalance to that logic. Once more it is the institutions of community and civil society—standing between the individual and the state—that turn out to be most needful in our time.

COMMUNITY AND IDENTITY ARE NOT the same thing. But the difference can be hard to grasp, because we have lately come to use the word "communities" to describe what are essentially just joint identities. A genuine community is not an intangible mass grouping (like "Jewish Americans"), but a concrete, tangible grouping (like "our congregation") that gives you a role, a place, and a set of relationships and responsibilities to other particular human beings. Community involves a mix of dependence on others and obligations to them, and so a connection with specific people with whom you share some meaningful portion of the actual experience of life in common.

From its earliest incarnations, some forms of American progressivism have sought to overcome the dependence that characterizes such communities by constructing some idea of a "national community" to replace them. The notion that you can only understand your place in American life by conceiving of yourself as living in the national community is not a communitarian idea, however, but a form of radical individualism, because in a nation as large as ours, it is not possible to live in actual community with the entire society. A community that large functions by giving essentially no one any real role in the lives of others. National cohesion, which can be very real and very valuable (and frequently has been in our country), is not the same as interpersonal community, and cannot ultimately substitute for it.[32]

A more human-sized community is not an abstract idea but a concrete reality. It can draw us out of ourselves not by giving us a broad, mass identity in common with all others (who stand in the same relation as we do to the whole, but who have little direct relation to us), but by giving us specific, tangible connections with particular others. It thus offers some ballast against the individualism of our time that would function not by centralizing and consolidating, but by working with the grain of diffusion and making the most it.

The liberalization of the 1950s and 1960s made it very difficult for the consolidated US economy to keep functioning well in the 1970s, and the solution was more, not less, liberalization of the economy. Something similar appears to be true of the culture. Our mainstream culture has been ravaged by the fracture and diffusion of the postwar era, but what it now requires (or rather, all that it will for now accept) is more, not less, diffusion. On both fronts, the civic purpose of greater localism and decentralization would not be so much to pull people down from the national level, but to pull them up out of an isolating individualism in a way that only vibrant near-at-hand communities can.[33]

But perhaps most important of all, the reinvigoration of near-at-hand communities of moral purpose would be particularly well suited to the kinds of cultural challenges we face in the age of individualism. We have seen that the scourge of entrenched poverty and the threat of immobility are functions of not only economic but also cultural factors that are deeply rooted. Transforming the lives of Americans stuck in poverty, or suffering the effects of estrangement from the core institutions of human flourishing, will therefore ultimately require more than material support. It will also require changes of behavior and habit and the building of new social capital. This cannot be done through a uniform social policy that injects subtle financial incentives into people's lives to nudge them into making different choices. That might change people's decisions about whether to work, or how to consume, but it is much less likely to change their judgments about whether to marry, or whether to turn their lives around for the sake of their children. Public programs aimed at encouraging those sorts of decisions by the careful management of incentives have a very poor track record.

Decisions like those are much more likely to be influenced by the expectations and mores of the surrounding culture. We stand a chance of helping people change their behavior by enabling them to live in communities with norms that encourage better behavior—to live in a culture in which the most obvious and socially acceptable thing to do in a given circumstance is also the morally preferable choice. That kind of culture can only be created by a whole community, and this is why embodying social conservatism in concrete communities may be the most promising avenue for addressing, over time, the kinds of entrenched social dysfunction that too many Americans now confront. In the absence of a consolidated, single national culture, it is much easier to imagine local, bottom-up moral subcultures creating the circumstances necessary for social renorming and moral revival. Indeed, we can do more than imagine: we can find many instances of just that all around us.[34]

There is not much that public policy can do to create communities that do a better job of encouraging constructive behavior: it could, however, do less harm, and it could leave room for such communities to form, and protect the space in which they take root and grow. That is why federalism and localism matter, why community matters, why religious liberty matters, and why limiting centralization matters. And it is also why all of these matter not as alternatives to a healthier national culture, but as prerequisites for it. The point of a subcultural conservatism (and, in time, presumably, also a subcultural liberalism) is not withdrawal or quietism, but an emphasis on community—on local sources of solidarity rooted in common moral premises—as a way of forming human beings and citizens who can then contribute to their society as well as to their community.

This does not mean that we should give up on national unity or pride. Quite the contrary. But it does suggest that what is required to address the particular excesses and troubles of our age is a new rootedness that will be communal before it is national. This is likely to be true for essentially everyone, but its truth is especially evident to those who do not partake of the cosmopolitanism of our individualist age. In our time, a healthy national identity may have to be constructed for each of us from the bottom up.[35]

The promise of this era, in cultural terms just as in economic terms, is the promise of diversity and choice. The danger of this era, in cultural just as in economic terms, is the danger of polarization and division. And the work of maximizing the promise while minimizing the danger—of enabling more of our fellow citizens to live out their own American dreams without losing the essential unifying power of a commonly held American Dream—is a foremost challenge for our politics in the coming years.

As usual, our political life lags behind our culture and economy in America. Decentralization has not gone nearly as far in politics as in the rest of our society; diversity has yet to be matched by subsidiarity. Our politics remains under the sway of nostalgia for that midcentury golden age—temporarily suspended as it was between an era of consolidation and an age of liberalization, and therefore now essentially irrecoverable. Most of our political leaders, on the Left and the Right alike, thus find themselves hard pressed to understand the polarization of our politics, even as they must play by the rules it has created. And they find it very difficult to grasp the diffusion transforming other facets of our society.

We cannot regain our bearings until that changes. If we are to create the conditions necessary for a revitalization of broadly shared prosperity and for a resurgence of decentralized cultural vitality, our politics will need to overcome its dysfunctions and to help us grow more unified by diversifying.

7

ONE NATION, AFTER ALL

EVEN IN A BITTERLY DIVIDED era, everyone seems to agree on one thing: Washington isn't working. Many people blame polarization itself for our political dysfunction—or rather, they blame the people on the other side of the partisan divide from themselves. If only they didn't stand in the way so stubbornly, things could finally work out. That's a natural enough view, and all of us fall prey to it now and then. But the frustration with our national politics is now remarkably universal. It fans populist anger while driving elites to despair. It persuades progressives that America is stuck while convincing conservatives that we are rushing in the wrong direction. It manages to make people on all sides of most issues feel as though they are under siege.

As we have seen, our frustration is driven in part by a failure of diagnosis—a failure of self-knowledge, which in turn is rooted in a widespread nostalgia for midcentury America. This nostalgia distorts our understanding of where we are and how we got here, thereby blinding us to some defining features of the present. It keeps us from seeing the good as much as the bad, and persuades too many in our politics to double down on tired formulas rather than look for ways to build on the very great strengths of twenty-first-century America to address its serious weaknesses. That nostalgia therefore makes it difficult not only to see a path out of our economic and social challenges but also to see a way past our divisions and to recover some genuine unity amid our raucous, fractured diversity.

Charting a path toward recovery will therefore require us to come to terms with some basic realities. We need to acknowledge that the age of consolidation in America is long over, and is not about to return. We are now a highly diverse and multifarious society defined by its profusion more than its solidity. That means we are fractured and divided, and always pulling ourselves apart. But it also means that we are a layered, varied, and dynamic society that ought to use its sheer multiplicity as an instrument of problem solving.

Just how to do that is one of the great challenges confronting our politics in the coming years. Perhaps the most significant way in which Washington isn't working, then, is that our political system has failed to rise to that challenge—or even really to acknowledge it. Using our multiplicity to our advantage would mean overcoming the binary approach that allows us only two options for thinking about our society: centralized consolidation or atomizing individualism. The former prevents us from benefiting from a vast array of problem-solvers, while the latter badly undermines our unity and social order. But our political vocabulary, built up over a century of coming together and then pulling apart, misleads us into thinking that consolidation and individualism exhaust the possibilities before us.

In practice, we have pursued these two extremes together. And in fact, they can probably only be pursued together. As Alexis de Tocqueville noted in the nineteenth century, as Robert Nisbet noted in the twentieth, and as our own experience has demonstrated, hyper-individualism and excessive centralization are not opposite inclinations but complementary impulses. As a centralizing government draws power out of the mediating institutions of society, it leaves individuals more isolated; and as individualism further erodes the bonds that hold civil society together, people conclude that only a central authority can pick up the slack. That dangerous feedback loop keeps us from seeing the possibility of other sorts of solutions to the problems we face.

Our national politics is stuck in this cycle. On the one hand, it is dissolving and diffusing: public trust in our governing institutions has been in a long-term decline; it has never been lower since the invention of polling. Our two major parties have been weakened, and our politics is more polarized—like our economy and culture.[1]

But on the other hand, we have tended to respond to these diffusing forces by increasingly consolidating the remaining power of government in our centralized, national state. Federal regulatory power has become more concentrated in the past few decades, even where its reach has been reduced by deregulation. Federal spending has grown faster than the economy and faster than state and local public spending. The federal government increasingly treats states and localities like appendages, and civil society like a federal proxy, at best—and sometimes like an outright adversary. Washington's dominance over some key sectors of the nation's life—particularly health care and education—has expanded apace.

Thus, the distinctive political failures of our era are functions of increasingly centralized administration in an increasingly decentralized society. Many of our most pressing problems lie at the nexus of institutional rigidity and social disintegration, each compounding the other, and so are embodied in an unsettling mix of paralysis in government and disunity among the governed. The Left and the Right both bear some blame for this, since they have allowed themselves to become in large measure partisans of centralizing government and of radical individualism, respectively. Their arguments are, in effect, about whether our government should do more or less of the same, and it is not hard to see why the public often finds these debates pointless.

This pattern in our politics not only frequently renders our federal government incompetent, but also stands in the way of the sorts of solutions that our twenty-first-century problems demand—the sorts of solutions toward which the prior two chapters began to point. Such solutions would seek to treat the excesses of individualism not through greater centralization of our institutions, but through greater *de*centralization of them, and to mitigate both over-consolidation and hyper-individualism by revitalizing the mediating layers of society.

These are the sorts of solutions most necessary for confronting our cultural and economic problems. But they are particularly urgent at this time in our political life, for reasons both practical and philosophical: they are required both to help our governing institutions work a little better and to help sustain the preconditions for our free society and for meaningful national unity in an age of fracture.

THAT OUR GOVERNING INSTITUTIONS AREN'T working very well is easy enough to see. Voter frustration with those institutions—from Congress to the federal bureaucracy to state and local public agencies—contributes mightily to the uneasy mood of the moment. And the academic study of American public administration is increasingly the study of decay. Peter Schuck, a veteran student of the federal bureaucracy and legal system (and a self-proclaimed liberal) offers a particularly comprehensive overview of the problem in his 2014 book *Why Government Fails So Often.* He concludes that almost no federal program could pass a cost-benefit analysis and that, as he writes, "the most striking feature of this failure— other than its sheer frequency and pervasiveness—is how deep and structural its causes are."[2]

But there is actually a fair amount of disagreement about those causes. Many scholars of American government, and many concerned citizens too, especially on the Left, contend that our problems require a kind of repetition of the progressive era—that our system is not sufficiently centralized, our government's chief executive is not sufficiently powerful, and our bureaucracy is not sufficiently empowered to address the complex problems we confront. Some even argue that we need to abandon America's constitutional order in favor of a parliamentary system that would allow for more consolidated control and responsibility.[3]

Others argue that polarization itself is killing our governing institutions. In the absence of a broad consensus about the goals of government, our public bureaucracy becomes a kind of political football—a constant object of debate rather than an instrument for advancing the public will—and our political institutions become theaters of aimless combat rather than venues for making governing decisions.[4]

Political polarization has certainly increased significantly in America in recent decades, and the ideological salience of the parties has grown, too. We have a party of the Left and a party of the Right in our national politics today to a greater degree than at almost any point in our history. And we also have an exceptionally unconstructive set of policy debates, which has made the politics of the twenty-first century especially frustrating and intensified the nostalgia many Americans feel for times of greater comity. But while it is true that dysfunction fuels nostalgia, it is also true that nostalgia generates dysfunction. Our polarized parties are now exceptionally backward-looking. They are offering the public a choice of competing nostalgias, neither of which is well suited to contending with contemporary American challenges. Surely at least part of the reason why they don't reach many practical compromises is that neither of them is actually offering many practical prescriptions.

It would be easier to reach workable bargains between distinctly conservative and liberal platforms suited to our circumstances than it is to find agreement between partisans of a rerun of the agenda of 1965 and those of a rerun of the agenda of 1981. But instead of applying their increasingly distinct worldviews to contemporary problems, each party has tended to understand its own increased coherence as an argument for persisting in old policy ideas—for completing the inherited checklists of the Right or Left. Each party so powerfully identifies its political objectives with a particular moment in our past that neither is inclined to apply its insights to today's different circumstances. The name of this problem is nostalgia or anachronism, not polarization.

American politics has been deeply polarized and divided before. The mid-twentieth-century consensus was quite exceptional. As political scientists David Brady and Hahrie Han noted in 2014, "today's polarization is a return to the historic norm of polarization," so that "simple claims about polarization per se being problematic or polarization itself being the explanation for Congress's inability to solve problems oversimplify the historical reality." What is more distinct about our time is our nostalgic disposition, not our lack of agreement.[5]

Because both parties are channeling that nostalgia, moreover, their objectives and priorities tend to be embodied less in concrete policy proposals and more in a vague and aimless frustration, which often manifests itself as populist anger. The form and vocabulary of this anger are expressions of the nostalgia in which it is rooted: they often end up directing themselves to something they call "the establishment"—a very mid-twentieth-century notion, borrowed (even by conservatives) from the postwar radical counterculture. The establishment is precisely what has been falling apart in our society over the past half-century and more. And yet on both the Left and the Right, political frustration is now forcefully directed against the party establishments and the political establishment as a whole. That establishment exists, but, as we have seen in the preceding chapters, it has been growing progressively weaker for decades. Indeed, one of the foremost challenges now facing our society is the challenge of thriving in the absence of a trusted, powerful establishment.

We thus find ourselves in a relatively populist moment in American politics not because the establishment is particularly strong, but precisely because it is weak. Its very weakness makes our establishment contemptible and hard to respect, and its having lost most of its power makes any power it continues to hold more, rather than less, obnoxious.[6]

The same is true of corporatism, or cronyism, in our politics. It, too, has plainly declined in prevalence and power since the middle of the twentieth century, but the significant amount that remains has grown far less tolerable in our diffuse society, distrustful as it is of big institutions and elite collusion. This is mostly to the good, in both cases. We should combat cronyism, which corrupts our politics, and we should generally welcome a populist spirit in our democracy. But we must also be careful to avoid allowing both causes to become mere channels for corrosive cynicism.

Managing that balance will require us to live in the twenty-first century: to overcome our nostalgia, to become better acquainted with how our society is changing and what problems it now faces, and to think about ways of addressing those problems that are suited to how we now live. A great deal of our political dysfunction could be alleviated by seeing modernization, rather than regression, as the means of national restoration.

When it comes to our political parties, such a turn toward the future would mean, first and foremost, modernizing our diagnoses of the nation's present circumstances, and revising our policy agendas based on that analysis. As we saw in the previous two chapters, much of this work would need to involve an agenda of federalism and subsidiarity and a greater inclination to use public policy to enable ongoing, incremental learning on the ground that functions by letting people make choices rather than imposing centralized solutions.[7]

Second, this work would require us to modernize the parties' institutions—perhaps especially the presidential nominating process (created rather carelessly in the early 1970s) and the parties' procedures for candidate recruitment and selection. These, too, were generally built three or four decades ago. They could benefit from institutional reforms rooted in a sense of how our society has changed since then.[8]

But our politics has lost the knack for institutional reform, because our nostalgic mindset leaves us at once apprehensive about how things are changing and unable to imagine structural improvements that would make for appropriate responses. Our faith that decay can't be helped except by the wholesale re-creation of a lost past too often keeps us from acting.

A similar pattern is evident in the dysfunction of the foremost institution of our system of government, the US Congress. Anyone who has observed the workings of Congress in the past decade would have to conclude that the institution is paralyzed. But the common notion that it is paralyzed by partisanship ignores the history of Congress—which is, if anything, a history of partisanship. Midcentury America was, again, an exception to that pattern. But the US Congress has not generally been as paralyzed as it is now even when it has been quite polarized.[9]

The conventional wisdom about congressional dysfunction is that Congress is hopelessly riven between ideological purists (especially among Republicans) and more practical and realistic meliorists (of both parties). But having spent an enormous amount of time with members of Congress and their staffs over the past decade, I believe that the real divide is often not ideological but experiential—a difference between newer members and those who have been in Congress for many years and therefore witnessed the last form of an effective legislative process in action and consider it the norm.

Congress has experienced in recent decades what many of our other governing institutions have experienced: a process of fragmentation. The power of the committee system, which once stood at the core of Congress's substantive work, has been badly degraded in the past several decades both by more assertive central leadership in both houses and by more independent-minded backbenchers. And, in more recent years, the latter of these trends—the rise of backbenchers who chafe against leadership mandates—has weakened that centralized leadership. The power of all intermediaries between the top party leaders and particular members has been diminished (through term limits on committee chairs, for instance, and greater leadership control of the agenda). The power of the leadership over those more atomized members has also diminished, especially since the elimination of "earmarks" in 2011, which has left the leadership powerless to offer public dollars for a member's district or a senator's state as an enticement for his or her vote.

This doesn't mean that Congress can't function again, but it does mean that Congress can't work the way it used to. In fact, the sort of process that yielded major legislation in the second half of the twentieth century hasn't really worked in Congress since around the time of the passage of the No Child Left Behind education bill in 2001, or perhaps the Medicare Modernization Act of 2003. Since then, and therefore for most of this century so far, major legislation has tended to be intensely partisan. It has been crafted by leadership largely in secret, has been pressed through quickly and bluntly, and above all, has been exceedingly rare. Even when it has passed (as with the Affordable Care Act in 2010, or the stimulus legislation in 2009), the course of its enactment has not felt to anyone like a healthy legislative process.

Members of Congress who were not elected before about 2003 have simply never experienced what the old-timers consider a healthy legislative process. They do not know its rhythms and patterns, the sense that a large measure is gradually moving and building momentum, the idea of a bill that will ultimately aim to draw a bipartisan coalition through barter and favor, earmarks and pork. Not having seen such a process succeed, they do not consider it the norm to which Congress should strive to return—and indeed, when they hear of that process, it often strikes them as unattractive, if not appalling.

By now, most members of both houses have joined Congress since that process was last the norm. And the institution has changed in ways that make that norm unlikely to return. But older members—including most of Congress's leaders in both parties—continue to view the old process as the definition of normality, and to wait and work for its return, rather than to seek new patterns of legislative effectiveness. This situation has created a deep division of expectations among members, and particularly among Republicans, since many more of them are newer to Congress. More junior members in both houses want institutional reforms, while more senior members want to recover the old ways of doing business. Congress is therefore now paralyzed in large part precisely because of a counterproductive nostalgia: because some of its most powerful members can only imagine a functional Congress on an old model that is not coming back, and that we should not want back.

A consolidated, secretive, corporatist process driven by authority and seniority and oiled by earmarks just does not seem to be the wave of the future in Congress. Where there has been some light and hope on the policy front on Capitol Hill lately, it has come instead from bottom-up networks of members advancing creative ideas largely outside the bounds of the old process and forcing them onto Washington's agenda—though for the most part not yet into law.

These hints of a new approach have been evident mostly among Republicans in the Obama years (as they are just more likely to arise within the party that does not control the presidency), in policy areas from taxes to welfare to health care to transportation and education. This new way of thinking has drawn the involvement of a few creative committee chairs, especially in the House of Representatives, and appeals to Speaker Paul

Ryan as well, but it has mostly been driven by backbenchers who often were not even members of the relevant committees. And here and there we have also seen some inklings of a bipartisan, networked legislative process, especially around criminal-justice reform and higher education.

There is a long way to go before this new approach to legislation might become the norm, and it cannot happen without some structural and institutional changes. Such changes will not make the parties less polarized or the leadership more centralized: instead, they will enable Congress to abide diffusion and seek ways to make it constructive—especially by re-empowering the formal committees of both houses and by better enabling less formal networks of members to produce legislation. In Congress, just as in the larger society, atomization and centralization are two sides of the same coin, and a better alternative can be found in mediating structures.[10]

But reshaping politics and government in this way will not be easy. It will require both parties to confront not only the fragmentation of some key institutions but also the countervailing pattern of the centralization of power in Washington. Even as our governing institutions have been weakened by the deconsolidation of the larger society, they have also been given more authority and control by that same society. Empowering disintegrating institutions would seem to be a recipe for trouble, and it has been.

This side of the equation—the centralization of power that is the counterpart to the greater individualism of the culture—has been apparent in the damaging dysfunction of many familiar federal programs. It is perhaps most prominently evident in health care, where the absurdly over-centralized Medicare system prevents badly needed innovation from taking place—and the Affordable Care Act is now exacerbating that problem. And it is evident as well in two related trends: in the growth of executive power relative to legislative power at the federal level, and (especially) in the empowerment of the federal government relative to state and local governments and to society at large.

The fracturing of all institutional power affects all of our governing institutions, debilitating them to varying degrees until they can adapt. But the branch of the government least amenable to being fractured—the unitary executive—has been undermined the least, and so has grown relatively stronger. In domestic affairs, the power of the executive branch is now wielded directly out of the White House to a greater degree than at any point in our history, not only because of President Obama's distinctly belligerent overreaching, but because of the efforts of presidents (and the willing collusion of Congresses) of both parties over several decades. This doesn't mean the executive branch is more competent or capable than it once was: the prowess of most federal agencies clearly has decayed. But even as their capacity to act has degraded, their power to act has grown. The age of societal diffusion has been an age of consolidating executive power.

But it has, to an even greater degree, been an age of consolidating *federal* power. Congress may be frequently dysfunctional, and the executive agencies may often be incompetent, but the reach and scope of federal power have nonetheless expanded in our time. The federal government now engages in more direct intervention, through spending and regulation, in the daily lives of Americans than it ever has in peacetime. State and local governments (and much of the nonprofit sector) have increasingly become mere federal agents, especially in health care, welfare, and (if to a significantly lesser extent) education. Some point to this use of proxies as a kind of devolution; in fact, it is not a devolution of power but an exercise of it. It involves a type of delegation through contracting and mandates, but it is not subsidiarity, and is often its opposite.[11]

This pattern has left America's system of federalism in disarray. For half a century and more, federal programs have been designed in ways that abuse the relationship between the federal government and the states—offering large sums of money to state governments in return for effectively deputizing them as enforcers of federal policy decisions. From Medicaid to the highway trust fund to primary and secondary education programs, the federal government has used its resources to turn the fifty sovereign states into something more like federal accessories. State budgets have long since become dependent on this style of federalism, and the capacity of state and local policymakers, and even of civil society, to truly experiment with new approaches to social policy has been badly diminished as a consequence.

The resulting dearth of genuine experimentation, both public and private, weakens our ability to address public problems and improve public services. It makes public agencies at all levels of government less competent. But that very incompetence often leads many politicians and citizens to call for more consolidated power—in Washington, and in the executive—in the hope that it might remedy incompetence. As a result, the middle layers of society—the very spaces and institutions in which the solutions to our twenty-first-century travails will need to be worked out—are routinely circumvented and collapsed.

To end this vicious cycle, we will have to see that political power needs to be dispersed just as other forms of power have been. The twentieth-century welfare-state approach to American government does not offer the answers America needs to the sorts of problems we have been tracing in these pages. We require a new, modernized definition of success—a new and better model of effectiveness, suited to our strengths and directed to our weaknesses. If we Americans are to see past our nostalgia and begin to address the kinds of challenges that have been leaving us so anxious in this century, we will need to look more frequently to genuine subsidiarity. That would be a response to radical individualism and to excessive centralization that would help to put governing power where our diverse country might best use it.

We have seen why an increasingly specialized economy requires policy mechanisms that adapt from the bottom up, and why an increasingly subdivided culture requires more empowered communities and subcultures. We therefore also ought to see why public policy in twenty-first-century America needs to be more diverse, dispersed, and diffuse. This would not mean returning to a premodern division of labor in government, as critics of the devolution of power often assert. Given how far we have come down the road of consolidation over the past century, a revival of subsidiarity in our national life would surely have the character of a kind of practical revolution, even if it were carried out incrementally and gradually (as it must be). But it is essential that such a revival be pursued not as a return to past practices but as an advance to new and better-adapted ones.[12]

Moreover, a revival of subsidiarity must rest not merely on the argument that federalism and localism are how Americans used to do things, but on the argument that federalism and localism are the ways we would be wisest to govern ourselves now, given our particular strengths and weaknesses. That argument would need to make a case for recovering our constitutional system by showing how that system will serve us well now and in the future.

Reemphasizing federalism and subsidiarity would not necessarily always make for more efficient administration. State and local governments and the institutions of civil society are hardly always models of effectiveness. But the federal government isn't, either. The point is not to find the ideal administrator—that is a fool's errand. Public administration in a complicated free society will always be a challenge. The point is that a greater diversity of problem-solvers would give us a greater chance of meeting people's needs; it would let us use our diversity as a tool while also combatting isolation and estrangement.

Honing an inclination to subsidiarity would offer us a way of thinking about solving problems together that begins in the neighborhood, in the church, in the school, in the community, and builds up. It would mean a political system and government better suited to meeting Americans where they are, better adapted to the range and variety of problems our country now confronts, better positioned to help us try solutions that arise in places as close to the problems as possible—and then to use our modern networked architecture of decentralized communication to teach and learn from others dealing with similar problems—and better able to revitalize our civic culture.

The latter point is especially crucial. Beyond its uses in the improvement of public administration, decentralization is increasingly essential to the basic health and unity of our free society. Injecting the middle layers of American life with more significance and power could help to detoxify our political culture a little: subsidiarity can contribute to a badly needed ethic of restraint and toleration in our national politics by reducing the pressure and the stakes involved in what Washington does.

And it would help our character as a people. The tendency of extreme individualism to be joined to extreme centralization is, perhaps above all, a challenge to our national character, because it collapses the space in which we ultimately become virtuous citizens of a free society. Tocqueville, in considering the risks to the character of democratic citizens, took note of how individualism tends to undermine people's faith in their capacity for practical self-government. "They judge that as citizens become weaker and more incapable," he wrote, "it is necessary to render the government more skillful and more active in order to do what individuals can no longer do." But this idea becomes a self-fulfilling prophecy, in that an increased role for centralized power leaves citizens less able to work together at the local level to address their problems. "The morality and intelligence of a democratic people," he observed, "would risk no fewer dangers than its business and its industry if the government came to take the place of associations everywhere."[13]

Why should the morality, intelligence, and character of the American people be threatened by the mix of individualism and centralization that now distorts our politics? The answer runs to the very heart of what it means to be a free society, bringing us to the core of the argument we have been tracing from the start. It helps us see why a society that collapses the space in which the mediating institutions function cannot long remain thriving and free.

THERE IS A WAY TO understand the trends we have been following—the growing fracture and diffusion of American life—as simply advancing the cause of liberty, and so as making our free society more free. By breaking down some concentrations of power, liberating the economy from the strictures of consolidated regulation, freeing people from the pressure to conform to oppressive moral norms, and unleashing a torrent of options and choices, the events of the past half-century have certainly made us more free in some important respects. And if the centralization of government power is directed to enabling that government to help us meet our material needs while we make our free choices, that, too, could make us yet more free in the end.

But this understanding of freedom, and therefore of the free society, is badly inadequate. It is a notion of freedom that, in distinct but related progressive and conservative forms, has grown pervasive in our time, and that also lies at the root of some of the biggest problems we have traced in these pages. Not all progressives share it, of course, but it is certainly the dominant understanding of freedom on the American Left. Many conservatives do not adhere to it, but a libertarian-leaning conservative form of it has nonetheless been prominent on the contemporary Right.

In its progressive (and dominant) form, this hyper-individualist, twenty-first-century notion of liberty begins from the straightforward premise that liberty consists of the individual's freedom from coercion and constraint—in essence, the freedom to shape one's life as one chooses. There will always be limits to that freedom, of course. But in this view most such limits are artificial and set up unjust barriers rather than natural and necessary constraints. Therefore, the proper mission of a liberal society is to remove as many of them as possible.

Some limits are material or economic. The simple fact of scarcity constrains what we can do. But this constraint does not apply equally to all. Some are rich and have ample resources to exercise their liberty, while others are poor and have few options. What is more, the efforts required to meet our material needs—work—often amount to constraints on our freedom as well. This is especially true for the less well-off. They're more likely to work at jobs they don't like for the sake of a paycheck. The liberal society tries to alleviate these constraints by redistributing wealth to some degree.

There are also social or traditional limits. Our society's established ways of doing things—especially in the sensitive realms of family, sexuality, and culture—unavoidably inhibit the freedom of people who would rather do otherwise. Here again the liberal society seeks to loosen or remove constraints, this time by enforcing an ethic of pluralism. Different moral and lifestyle choices are to be respected, provided they are freely made and do not come at the expense of other people's safety or freedom to choose. There are of course boundaries. For example, we harshly censure racism, and in some contexts elaborate taboos develop that critics deride as "political correctness." But the ideal is straightforward. Our society is more just to the degree that individuals are free from what are deemed artificial social constraints. It's for this reason that some progressives see political correctness as ministering to a greater freedom.

Still other limits are political. These often combine the other two types of limits. Progressives suspect that our politics too often answers to powerful interests that seek their own benefit by abusing the weak, or that strive to enforce their own moral views upon dissenters. Therefore, we should limit such abuses of power and protect people's freedom. In essence, our society should be arranged to ensure that as many as possible of our binding obligations are individually chosen, and that our lives are, to the extent possible, our own to shape. Getting to that point will sometimes require coercive actions by the state, especially to limit the power of those who would coerce or constrain the choices of others. Restrictions on campaign contributions provide one example, prohibitions against hate speech another. The liberal vision of freedom deems these limitations legitimate if they are aimed at expanding the realm and reach of individual autonomy overall.

The choosing individual is the foundation of this progressive vision of liberty, and all of society is to be constructed around that essential unit. This is the root of our expressive individualism. It could hardly be stated more neatly than it was in Supreme Court Justice Anthony Kennedy's opinion in the 1992 abortion case *Planned Parenthood v. Casey*: "At the heart of liberty," he famously wrote, "is the right to define one's own concept of existence, of meaning, of the universe, and of the mystery of human life." All is to be made subject to the choosing individual, including the most profound of our human relations and obligations to others. All the world is "concepts," and to each his own.[14]

Conservatives raise a variety of objections to this understanding of the liberal society. But in recent years, many of the most common objections have not reached the root of the problem, because they have emphasized only the fact that the range of government coercion the progressive view of liberty permits is much too broad. The conservatives (and all the more so libertarians) who emphasize this point tend to ground their complaints in the same radical individualism as the progressives they oppose. They don't object to the Left's view of liberty, they just think the Left betrays it. They insist, for instance, that public redistribution of wealth is a greater constraint on free choice than the economic want it is meant to address.

The same goes for campaign-finance laws, speech restrictions on college campuses, and many other progressive efforts to limit liberty for the sake of greater liberty.

Their individualism leads some on the Right to this view in part because the American conservative idea of liberty is often mediated by the concept of rights, and especially property rights. The fact of economic want is not a violation of these rights. Poverty in this sense does not necessarily involve injustice. By contrast, government redistribution of property can directly impinge on our rights of ownership, and so can easily be seen as unjust. Some conservatives therefore assert that an idea of liberty grounded in individual rights is superior to the progressive approach that seeks an overall increase in individual autonomy. Rights, especially property rights, impose meaningful limits on the power of the state, which is uniquely positioned to constrain our liberty.

This highly individualist conservative idea of liberty is less concerned with giving different people equal power to make their choices matter, and more concerned with letting every individual do what he wishes with what he has—provided he does not take from others. This is an ethic of protection rather than provision. A society cannot overlook the well-being of the poor, of course, and most conservatives acknowledge the need to use the power of government to make sure people's basic needs are met. But they regard doing so as part of our general obligation to keep our fellow citizens from deprivation. It has nothing to do with liberty, and so is not fundamental to what makes a free society free.

The individualist progressive therefore sees freedom as a power to act, while the individualist conservative or libertarian sees freedom as an absence of restraint. This is a real difference—a lot of our political debates turn on it—but it can too easily obscure a deeper agreement: that a free society is simply a collection of individuals who are free of coercion or constraint, and nothing more.

This view of liberty fits the society we have become over the past half-century like a glove. Its growing prominence has been driven by our fracture and diffusion, and in turn has further empowered those forces. It is the conceptual counterpart to the social and cultural evolution we have followed. But this means it also suffers from the same failings, and therefore that it highlights the problems with that broader evolution. Simply put, the progressive and conservative versions of this twenty-first-century idea of liberty take the free human person largely for granted. They assume society begins with such individuals, rather than that it produces them.

Taking that choosing person for granted was a luxury we might have thought we could afford in America's midcentury golden age, when a highly consolidated (perhaps even excessively ordered) society was beginning to liberalize. But all the trends we have been tracing suggest we should take that person for granted no longer. Our highly individualist, liberationist ideal of liberty is possible only because we presuppose the existence of a human being and citizen capable of handling a remarkably high degree of freedom and responsibility. We do not often enough reflect on how extraordinary it is that our society actually contains such people. A population of citizens generally capable of using their freedom well is the greatest achievement of modern civilization—greater even than the US Constitution and the market system, which depend upon such people. That achievement is the prerequisite for the free society, not only at its origin but in every generation. It is what makes the illusion of complete autonomy even minimally credible.

And yet, we clearly fail to appreciate it. It is a very dangerous thing to take the preconditions for our way of life for granted, especially when the centrifugal forces pulling at our society increasingly undermine those preconditions. But what exactly are those preconditions? What, indeed, does it take to make the freely and rationally choosing man or woman possible?

An idea of liberty is an essential part of the answer. But it is not the individualist notion of liberty we have just traced. Surely liberation from coercion alone does not prepare us for the practice of liberal freedom. To liberate us purely to pursue our wants and wishes is to liberate our appetites and passions. But a person in the grip of appetite or passion couldn't be our model of the free human being. Such a person is not someone we would easily trust with the exercise of great political and economic freedom.

The liberty we can truly recognize as liberty is achieved by the emancipation of the individual not just from coercion by others but also from the tyranny of his unrestrained desires. This is hardly a novel insight, of course: Socrates helped his students grasp it twenty-five centuries ago. Judaism, Christianity, and Islam are rooted in it. But it is a truth our high self-esteem sometimes makes us forget.

This older idea of liberty requires not only that people be free to choose, but also that they be able to choose well. Such liberty arises when we want to do more or less what we ought to do, so that the moral law, the civil law, and our own will are largely in alignment, and choice and obligation point in the same direction. To be capable of freedom, and capable of being liberal citizens, we need to be capable of that challenging combination. And to become capable of it, we need more than the liberation of the individual from coercion. We need a certain sort of moral formation.

To achieve that formation in a free society—where we do not want the state to direct or compel it—requires that we commit ourselves to more than our own will and whim. It requires a commitment precisely to the formative social and cultural institutions that we have seen pulled apart from above and below in our age of fracture. They are where human beings become free men and women ready to govern themselves.

The family is the first and most crucial institution of moral formation. It is above all the nursery of the next generation, which enters the world incapable of exercising liberty and plainly in need of both protection and instruction. And it is proof against the notion that all human relations can be turned into matters of choice. To live as fathers and husbands, wives and mothers, children and siblings, is to live lives shaped by duties and obligations that sometimes grate but often bring joy. This is why the family is best suited to creating individuals freely discharging their responsibilities—the very foundation of any free society. But when we lose sight of the need for the formation it enables, the family can easily come to seem instead like a constricting social form that is justified, at best, as a reliable way to meet some basic material needs—which could surely be met in other less oppressive ways.

Work is another crucial means of shaping us for liberty. Like the family, it has an obvious material utility, enabling us to support ourselves and our families financially. But work also buttresses dignity, inculcates responsibility, encourages energy and industry, and rewards reliability. It can help form us into better human beings and better free citizens. To see only its material utility is to imagine that work, like family, could be replaced by more efficient forms of distribution. If work is nothing more than a means to financial support, nothing is lost if we provide for the needs of those with meager means in ways that do not require those who can to enter the workforce—and so we now often do.

An excessively utilitarian understanding of the human good also inclines us toward a thin, unedifying notion of education. Even (or perhaps especially) in higher education, we are increasingly squeezing out liberal learning to make room for more skills training and technical degrees. We surely need technical education, but that cannot be all that education means. Liberal learning is out of step with our times because it offers us not vocational skills but the shaping of habits of thought and practice. It forms our souls through exposure to beauty, to truth, and to the power of the sublime that we can only glimpse through the mediation of rare artistic genius. It is, in this sense, closer to an aristocratic idea of leisure than to the modern idea of training, which is why it offers an essential corrective to the excesses of our way of life.

Civic engagement can also help us learn to use our freedom in practice. By enabling us to make a difference in the lives of our neighbors through common action, it can help us see the limits of both radical individualism and hyper-centralization. By a utilitarian measure of administrative efficiency, local action could sometimes (though not always) seem inferior to some federal programs. But in terms of preparing us for the burdens of liberty, it can be invaluable.

But the ultimate soul-forming institutions in a free society are frequently religious institutions. Traditional religion offers a direct challenge to the ethic of the age of fracture. Religious commitments command us to a mixture of responsibility, sympathy, lawfulness, and righteousness that align our wants with our duties. They help form us to be free. That is not why they draw the allegiance of liberal citizens, of course: people are drawn to what they understand to be the truth their faith reveals. But the role of religious institutions in enabling our free society to thrive is nonetheless an additional important reason for that *society* to value and protect them.

Being valued and protected is what these mediating institutions all require from the larger society. And in return, they help to form us as free citizens who can live together—not by agreeing with one another about everything (as different institutions and communities can inculcate quite different ethics), but by living out the genuine potential, and recognizing the real limits, of human liberty in practice.

Of course, not everyone has the good fortune of a flourishing family, or the opportunity for rewarding work, or a liberal education, or a humbling faith, let alone all of these at once. In our time, in particular, many people are not only estranged from some of them but are denied the chance to encounter them. But some combination of these soul-forming institutions is nonetheless within the reach of most, and the work of reinforcing them, sustaining the space for them, and especially putting them within the reach of as many of our fellow citizens as possible must be among our highest and most pressing civic callings. That calling, rather than a hyper-individualist liberationism, should be the organizing principle of our political life, helping us see what to conserve and how to progress.

And yet, as we have seen, it is our attachments to these very institutions that have been most degraded in modern America. The progress of the ethic of diffusion and liberalization has meant growing estrangement from precisely these prerequisites for human flourishing, especially among the least advantaged Americans. And the well-intentioned responses of our government to the material deprivation often created by that dislocation have frequently only worsened the very same estrangement.

It could hardly avoid doing so, since family, work, community, and religion are what fill the middle layers of our social life. So while individualism pulls at them from below, centralized government pulls at them from above, hollowing out the middle spaces where a free society forms its citizens.

This is, then, just another way to tell the same story laid out in previous chapters, but from the perspective of the evolution of our public philosophy and our social and political institutions, which has naturally
accompanied the evolution of our economy and culture. And it points
toward the same conclusion—highlighting the need for a revival of our
mediating institutions as a way to preserve and build upon the benefits of
our society's liberalization and diversification while addressing the costs of
its fracture and diffusion.

But putting the problem in these terms also highlights the need for
political arguments that might give voice to the case for such an approach
to national renewal. Changing how we think about the structure of our
society will require also challenging how we now tend to understand freedom—and therefore how we understand much else. A fuller idea of freedom than the one we now incline toward turns out to be a precondition
for the actual practice and preservation of freedom in our time. So a public argument about the mediating institutions is essential to confronting
the kinds of problems we have been tracing in these pages.

In time, both the Left and the Right will need to formulate their cases
to the nation in this vocabulary of the human scale. The Left certainly has
a lot to work with in constructing a progressivism of the mediating institutions, including a rich tradition of community activism, labor organizing,
political engagement, and economic localism. But it will have to overcome
a social vision that is by now deeply rooted and powerfully dominant among
liberals: the idea that the only genuine liberty is individual liberty, and that
the only legitimate authority is the authority of the national government.

The Right has a great deal more to work with. And there is reason to
think that conservatives will get there first and will find that they are exceptionally well armed to help revitalize and modernize America in the age
of fracture. For reasons that run very deep, the Right is particularly well
positioned to see the limits of a hyper-individualist understanding of the
free society and the practical and philosophical necessity of our mediating
institutions.

By reconnecting with the roots of its conservatism, today's Right can
therefore make the case for the recovery of an inclination to subsidiarity

as a means of mitigating both the administrative dysfunction of our government and the oversimplification of liberty that has characterized twenty-first-century America.

IT MAY SEEM PECULIAR TO suggest that conservatives may well be the first to look forward and adapt. There is, after all, something inherently nostalgic about any form of conservatism. What we now require of our politics will involve some significant changes, and a disposition toward adaptation and adjustment. Why should conservatives be better able than liberals to offer that?

The answer has to do with the substance of the changes our society has undergone and with the character of the reforms we need. Both, as we have seen again and again, should send us looking to the middle layers of society for answers. And conservatism is—or rather can be and should be—the political philosophy that understands society as what happens in those mediating structures. The reasons for that reach to the ideological core of the modern Right.

American conservatism has always consisted of a variety of schools of social, moral, political, and economic thought. But they are nearly all united, in a general sense, by a cluster of anthropological assumptions. Conservatives tend to see the human person as an incorrigible mass of contradictions: a fallen and imperfect being created in a divine image, a creature possessed of fundamental dignity and inalienable rights, but always prone to excess and to sin, and ever in need of self-restraint and moral formation. This elevated yet gloomy conception of man, deeply informed by the peculiar, paradoxical wisdom of the West's great religions, often distinguishes conservatives from libertarians and progressives alike, and sits at the core of most conservative thinking about society and politics.

It leads, to begin with, to low expectations of human affairs, away from utopianism, and to a sense that the most profound and basic human problems recur in every generation because they are intrinsic to the human person. That fallen character of man suggests that, left to itself, the default condition of the human race is more likely to be miserable than happy, and that failure in society is more likely than success. We conservatives are therefore often far more thankful for success in society than we are outraged by failure. And so we look to build on what is working more often than we seek to start from scratch.

Progressives tend to feel differently because their expectations are often higher. They are more open to the possibility of permanently overcoming some human limitations, and sometimes think they have a formula for doing that, so the persistence of failure infuriates them. When conservatives are outraged, it is generally at seeing something valuable lost; progressives are more commonly outraged at the obduracy of the status quo. A good and just society surely requires both inclinations.

An appreciation of and gratitude for what works in society, and an inclination to address our failures by building on successes, give conservatives a high regard for long-standing social institutions—those that have been valued by generations of people dealing with the same kinds of basic human problems we now face. It is a key reason why conservatives are traditionalists, inclined to be protective of established ways rather than quick to throw them aside.

Those customs and institutions that have stood the test of time (which is really a recurring trial-and-error process, generation after generation) are likely to be best adapted to help us address timeless human challenges and meet enduring human needs, and therefore to enable genuine progress. They are likely to possess more knowledge than we can readily perceive, and more than any collection of technical experts, however capable, is ever likely to have. And, of course, such institutions—families, communities, civic and religious groups, markets, and more—make up the mediating layers of a free society.

An appreciation of those middle layers is therefore one of the things that most often sets conservatives apart from progressives. Because they often reject the legitimacy and suspect the motives of many of our mediating institutions, contemporary progressives tend to make arguments for government action that implicitly assume, without expressly defending, a view of society as consisting of individuals and a state. So, for instance, in his Second Inaugural Address in 2013, President Obama argued that the demands of a changing world make a greater reliance on government unavoidable, because the only alternative is a radical and simple-minded individualism:

> For the American people can no more meet the demands of today's world by acting alone than American soldiers could have met the forces of fascism or communism with muskets and militias. No single person can train all the math and science teachers we'll need to equip our children for the future, or build the roads and networks and research labs that will bring new jobs and businesses to our shores. Now, more than ever, we must do these things together, as one nation and one people.[15]

This emaciated understanding of the life of our nation is precisely why the Left is for now poorly equipped to help America adjust to twenty-first-century realities. In Obama's view, and that of many other liberals, there seem to be no meaningful middle layers of society. Our only modes of action appear to be as a "single person," or "one nation and one people." It is a view that flattens the complex, evolved topography of social life and leaves us no way out of the corrosive feedback loop of individualism and centralization.

The sociology of conservatism, which understands society as spun out of the family, the community, and the array of mediating social structures that shape relationships among individuals, should move the Right to fervently resist that flattening. It should move us to seek progress through society's evolved, traditional institutions, rather than around them or in spite of them, because those institutions answer to the enduring character of the human person.

And that correspondence between the human person and the complicated social institutions that give our society its form means, in turn, that there is no easy way to effectively replace the mediating institutions. The alternative to working through the middle layers of society to address our problems is working through synthetic and artificial social structures created by brute exercises of technical expertise empowered with state authority. In other words, the alternatives to our traditional mediating institutions are government programs rooted in the sociology of progressivism.

We now live amid a profusion of such programs. They are the pillars of the liberal welfare state. They were designed with the best of intentions: each is expected to answer a real social need that some progressives believed could no longer be met by the mediating institutions of society. And they have surely done a great deal to help people in need. But, as we have seen, they are increasingly poorly suited to the kinds of problems our society faces in this era of fracture and diffusion—when the capacity for centralized social management, which has always been very limited, grows more so all the time.

An appreciation of that limit links the Right's vision of society to its theory of administration. Because conservatives tend to believe that society's knowledge, gained over generations of trial and error, is contained in the forms, structures, and ideals of its institutions, they tend to expect those traditional institutions ultimately to be more functional and adaptable than even the best-engineered public programs. Conservatives tend not to share in the progressive confidence in technical expertise, because they doubt that any group of experts could ever have enough knowledge to pull off the feats of management and administration that our government is now frequently expected to achieve. Institutions that channel social knowledge from below and address human needs at a personal level are more likely to adapt to problems and circumstances and to find solutions.

That bottom-up channeling of knowledge is what many of our society's mediating institutions do much of the time. And it is a role they could play in helping to address some of what we generally think of as public policy problems as well. Presented with a classic policy problem (like how to improve schooling, reduce poverty, or lower health-care costs), an approach that sought to empower rather than crowd out the mediating institutions might allow different service providers to try different ways of meeting the need in question (like providing schooling or insurance), enable recipients or consumers of those services to decide which approaches work for them and which do not, and keep those that work and not those that fail.

Conservatives today are well positioned to propose different ways of moving from the welfare-state model to precisely this kind of mediating-institution model of policy in different arenas of public policy. They already routinely propose such reforms in some key areas, such as education, health care, and welfare, and it is where conservative ideas point on the full range of domestic policy questions.

Conservatives now need to help the public see just what we have to offer on this front, and why it makes for a particularly good fit for the challenges America confronts. Conservatives should therefore enter into the details of public-policy debates, and not limit themselves to the level of abstraction. Some conservatives recoil from such details, taking arguments about them to be concessions to the technocratic mindset they reject. But in fact, engaging in such debates is the only way to effectively transform our governing institutions—to imbue them with an anti-technocratic modesty that makes possible continuous improvements against a background of constructive stability.[16]

In America, such engagement with the details of policy is particularly important because it can also be a means of rescuing the character of our public institutions from some destructive distortions. The US Constitution, as both its structure and the writings of its framers make clear, is rooted in just the sort of skeptical view of human nature and human power that now often characterizes conservatism, and it advances precisely the view that the government (and the Constitution itself) exists to create a protected space within which society can flourish, rather than to fill that space or command what happens in it. That is why the Right tends to view the boundaries established by the Constitution as liberating (or as creating a space for us to thrive), while the Left tends to view them as constricting (or as keeping the government from acting decisively and moving the country forward).

American progressives have often been dissatisfied with the modest role assigned to the federal government in our system, and have sought innovations in public administration that would advance a more assertive role for it. We have seen why such federal assertiveness, which is the counterpart to radical individualism, needs to be restrained. A key task of conservative reformers today is to recover the more humble idea of American government at the core of our system. They must do so by starting with that system as they find it; there is no other choice. Championing changes in modern government must not be confused with a willingness to abide the presumptions that have distorted that government for many decades.

The modernization of our institutions that is now so badly needed will therefore have the character of a recovery—not a return to the past, but a revival of the timeless principles and premises that undergird our system of government. And among those principles and premises is the fact that our free society requires a flourishing private culture of moral formation for liberty, which in turn requires that we prize and defend the institutions that engage in such formation at a personal level.

American conservatism has long been the party of the mediating layers in our politics, in deed if not always in word, resisting the twin pressures pulling those institutions apart from above and below. What we now think of as fiscal conservatism, with a more libertarian bent, has struggled to resist the pressure to collectivize and centralize our national life, restraining federal power and insisting on its limits. What we now think of as social conservatism, with a more communitarian bent, has struggled to resist the pressure to disaggregate our national life, restraining our expressive individualism and insisting on the importance of family, faith, work, and community. They have frequently worked together not only because they have common adversaries, but also because they often (though not always) share a common vision of the good.

But as a political movement, American conservatism is now much more in the habit of emphasizing the rhetoric of opposition to excessive centralization than the rhetoric of opposition to excessive individualism. Prominent conservatives, including politicians, have frequently made an explicit case for the mediating, human-level institutions, and for understanding even the Right's case against centralization as a defense of those institutions. But the modern Right's formative experiences in the struggle against communism, and its vital, continuing struggle against the consolidating welfare state, have made a kind of loose vocabulary of hyper-individualism the lingua franca of conservatism.[17]

Today, when our deepest national problems have more to do with dissolution than with constriction and conformity, the Right needs to recover the language of conservative communitarianism—to make the case for the middle layers—both when waging the essential fight against statism and when making the difficult case against radical individualism. We need to refine and clarify our defense of the dense, thick forms of American citizenship that are only possible in the middle and that have long been thinned and diluted by both over-centralization and hyper-individualism.

This is why conservatives, as the partisans of the mediating institutions in our politics, could be uniquely well positioned to take the lead in helping America out of its twenty-first-century funk. They have much work to do to get there, but they have a shorter road to travel. Liberals will likely ultimately find their way to a left-leaning version of such an agenda as well. But they start further behind, because they are not only blinded by nostalgia (as conservatives tend to be as well), but also too frequently committed to precisely the vision of society—the vision of an America consisting of individuals and a government—that now needs to be overcome.

The first glimmers of a way out of our frustrations are likely to look like a conservative agenda of modernization through subsidiarity, a revival of federalism, and a commitment to a robust pluralism of moral subcultures.

ULTIMATELY, AND PERHAPS MOST IMPORTANT, such an agenda will also need to draw us together again in an age of division and fracture. In its conservative and its liberal forms, it will need to help us as Americans begin to rediscover what unites us, and why a restoration of the mediating layers of our society would also be a restoration of a robust idea of citizenship.

Our idea of citizenship has, after all, been strained and thinned for decades by the forces pulling us apart. And the frustration that now pervades our politics suggests that these strains have put us at risk of both a loss of national cohesion and a dangerous overreaction to that very loss—at risk, that is, of both a loss of our edifying nationalism and the rise of a more pernicious form.

Nationalism can easily take toxic forms, especially in times of change and growing diversity and liberalization—cultural and economic. And it can suffocate the mediating institutions, as it did in America starting early in the twentieth century. But Americans have always also had recourse to a more wholesome and constructive nationalism, because our nation is to an exceptional degree a creedal nation with high expectations of itself. American nationalism need not merely be a love of what our country has been (though it is that), but can at the same time also be a love of what our country ought to be—a love of the ideal that we have always held out before ourselves as the American possibility, even if we have never fully realized it.

But that ideal, put forward in the Declaration of Independence and pursued ever since in a variety of ways by Americans of all races, religions, and political persuasions, is most accessible when we allow the mediating layers of our culture and society to flourish. It is not a vision of radical individualism or of consolidated statism. It is a vision of the free society rooted in an understanding of liberty that depends upon our institutions of moral formation and on the kind of person they produce—the citizen fit for virtuous freedom. It is an ideal rooted in natural rights but put into practice by free men and women who are not merely natural but also social achievements.

American citizenship is not simply the application of that shared ideal, of course. It is not just philosophy in practice. Our society is held together not only by the principles of equality and freedom but also by the shared triumphs and tragedies of American life and by the experience of unity amid diversity—of becoming one out of many not by denying our differences, but by rising above them when we are called.

That idea of American citizenship has been undermined first by the excessive consolidation of the early twentieth century and then by the excessive individualism of the past half-century. The combination of the two has contributed to a distorted understanding of both freedom and authority, and therefore of political life—leaving us with a radically individualistic ideal of liberty and a highly centralized, statist understanding of legitimate authority. But the most profound forms of freedom and authority fill the spaces in between the individual and the state, and both individual freedom and national power are functions of what happens in those spaces. Reviving our commitment to those intermediate layers of our society would therefore help to revive both freedom and authority in American life, and with them American citizenship.

The goal of a robust subsidiarity should therefore not be to have Americans living in parallel, but to better enable us all to live together. As a community is made of families, so our great nation must be built up out of communities, each forming its citizens to seek the good—and so to help the whole to seek the common good. This is how the principles of our founding, together with the active recollection of what is most worthy in our history, can help to draw the best out of our distinct communities. That is why a nationalism that aspires to fulfill the promise of our country requires a nation rooted in its morally meaningful communities. Only such a nation can form its citizens to be capable of standing unified and free in dedication to the noblest of all political propositions.

Our continuing mutual commitment to the proposition that all men are created equal, the truth that holds us together as Americans, is therefore not merely an appeal to some abstraction. Rather, it has been a common touchstone—hearkened to in our moments of greatest pride and held up to shame us out of our greatest faults and moral failings as a nation. It is a nexus of national memory and obligation in no small part precisely because it speaks to the role properly played by the nation in our lives. It calls upon the virtues we can only develop as free people formed in our distinct communities, but it would have us exercise those virtues in the service of a calling so high as to now and then draw us beyond those distinct communities.

An alertness to that kind of national calling and its meaning is frequently a function of precisely our common recognition of communal diversity amid human equality. As the political philosopher Peter Berkowitz has argued, "only a citizenry in the habit of tolerating a multiplicity of outlooks and ways of life—and in the habit of recognizing one another as equal in freedom—will be capable of honoring constitutional imperatives and effectively operating the organs of constitutional government."[18]

And only such a citizenry, too, will be able to resist the excesses of our age of fracture, and to see the need for balance, and for limits. Often, what we all require most are reminders of the truths that modern life too easily makes us forget. The institutions of our society offer those—compelling us to confront the limits of choice, the extent of our deepest more-than-chosen commitments, the necessity of reciprocity, the humanity of our neighbors, and the depths of our dependence and therefore of our obligations. But it is perhaps in particular our national institutions, and our common citizenship, that remind us of another set of easily forgotten truths—about the equal dignity and rights of all, and the unique commitment of this almost chosen people to embody and defend them. As we wrestle with a variety of social, economic, and political challenges in the coming years, we ought to strive to keep that amalgamating memory and unifying conviction in mind, and to pursue our other goals in ways that strengthen, rather than weaken, our common commitment to it.

The centralization of our political life is one obstacle to keeping that commitment strong. It compels us to take up nearly all public questions at the highest level of government, and so at too great a distance from the concrete relationships with one another that make genuine mutual respect a possibility. And it encourages a spirit of strife, a sense of constant combat on every front, which keeps us from simply enjoying our common life together and letting it call us higher. The simultaneous advance of a spirit of radical individualism is another obstacle to keeping ourselves focused on that commitment. It causes us to see our fellow citizens as outsiders in the world we seek to create around ourselves, rather than as friends and neighbors in communities we share.

Our vast, extended republic has always faced the challenge of remaining one nation while remaining free, and so has always confronted the twin temptations of consolidation and individualism. It sought originally to avoid that dual trap by constraining the national government and empowering states, localities, and civil society. Americans were once keenly alert to the risks of what James Madison called "an extension of the Federal powers to every subject falling within the idea of the 'general welfare.'"[19]

At the same time, the most perceptive observers of our society have also long been worried about what Alexis de Tocqueville described as the tendency of democratic individualism to "place men beside one another without a common bond to hold them." The danger inherent in both those excesses is the danger of flattening down the layers of our social life so that only loose individuals and a national state would remain. Both Madison and Tocqueville, like many other keen students of American democracy, proposed empowering the middle layers of society in an effort to combat these tendencies, and that is frequently what America has done: restrain the national government and empower the institutions of family, community, local authority, and civic action.[20]

This cannot always work, of course. There are limits, and there are times when national action is the only way to achieve a national purpose. Subsidiarity means entrusting power to the lowest level that can effectively use it to the good, not simply to the lowest level. But it also means that national action should therefore be an exception, not the norm.

To address our frustration, then, we will need to work to recover the insights that have at other moments of uncertainty guided our country's efforts to forge a geographically, culturally, and economically disparate people into a cohesive nation. But we will need to explore how those insights could be applied to our novel, twenty-first-century circumstances—to build upon our dynamism and diversity while combatting the aimlessness, isolation, social breakdown, and stunted opportunities that now stand in the way of too many Americans.

There will be no simple, wholesale solution to our problems but rather a diverse and variegated mix, expressing in different settings and circumstances different sets of priorities, different diagnoses, and different assessments of value. Subsidiarity means no one gets to have their way exclusively. And that is what freedom means, too. As Robert Nisbet put it half a century ago, a genuinely free society is free because "its power will be limited by associations whose plurality of claims upon their members is the measure of their members' freedom from any monopoly of power."[21]

This is a freedom to be exercised at the interpersonal level. Our national revival will ultimately depend on our ability to revive human-sized institutions of various forms and characters: familial and communal, social and political (of all parties and stripes), charitable and commercial, educational and spiritual, sacred and profane. We will recover our strength and also our unity by living more of our lives at eye level with one another.

That, in the end, is perhaps the deepest reason why a recovery of the model of community as the basic pattern of American life holds out the promise of overcoming the divisions of our age of fracture without surrendering the advances of our era of liberalization and diversity. It can help us live out our American citizenship as a culmination of the virtues we build in our communities. It can contribute to a spirit of forbearance in our political life, by lowering the stakes a little. It can help build stronger habits of engagement and participation at the local level, where, too often, meeting spaces now stand empty, because what happens there is not allowed to matter. Our free society and the essential work it does—including both the effective defense of individual rights and liberties and the effective advancement of national goals and ideals—can only be sustained through the mediating institutions that simultaneously break up concentrated power and pull together isolated individuals.

If we can break the stranglehold of midcentury nostalgia on our common life, we will come to see that the politics of restoration we require will be a politics of subsidiarity. That does not make for a neat and simple checklist of actions to take. It would surely involve some significant transformations of some of our welfare-state institutions. But it would also involve more subtle changes and a different way of thinking about public policy in our day-to-day politics as we go about addressing the kinds of problems our political system is always called on to take up. It would involve a change of emphasis, a new set of instincts and defaults, a different way of approaching our problems and imagining solutions, and a new patience with our country's sheer multiplicity, and therefore a new openness to our country's incorrigible ingenuity. It will mean that not every problem becomes an argument for a federal program, that exceptions become the norm, and that our expectations of policy are lowered while our expectations of each other rise.

To translate that general disposition into specific policy reforms will be the work of the coming generation. It is work that has clearly begun in our politics, but that has not yet taken center stage. If it does, it can help our political system become a better fit for our unbundling economy and our diversifying culture, and so can help our politics become less frustrating and more useful. And it can enable our government once again to play its proper supporting role in the life of our ever-changing, always moving, anxious, eager, endlessly marvelous country.

ACKNOWLEDGMENTS

This book has been a labor of love for me. But it has meant just plain old labor for others, whose support, guidance, good will, and patience really made it possible. It has therefore left me with enormous debts of gratitude.

Several friends and colleagues have gone above and beyond in helping me think through the themes of this book. Ramesh Ponnuru, a close friend and frequent partner in crime, has helped me make sense of a complex time and also offered an example of an intelligent, principled, rigorous, and civil public conservatism that has inspired me and many others. Reihan Salam, another dear friend, has allowed me to abuse his patience and mooch off his fierce intellect over many hours of talking through the book's assorted arguments. He also did me the enormous favor of reading through the manuscript and offering immensely useful comments and corrections. Several other good friends and colleagues did the same, either thinking through elements of the argument with me or reading parts or all of the text and improving the final product immeasurably. They include Adam Keiper, Peter Wehner, Scott Winship, Adam White, Peter Lawler, Emily Schultheis, Andrew Evans, Ben Silver, and Scott Galupo. I have also learned a great deal that was of value to the book, and to much else, from many conversations in recent years with Leon Kass, Michael Gerson, Ross Douthat, David Brooks, Matthew Continetti, Michael Connolly, Andrew Bremberg, and other wise friends. None of these guides and advisers bears any blame for this book's many faults, which persist despite their best efforts. But whatever is worthwhile in these pages has undoubtedly been learned from them.

I am also deeply indebted to and grateful for a loose assortment of friends and colleagues with whom I have spent the past several years working, learning, and thinking. Many of them (including some of those just noted) have come to be called "reform conservatives," whether they like it or not, and their work has been paving the way for an American renewal. They have been ably gathered of late under the auspices of the Conservative Reform Network (shepherded by April Ponnuru, John Murray, Kate O'Beirne, and Neil Bradley), but have also made their mark in the world of public policy, in the academy, in journalism, and in politics. I have been privileged and humbled to be in their company.

I am grateful, as well, to a number of magazine editors who have allowed me to think out loud in their pages in recent years about some of the broad themes taken up in this book. These include Rich Lowry of *National Review*, Bill Kristol of the *Weekly Standard*, John Podhoretz of *Commentary*, and R. R. Reno of *First Things*, among others. All four have done a great deal to advance the intellectual culture of the Right, and of the country, in recent years, and their publications offer admirable models of what a journal of opinion can accomplish for a free society.

These magazines are always nice places to visit, but I am even more grateful for my professional home. Since 2007, I have been fortunate enough to be allowed to hang my hat at the Ethics and Public Policy Center in Washington, DC, and much of my work on this book was done there. It is an island of collegiality and intellectual engagement in a city where both are too often lacking, and for that I am enormously indebted to its president, Ed Whelan, and to my colleagues. Since 2009, I have also been lucky enough to serve as editor of *National Affairs* magazine, and my wonderful team of colleagues there has made it a joy—my thanks to them all. Neither this book nor my other work in recent years could have been possible without the generous support, encouragement, and guidance of Roger Hertog, for which I am deeply grateful.

At Basic Books, I have been particularly fortunate to work with Lara Heimert, who is both the publisher and a master editor. Anyone who henceforth asks me what book editors do will be shown what this book was before Lara improved it and what it then became, and will be left with no doubt about just how invaluable good editors are. Alia Massoud and Leah Stecher made sure the process stayed on track, among much else. Katherine Streckfus's thoughtful and exacting attention left the text far stronger and cleaner, and Melissa Raymond expertly saw the book through production. The entire team at Basic has never been anything short of superb. I am very grateful to them all.

My greatest debt, however, is, as always, to my family. I am grateful to my parents for more than I could ever say. I am grateful to my children, Maya and Sam, for making sure I never took this work, myself, or anything else too seriously. But, above all, I am grateful to, and grateful for, my wonderful wife, Cecelia, who is so much more than I deserve. She is, to put it plainly, the best human being I know. The only proof I have that she may not be simply perfect is her questionable choice of spouse. I dedicate this book to her with love and admiration.

NOTES

Introduction

1. Alexis de Tocqueville, *Democracy in America*, Harvey Mansfield and Delba Winthrop, trans. (Chicago: University of Chicago Press, 2000), 673.

Chapter 1: Blinded by Nostalgia

1. Barack Obama, "Remarks by the President in State of the Union Address," January 25, 2011, White House, https://www.whitehouse.gov/the-press-office /2011/01/25/remarks-president-state-union-address.

2. Mitt Romney, "Address Accepting the Presidential Nomination at the Republican National Convention in Tampa, Florida," August 30, 2012, American Presidency Project, www.presidency.ucsb.edu/ws/?pid=101966.

3. Rick Santorum, *Blue Collar Conservatives: Recommitting to an America That Works* (New York: Regnery, 2014), 11.

4. Elizabeth Warren, "Democratic National Convention Speech," September 5, 2012, ABC News, http://abcnews.go.com/Politics/OTUS/transcript-elizabeth -warrens-democratic-convention-speech/story?id=17164726.

5. Paul Krugman, *The Conscience of a Liberal* (New York: W. W. Norton, 2007), 3.

6. Robert Putnam, *Our Kids: The American Dream in Crisis* (New York: Simon and Schuster, 2015), 1.

7. Lane Kenworthy, *Social Democratic America* (New York: Oxford, 2014), 2–3.

8. Barack Obama, *The Audacity of Hope: Thoughts on Reclaiming the American Dream* (New York: Crown, 2006), 38. Obama seemed to recognize that these recollections were at least a little too rosy, but six years later, as president, he offered a similar ode to the old consensus. "Yes, there have been fierce arguments throughout our history between both parties about the exact size and role of government— some honest disagreements," he told an audience in Cleveland, Ohio, in 2012. "But in the decades after World War II, there was a general consensus that the market couldn't solve all of our problems on its own. . . . In the last century, this

consensus—this shared vision—led to the strongest economic growth and the largest middle class that the world has ever known. It led to a shared prosperity."
Barack Obama, "Remarks by the President on the Economy—Cleveland, OH,"
June 14, 2012, White House, https://www.whitehouse.gov/the-press-office/2012
/06/14/remarks-president-economy-cleveland-oh.

9. Charles Murray, *Coming Apart: The State of White America, 1960–2010* (New
York: Crown Forum, 2012), 11. Murray's emphasis, which hits upon a crucial point,
as we shall see in the chapters to follow, is on the ways in which America has
changed since that time by becoming less consolidated—less uniform and more
varied, less centralized and more fractured. Some of this has been to the good,
Murray acknowledges, but ultimately it has brought on social changes that, if left
unchecked, "will end what has made America America" (p. 12).

10. This century so far has seemed to some Americans eerily reminiscent of the
1970s, and some on the Right, in particular, have suggested that this means that
something like the American renaissance of the 1980s is both possible and necessary
now. As conservative author, publisher, and presidential candidate Steve Forbes put
it in 2011, "today we are once again beset by a Carter-esque malaise, wherein we
must accept abnormally high unemployment and the notion that printing more
dollars is the way to recovery." Steve Forbes, "Reagan's Legacy and the Current
Malaise," *Wall Street Journal*, March 22, 2011.

11. For a debate transcript, see CBS News, www.cbsnews.com/news/democratic
-debate-transcript-clinton-sanders-omalley-in-iowa.

12. Sandra Colby and Jennifer Ortman, "The Baby Boom Cohort in the United
States," *Current Population Reports*, US Census Bureau, 2014, 2.

13. The term was likely coined by journalist Landon Jones in his book *Great
Expectations: America and the Baby Boom Generation* (New York: Coward-McCann,
1980), but has been widely used in the demographic literature ever since.

14. This outsized economic footprint is in part a function of the fact that the
bulk of the boomers are now in their prime working years; it will diminish fairly
rapidly in the coming decades as the relative size of the cohort diminishes and as
the boomers enter into retirement. See Colby and Ortman, "Baby Boom Cohort."

15. It is, of course, a particular subset of the boomer generation that tends to
define the attitudes we identify with the whole. White, well-off baby boomers are
the portion of that generation that became culturally dominant. It is important not
to overlook the rest of the cohort, and not to overstate the actual significance of
generational labels. But "baby boomer" is a meaningful moniker largely because
this unusually significant demographic subgroup thinks of itself as boomers.

16. Another insightful recent book, Francis Fukuyama's *Political Order and Political Decay: From the Industrial Revolution to the Globalization of Democracy* (New
York: Farrar, Straus and Giroux, 2015), offers a great example of why such an approach to understanding the state of the nation might be tempting, but also why
it might be dangerous. It is discussed further in chapter 7.

17. These figures are based on January 2015 data and projections from the Current Population Survey of the US Census Bureau, www.census.gov/programs-surveys/cps.html.

18. Peter Lawler, "The Tool of Selective Nostalgia," *First Things*, October 23, 2014, www.firstthings.com/blogs/firstthoughts/2014/10/the-tool-of-selective-nostalgia. Lawler's assorted essays and books, his disposition, and his mode of argument have all been profoundly formative for me, and have much to do with the nature of the argument advanced in this book.

19. Mark Henrie, "Understanding Traditionalist Conservatism," in Peter Berkowitz, ed., *Varieties of Conservatism in America* (Palo Alto, CA: Hoover Institution Press, 2004), 11. (Unless otherwise noted, italics appear in the original.)

20. Putnam, *Our Kids*, 2. I take Putnam to include himself among those who would *not* return to that past without major reforms, though his construction here is unclear.

21. Murray, *Coming Apart*, 7.

Chapter 2: The Age of Conformity

1. Alexander Hamilton, John Jay, and James Madison, *The Federalist Papers* (New York: Signet, 2003), 6–7.

2. Ronald Inglehart, *Modernization and Postmodernization: Cultural, Economic, and Political Change in 43 Societies* (Princeton, NJ: Princeton University Press, 1997).

3. Steven Gillon and Cathy Matson, *The American Experiment: A History of the United States*, vol. 2, *Since 1865* (New York: Wadsworth, 2009), 512.

4. A good example of this mode of early progressivism is Herbert Croly's influential book *The Promise of American Life* (New York: Macmillan, 1909).

5. As we shall see, this made a form of progressivism with somewhat different emphases a natural fit for a much more individualistic social ethic later in the twentieth century—and in both its collectivizing and its individualizing forms, progressivism often involved a diminution of the role and importance of small-scale institutions, from the family to community groups, and the assorted power centers of civil society.

6. A good example of this strand of early progressivism is Charles Beard's important book *An Economic Interpretation of the United States Constitution* (New York: Free Press, 1913).

7. From Roosevelt's 1910 speech "The New Nationalism," as published in Ronald J. Pestritto and William J. Atto, eds., *American Progressivism: A Reader* (Lanham, MD: Lexington Books, 2008), 211–223.

8. Ibid.

9. Croly, *Promise of American Life*, 236.

10. Ibid., 29.

11. For an in-depth discussion of this facet of the progressive era see, for instance, Thomas C. Leonard's *Illiberal Reformers: Race, Eugenics, and American Economics in the Progressive Era* (Princeton, NJ: Princeton University Press, 2016).

12. John Dewey, "The Future of Pacifism," *New Republic*, July 28, 1917.

13. Jonah Goldberg, *Liberal Fascism: The Secret History of the American Left, from Mussolini to the Politics of Change* (New York: Crown Forum, 2008), 108.

14. See, for instance, Harry N. Scheiber's *The Wilson Administration and Civil Liberties, 1917–1921* (New Orleans: Quid Pro Books, 2013).

15. Thomas Picketty and Emmanuel Saez, "Income Inequality in the United States," *Quarterly Journal of Economics* 118, no. 1 (2003). In an important 1992 paper, economists Claudia Goldin of Harvard and Robert Margo of the Massachusetts Institute of Technology termed this process "the Great Compression." See Claudia Goldin and Robert Margo, "The Great Compression: The Wage Structure in the United States at Mid-Century," *Quarterly Journal of Economics* 107, no. 1 (1992).

16. Alan Petigny, *The Permissive Society: America, 1941–1965* (New York: Cambridge University Press, 2009).

17. In his book *The Road to Character* (New York: Random House, 2015), journalist David Brooks offers a superb overview of this profound transformation of American attitudes after the war. I am indebted to him for these examples.

18. William F. Buckley Jr., "*National Review*: Credenda and Statement of Principles," reprinted in Gregory Schneider, ed., *Conservatism in America Since 1930: A Reader* (New York: New York University Press, 2003), 201–205.

19. Martin Luther King, "Transformed Nonconformist," November 1954, Martin Luther King, Jr., Papers Project, Stanford University, https://swap.stanford .edu/20141218225614/http://mlk-kpp01.stanford.edu/primarydocuments/Vol6 /Nov1954TransformedNonconformist.pdf.

20. Sharon Cohany and Emy Sok, "Trends in Labor Force Participation of Married Mothers," *Monthly Labor Review* (Bureau of Labor Statistics), February 2007.

21. William Branson, Herbert Giersch, and Peter G. Peterson, "Trends in United States International Trade and Investment Since World War II," in Martin Feldstein, ed., *The American Economy in Transition* (Chicago: University of Chicago Press, 1980), 184. Of course, the decimation of other advanced economies also had a countervailing effect by reducing demand for American goods abroad. But demand appeared to increase much faster in the wake of the war than the productive capacity of those economies could.

22. For a useful overview, see Brink Lindsey, "Paul Krugman's Nostalgianomics: Economic Policies, Social Norms, and Income Inequality," White Paper, Cato Institute, February 9, 2009.

23. See, for instance, Scott Winship, "Has Middle-Class Pay Risen as Much as It Should Have?" *Forbes*, May 12, 2015, www.forbes.com/sites/scottwinship/2015/05 /12/has-middle-class-pay-risen-as-much-as-it-should-have.

24. Picketty and Saez, "Income Inequality in the United States."

25. Gallup's historical figures can be found at "Trust in Government," Gallup, www.gallup.com/poll/5392/trust-government.aspx.

26. Perhaps the first to take note of this paradox was the keenest of all observers of our democracy, Alexis de Tocqueville. In reflecting on the dangers of hyper-individualism in a democratic society, Tocqueville wrote:

I want to imagine with what new features despotism could be produced in the world. I see an innumerable crowd of like and equal men who revolve on themselves without repose, procuring the small and vulgar pleasures with which they fill their souls. Each of them, withdrawn and apart, is like a stranger to the destiny of all the others: his children and his particular friends form the whole human species for him; as for dwelling with his fellow citizens, he is beside them, but he does not see them; he touches them and does not feel them; he exists only in himself and for himself alone, and if a family still remains for him, one can at least say that he no longer has a native country.

Above all these an immense tutelary power is elevated, which alone takes charge of assuring their enjoyments and watching over their fate. It is absolute, detailed, regular, far-seeing, and mild. It would resemble paternal power if, like that, it had for its object to prepare men for manhood; but on the contrary it seeks only to keep them fixed irrevocably in childhood; it likes citizens to enjoy themselves provided that they think only of enjoying themselves. It willingly works for their happiness; but it wants to be the unique agent and sole arbiter of that; it provides for their security, foresees and secures their needs, facilitates their pleasures, conducts their principal affairs, directs their industry, regulates their estates, divides their inheritances; can it not take away from them entirely the trouble of thinking and the pain of living?

This Tocquevillian paradox of individualism and centralization is a key theme of the coming chapters. Alexis de Tocqueville, *Democracy in America*, Harvey Mansfield and Delba Winthrop, trans. (Chicago: University of Chicago Press, 2000), 663.

27. Lyndon Johnson, "The Great Society," in Michael Nelson, ed., *The Evolving Presidency: Landmark Documents* (Washington, DC: Sage, 2015), 181.

Chapter 3: The Age of Frenzy

1. For a more extensive and quite profound examination of American life in the 1970s, I can hardly recommend enough David Frum's superb book *How We Got Here: The 70's* (New York: Basic Books, 2000).

2. Income volatility also increased substantially in this period. See, for instance, Scott Winship, "Bogeyman Economics," *National Affairs*, Winter 2012.

3. In his insightful book *The New Dollars and Dreams: American Incomes and Economic Change* (New York: Russell Sage Foundation, 1999), Frank Levy argues persuasively that spending on the Vietnam War was a chief contributor to this rise in inflationary pressures.

4. Indeed, Nixon had more or less run for the presidency on a platform of restraining and reversing the diffusion of American life that seemed to be getting out

of hand by the late 1960s, and his economic approach was closely linked to his cultural appeal to the "moral majority," as he termed it, and his attitude toward rising crime and disorder. Although liberalization and diffusion represented a core tendency, a generative fact, of American life in the wake of the war, it drew firm resistance in the form of various strains of populism and nationalism of the Left and the Right by the late 1960s, as it has continued to do ever since.

5. See, for instance, "Confidence in Institutions," Gallup, June 2–7, 2015, www .gallup.com/poll/1597/confidence-institutions.aspx.

6. It is worth stressing once more that this was a bipartisan effort, and not purely a Republican or conservative enterprise. Massachusetts senator Ted Kennedy, perhaps the most prominent liberal in the Senate in those years, was among its chief proponents.

7. This pattern of administrative centralization and institutional fragmentation will be taken up in more detail in chapter 7.

8. Tom Wolfe, "The 'Me' Decade and the Third Great Awakening," *New York*, August 23, 1976.

9. The exact boundaries of mainline Protestantism are a subject of some dispute, but it is generally agreed that at least seven denominations constitute the core mainline churches: the United Methodist Church, the Evangelical Lutheran Church in America, the Episcopal Church, the Presbyterian Church, American Baptist Churches USA, the United Church of Christ, and the Disciples of Christ.

10. On this point, see, for instance, Ross Douthat's book *Bad Religion: How We Became a Nation of Heretics* (New York: Free Press, 2012) and Joseph Bottum's *An Anxious Age: The Post-Protestant Ethic and the Spirit of America* (New York: Image, 2014).

11. Douthat, *Bad Religion*, 62.

12. These data are available at Jennifer Robison, "Decades of Drug Use: Data from the '60s and '70s," Gallup, July 2, 2002, www.gallup.com/poll/6331/decades -drug-use-data-from-60s-70s.aspx.

13. W. Bradford Wilcox, "The Evolution of Divorce," *National Affairs*, Fall 2009, 83.

14. Ibid.

15. George Akerof, Janet Yellen, and Michael Katz, "An Analysis of Out-of-Wedlock Childbearing in the United States," *Quarterly Journal of Economics* 11, no. 2 (1996): 277–317.

16. These effects, it must be noted, worked in both directions. A very large portion of the increased debt burden of the 1980s was actually the result of higher interest rates on the national debt, rather than of changes in the balance between spending and revenue.

17. As Michael Mandel put it in "Reagan's Economic Legacy," *Bloomberg Business*, June 20, 2004:

> [Reagan's] message of competitive markets, entrepreneurial vigor, and minimal regulation found a willing audience in an era of rapid technological change, where innovation was opening new opportunities seemingly every

day. Reagan's first term saw the creation of such future giants as Sun Microsystems, Compaq Computer, Dell, and Cisco Systems—the greatest entrepreneurial burst of new companies since the early 20th century. . . . Taken together, the changes Reagan championed in the tax system fostered innovation and entrepreneurialism even as they encouraged the development of venture capital and investment in human capital. And Reagan's willingness to push for more flexible labor markets and less regulation helped companies react faster to economic changes, including new technologies. As a result, the impact of the policies Reagan set out in the 1980s, which slowly worked their way through the economy, helped lay the groundwork for the Information Revolution of the 1990s.

18. Francis Fukuyama, *The Great Disruption: Human Nature and the Reconstitution of Social Order* (New York: Free Press, 1999), 15.

19. Robert Shapiro, "Income Growth and Decline Under Recent U.S. Presidents and the New Challenge to Restore Broad Economic Prosperity," Brookings Institution, March 2015, www.brookings.edu/~/media/research/files/papers/2015/03/05-income-growth-decline-economic-prosperity-shapiro/shapirov3.pdf.

20. In part, the decline was also a function of the entry of women into the workforce in large numbers—as women frequently outcompeted men for low-skill jobs that were not intensely physical.

21. Perhaps most prominent among such critics was Everett Ladd of the University of Connecticut.

22. People under these circumstances, Fukuyama wrote in 1999 in *The Great Disruption,*

> are increasingly distrustful of any authority, political or moral, that would constrain their freedom of choice, but they also want a sense of community and the good things that flow from community, like mutual recognition, participation, belonging, and identity. Community has to be found elsewhere, in smaller and more flexible groups and organizations where loyalties and memberships can be overlapping and where entry and exit entail relatively low costs. People might thus be able to reconcile their contradictory desires for community and autonomy. But in this bargain, the community they get is smaller and weaker than most that have existed in the past. Each community shares less with neighboring ones, and the ones to which they belong have relatively little hold. The circle of people they can trust is necessarily narrower" (pp. 90–91).

Chapter 4: The Age of Anxiety

1. Productivity growth did revive after that first recession of this century, and actually grew faster from 2000–2007 than it had in any business cycle going back to the 1960s. Growth in gross domestic product per capita was very low, however.

2. The standard unemployment rate measures the portion of Americans who are seeking work but do not have a job. The workforce participation rate is a measure of the portion of all working-age Americans who are working—and therefore offers a sense not only of how many Americans are unable to find work, but also how many are not even seeking it, and therefore might be thought of as altogether detached from the workforce.

3. McKinsey Global Institute, *Growth and Renewal in the United States: Retooling America's Economic Engine*, McKinsey & Company, February 2011. Today's immigrants, just like those of past waves of immigration, tend to possess lower skills and education than most native-born Americans. There is nothing unusual about that. But today's economy is different from the economy that met past waves of immigration in some crucial ways, perhaps most notably because a far greater portion of jobs require significant skills and education. This point will be taken up in more detail in chapter 5.

4. The scholar and journalist Walter Russell Mead has described the array of public and private institutions that made up the postwar order and the assumptions that underlay them as "the blue model," as it represents a deeply rooted liberal (and thus "blue-state") mindset about how institutions work. In "The Once and Future Liberalism," *American Interest* 7, no. 4 (2012), Mead wrote:

> In the old system, most blue-collar and white-collar workers held stable, lifetime jobs with defined benefit pensions, and a career civil service administered a growing state as living standards for all social classes steadily rose. Gaps between the classes remained fairly consistent in an industrial economy characterized by strong unions in stable, government-brokered arrangements with large corporations—what [economist John Kenneth] Galbraith and others referred to as the Iron Triangle. High school graduates were pretty much guaranteed lifetime employment in a job that provided a comfortable lower middle-class lifestyle; college graduates could expect a better paid and equally secure future. An increasing "social dividend," meanwhile, accrued in various forms: longer vacations, more and cheaper state-supported education, earlier retirement, shorter work weeks, more social and literal mobility, and more diverse forms of affordable entertainment. Call all this, taken together, the blue model.

This description is, as we have seen, more than a bit romanticized, but it contains much truth and it offers a useful summary of the fondly remembered ideal of midcentury America. Much of the infrastructure of American public policy was built to support this structure, and therefore appears increasingly anachronistic.

5. Arnold Kling and Nick Schulz have aptly termed these kinds of pseudo-governmental sectors "the new commanding heights" of the American economy. See their article "The New Commanding Heights," *National Affairs*, Summer 2011.

6. The Left has even made some efforts in this century to build new programs and institutions on that mid-twentieth-century model, especially through the Affordable Care Act, which has made the federal government the primary regulator of health insurance in America and created a system of lumbering, ill-designed benefits and mandates to increase access to subsidized insurance coverage. The law was enacted with a bare majority through appalling legislative chicanery, has remained exceptionally unpopular, and its implementation has required numerous administrative contortions of highly dubious legality. But the Left's insistence on pushing it forward at all costs has certainly been telling of the obduracy of the midcentury technocratic mindset in some liberal ranks.

7. See for instance, "Confidence in Institutions," Gallup, June 2–7, 2015, www .gallup.com/poll/1597/confidence-institutions.aspx. Two protracted and ultimately largely failed wars in the Middle East launched by George W. Bush's administration contributed to a continuing decline of confidence even in some of the most trusted of our public institutions: the military and defense establishments. Our domestic public institutions have fared worse still.

8. US Census data do suggest the possibility of a modest improvement in the out-of-wedlock birth rate since roughly 2007, which may suggest the beginning of a turn for the better on that front, though rates remain extremely high, and it is too soon to say whether a real downward trend is evident.

9. These figures are influenced by the aging of the population, though the trend plainly holds for working-age Americans as well.

10. As detailed further in chapter 6, this growth in the number of people describing themselves as religiously unaffiliated seems mostly to describe changing attitudes among people who were already loosely affiliated, rather than a loss of belief and attachment among practicing Christians. But the change is no less significant for being mostly a matter of self-description, and in fact may thereby play a greater role in changing social attitudes about religion in the public square.

11. See, for instance, Andrew Flowers, "Big Business Is Getting Bigger," Five Thirty Eight Economics, May 18, 2015, http://fivethirtyeight.com/datalab/big-business-is -getting-bigger. This point will be taken up at greater length in chapter 5.

12. In fact, today's largest corporations, while they generally are not the same as those of decades past (so that increasing competition has certainly felled some giants), account for a larger share of the economy than they have in several decades. As journalist Andrew Flowers noted, "The overall revenues of Fortune 500 companies have risen from 58 percent of nominal GDP in 1994 to 73 percent in 2013." Flowers, "Big Business Is Getting Bigger."

There has been a lot of talk about emerging trends in contract work in recent years, but actual evidence for the growth of a "gig economy" remains scarce at this point. Americans today do not seem more likely to be self-employed than they were in the past several decades. See, for instance, Josh Zumbrun and Anna Louie

Sussman, "Proof of a 'Gig Economy' Revolution Is Hard to Find," *Wall Street Journal*, July 27, 2015.

13. In "The Transformation of American Community," *National Affairs*, Summer 2011 (www.nationalaffairs.com/publications/detail/the-transformation-of-american-community), Marc Dunkelman further explains how technology has tended to intensify our closest and most distant social links at the expense of such middling relations. He writes:

> Consider, for example, how the past several decades have expanded our opportunities to invest more heavily in inner-ring relationships. Waving goodbye while running out the door in the morning no longer means you won't be in touch until dinner. Mobile phones and Blackberries allow spouses to keep tabs on one another throughout the day. Parents off on business trips can use Skype to read *Goodnight Moon* to their toddlers. College students can text their "helicopter" moms to consult about whether to order a burger or a salad in the cafeteria.
>
> At the same time, the past several decades have provided Americans with new opportunities to focus on the outer-ring relationships that most pique their interest. Sports fanatics need not read a general-interest newspaper, because blogs cover their preferred stories in greater depth. Television programs catering to broad audiences (think of *The Ed Sullivan Show*) are being replaced by networks (*Lifetime*, for example) focused squarely on particular sets of demographics. Local bookstores are suffering because readers can have titles shipped to them via Amazon, or better yet, directly to their iPads or Kindles.

14. We will consider this pattern in greater detail in chapter 6.

15. Our ability to grasp the pattern regarding disparate lives in different socioeconomic groups and its implications is hampered somewhat by the tendency to think of these trends in terms of economic inequality. The twenty-first century continued to see significant income inequality in the US economy, to be sure, but because inequality generally grows most quickly in prosperous economic times (because the wealthy grow wealthier more quickly in a strong economy, and their incomes are much more sensitive to market volatility than those of people further down the scale), the growth of inequality has actually been somewhat muted even as its persistence has perhaps become less tolerable to many.

Demographers often use levels of education as substitutes for social class when considering modes of living, because they tend to align closely with income and yet are not exclusively economic measures. These are a logical and plausible stand-in, and so I do employ them here, but it is worth noting one important problem with this measure: since educational attainment has been rising over time, those Americans who do not attend college today are a significantly smaller and worse-off group than those who did not attend college three or four decades ago.

This does not render the measure hopelessly distorted, but it does tend to exaggerate differences over time to some degree. This is why I have, for the most part, used that measure in comparing different groups of Americans today, rather than in drawing contrasts with the past.

16. These figures, from the US Bureau of Labor Statistics, are certainly influenced by the greater prevalence of college degrees among younger Americans than among older ones (and especially, in turn, by the inclusion of senior citizens in the data), but they provide a useful overview of the relationship between educational attainment and employment.

17. See Richard Fry, "New Census Data Show More Americans Are Tying the Knot, But Mostly It's the College Educated," Pew Research Center, February 6, 2014, www.pewresearch.org/fact-tank/2014/02/06/new-census-data-show-more -americans-are-tying-the-knot-but-mostly-its-the-college-educated; Philip Cohen, "College Graduates Marry Other College Graduates Most of the Time," *The Atlantic*, April 4, 2013, www.theatlantic.com/sexes/archive/2013/04/college-graduates -marry-other-college-graduates-most-of-the-time/274654.

18. On divorce rates, see, for instance, Claire Cain Miller, "The Divorce Surge Is Over, But the Myth Lives On," *New York Times*, December 2, 2014, A3. Data on birth rates are from the federal Centers for Disease Control and Prevention, "National Survey of Family Growth," www.cdc.gov/nchs/nsfg.htm.

19. See Nicole Neroulias, "Church Attendance Dropping Among Less-Educated White Americans," Huffington Post, August 25, 2011, www.huffingtonpost.com /2011/08/25/church-attendance-dropping_n_937138.html.

20. This specialization is taken up in detail in chapter 5.

21. The shape of these charts might suggest a further point: it could be taken to imply that we are living in circumstances analogous to those at the end of the nineteenth century or the beginning of the twentieth. In some limited ways, there is surely something to this. Our politics these days resembles the divisive and partisan political life of the late nineteenth century more than that of almost any point in the twentieth. Our cultural diversity makes us very different from the America of the mid-twentieth century, but not so different from that of the late nineteenth century. An economy marked by many free agents working independently and out of their homes, rather than attached to discrete and uniformly defined jobs and employers, is also a kind of return to preindustrial norms—and will in time likely require major changes to the safety net of rules and benefits meant to protect workers from risk, but designed for twentieth-century labor arrangements. Our intense income disparities, meanwhile, hearken to the early industrial age. A cultural and media environment that consists of a profusion of narrow options more than a small number of broad mass voices also recalls that earlier time in America. We have something to learn from nineteenth-century America about how to make these unfamiliar patterns work for us, to be sure, but only so much. The trends we have been living through have not added up to a return. We are arriving at this

diffuse and deconsolidated state having experienced and been shaped by the twentieth century—having modernized, democratized, technologized, and liberalized in ways that Americans a century ago could not have imagined. We can learn from their experience, but we cannot—and should not want to—re-create it.

22. I refer here to Federalist No. 10, where Madison famously offers "a Republican remedy for the diseases most incident to Republican Government," because he believes no other kind of remedy could be acceptable to Americans.

23. We need hardly look further than the Affordable Care Act, enacted in 2010 to bring our health-care system to the standards of 1965, for an illustration of this point.

24. We can find some forms of such a vision in all parts of our politics, but it has been most characteristic of American progressivism and remains so. Former Democratic congressman Barney Frank of Massachusetts voiced one version of it at the Democratic National Convention in 2012, telling the audience that "there are things that a civilized society needs that we can only do when we do them together, and when we do them together that's called government." He was thus suggesting that all non-individual action is, in essence, government action. President Obama voiced such a view even more starkly in his Second Inaugural Address in 2013, noting that a more empowered federal government was necessary, "for the American people can no more meet the demands of today's world by acting alone than American soldiers could have met the forces of fascism or communism with muskets and militias. No single person can train all the math and science teachers we'll need to equip our children for the future, or build the roads and networks and research labs that will bring new jobs and businesses to our shores. Now, more than ever, we must do these things together, as one nation and one people."

Our only possible means of addressing our problems, in this desolate vision of American life, is for each of us to act as a lone, isolated, "single person" or for all of us to act as "one nation and one people." There is apparently nothing in the middle; there are no joint projects that are not national, government-centered projects. The American Left has many resources at its disposal for overcoming this corrosive and dangerous view, and it is certainly not how all contemporary progressives think. But it is a kind of mental reflex that persists.

Chapter 5: The Unbundled Market

1. Adam Smith, *An Inquiry into the Nature and Causes of the Wealth of Nations* (New York: Modern Library, 1994), 11.

2. Lawrence H. Summers and Ed Balls, *Report of the Commission on Inclusive Prosperity*," Center for American Progress, January 15, 2015, 7–8, https://www.americanprogress.org/issues/economy/report/2015/01/15/104266/report-of-the-commission-on-inclusive-prosperity.

3. Jason Furman, *A Brief History of Middle Class Economics: Productivity, Participation, and Inequality in the United States*, Center for Economic and Policy Re-

search, February 20, 2015, www.voxeu.org/article/brief-history-middle-class
-economics; Joseph Stiglitz, *Rewriting the Rules of the American Economy: An Agenda for Growth and Shared Prosperity* (New York: Roosevelt Institute, 2015), 19. In 2012, President Obama said much the same himself. "Over the last few decades," he told an audience in Cleveland, "the income of the top 1 percent grew by more than 275 percent, to an average of $1.3 million a year. Big financial institutions, corporations saw their profits soar. But prosperity never trickled down to the middle class." Barack Obama, "Remarks by the President on the Economy," June 14, 2012, https://www.whitehouse.gov/the-press-office/2012/06/14/remarks-president-economy-cleveland-oh.

4. For a thorough review of the key claims in the Left's core narrative of gloom, see, for instance, Scott Winship, "Bogeyman Economics," *National Affairs*, Winter 2012.

5. For an overview of the facts regarding retirement savings see Andrew Biggs and Sylvester Schieber, "Is There a Retirement Crisis?" *National Affairs*, Summer 2014.

6. This critique of progressive policy thinking has been advanced most prominently by the Manhattan Institute's Scott Winship in recent years. See "Bogeyman Economics," cited above, among his many other essays, studies, and articles.

7. Ginni Thomas, "Economist: 'It's 1979 All Over Again' in America," *Daily Caller*, September 5, 2015 http://dailycaller.com/2015/09/05/economist-its-1979-all-over-again-in-america. See also Larry Kudlow, "The GOP Needs a 5 Percent Growth Target," National Review Online, May 29, 2015, www.nationalreview.com/article/419088/gop-needs-5-percent-growth-target-larry-kudlow; Steve Forbes, "Reagan's Legacy and the Current Malaise," *Wall Street Journal*, March 22, 2011. Numerous other examples could be cited.

8. The tendency to treat the particular planks of the Reagan agenda as general principles rather than specific applications of principle has also led some contemporary conservatives to insist that the threat of hyperinflation must be just around the corner now, even in a time of exceedingly low general price inflation.

9. Smith, *Wealth of Nations*, 64.

10. That globalization itself is continuing to intensify is not an undisputed fact. By some measures, global trade has been decreasing in recent years, though many economists attribute these findings to a failure to account correctly for global gross domestic product. Nonetheless, the effects of globalization on the level of specialization of our economy are plainly more intense now than they were a generation ago.

11. David Autor, "Polanyi's Paradox and the Shape of Employment Growth," draft prepared for the Federal Reserve Bank of Kansas City's economic policy symposium on "Re-Evaluating Labor Market Dynamics," August 21–23, 2014, in Jackson Hole, Wyoming, online at http://www.nber.org/papers/w20485.

12. The shrinking of the middle class was mostly driven by rising incomes in the last four decades of the twentieth century. The picture has been more mixed (and driven to a greater degree by declining incomes) in the twenty-first century. See, for instance, Alicia Parlapiano, Robert Gebeloff, and Shan Carter, "The Shrinking American Middle Class," *New York Times*, January 26, 2015, www.nytimes.com/interactive/2015/01/25/upshot/shrinking-middle-class.html.

13. See, for instance, Gianmarco I.P. Ottaviano and Giovanni Peri, *Immigration and National Wages: Clarifying the Theory and the Empirics*, National Bureau of Economic Research, July 2008, www.nber.org/papers/w14188. A slightly more recent study conducted by Heidi Shierholz for the Economic Policy Institute yielded very similar results. See Heidi Shierholz, "Immigration and Wages: Methodological Advancements Confirm Modest Gains for Native Workers," EPI Briefing Paper #255, February 4, 2010, www.epi.org/publication/bp255.

14. The same logic occasionally arises in debates about the future of our public entitlement systems, as existing retirees and near retirees are left alone in most reform proposals while changes are suggested for younger people now paying into the system. This makes sense, as the kinds of protections possible in a consolidated economy are not plausible in ours, and the new approach to such benefits (especially when it comes to defined-benefit programs in the public and private sphere) can often be better for beneficiaries in the long run. But the nature of this change means that the baby boomers are often being allowed to keep the more straightforwardly generous terms of a prior era while the younger Americans who are paying their bills are being promised something less familiar, at the very least. This preferential treatment for the boomers at the expense of their children and grandchildren is a defining feature of contemporary American life.

15. Megan McArdle, "U.S. Workers Brought the 'Great Reset' on Themselves," Bloomberg View, May 19, 2015, www.bloombergview.com/articles/2015-05-19/u-s-workers-brought-the-great-reset-on-themselves.

16. Other kinds of arguments for emphasizing inequality—for instance, that it is a threat to our democracy, or inhibits opportunity, or leads to financial instability—are similarly poorly supported. On all these fronts see, for instance, Scott Winship, "Overstating the Costs of Inequality," *National Affairs*, Spring 2013.

17. These figures put us in the same neighborhood as most other developed nations. Scholars disagree about whether relative mobility in the United States is meaningfully lower than in Canada and parts of northern Europe or roughly the same, but no one now argues (as Americans once used to believe) that we are uniquely mobile. See, for instance, Markus Jäntti, "Mobility in the United States in Comparative Perspective," *Focus* 26, no. 2 (2009): 38–42.

18. "Pursuing the American Dream: Economic Mobility Across Generations," Pew Charitable Trusts, July 2012, www.pewtrusts.org/en/research-and-analysis/reports/0001/01/01/pursuing-the-american-dream.

19. These areas have been of particular interest to a group of reform-minded conservative policy experts in recent years, whose work on this front may be found in the archives of the journal *National Affairs* (which I edit) and in a collection published in 2014 by the Conservative Reform Network in book form called *Room to Grow: Conservative Reforms for Limited Government and a Thriving Middle Class*, available at http://conservativereform.com/roomtogrow.

20. Andrew Kelly, "Higher Education Reform to Make College and Career Training More Effective and Affordable," in *Room to Grow*, 49.

21. Ibid., 57.

22. This point is particularly important because the available evidence increasingly demonstrates that simply expanding the scope of loan and grant aid tends to inflate tuition costs, and therefore can be dangerously counterproductive. See, for instance, Grey Gordon and Aaron Hedlund, "Accounting for the Rise in College Tuition," National Bureau of Economic Research, September 28, 2015, www.nber .org/chapters/c13711.pdf.

23. The work of these thinkers can be found in particular in the pages of the quarterly journal *National Affairs*. They are also prominent in most of the key conservative think tanks in Washington and are frequently featured in other conservative journals of opinion, such as *National Review, The Weekly Standard*, and *Commentary*.

24. See, for instance, Steven Teles, "Kludgeocracy in America," *National Affairs*, Fall 2013, and John DiIulio, *Bring Back the Bureaucrats: Why More Federal Workers Will Lead to Better (and Smaller!) Government* (Philadelphia: Templeton Press, 2014).

25. Mike Konczal, "No Discount: Comparing the Public Option to the Coupon Welfare State," New America Foundation, December 2012, https://static.newamerica .org/attachments/4165-no-discount-comparing-the-public-option-to-the-coupon -welfare-state/Konczal_Mike_PublicOption_NAF_Dec2012.73ec1576c8a14f248cf79 2a954387e36.pdf.

26. C. W. Mason, "Public Options: The General Case," The Slack Wire, September 5, 2010, http://slackwire.blogspot.com/2010/09/public-options-general-case .html. This view takes account of the price effects of subsidies, which conservatives often highlight with regard to the effect of student loans in higher education, for instance, but often ignore even in the closely related arena of K-12 school vouchers, let alone in areas further afield.

27. Eric Schnurer, "When Government Competes Against the Private Sector, Everybody Wins," *The Atlantic*, March 11, 2015, www.theatlantic.com/politics/archive /2015/03/when-government-competes-against-the-private-sector-everybody-wins /387460.

28. I point to the prospect of a "public-options progressivism" here not to endorse it, which I decidedly would not, but to suggest that it is a plausible direction for the twenty-first-century Left, and that there are reasons to think it is where

progressivism and the administrative state might be headed in the coming decades. Conservatives would resist and reject this approach for a variety of reasons: among others, such an approach confuses the role of the state in markets, combining elements of the role of a referee and that of a player in market competition in ways that will likely prove unsustainable; it almost certainly could not avoid showing preference to the relevant public options over private competitors and supporting them with implicit subsidies and advantages; and public options would not be subject to the kinds of life-or-death pressures faced by private companies that will simply go out of business when they fail—public providers of goods might lose market share if they fail to attract customers, but they would not confront the same fundamental competitive pressures. Ultimately, progressives often propose this strategy because they believe the public option would be superior to the competing private options, and they would likely find it difficult to avoid tipping the scale to make that so. All of this would raise serious risks of creating dangerous market failures and distortions rather than alleviating them.

29. Although this sharpening of ideological aims might tend to sharpen substantive policy differences between the parties, I suspect it could at the same time mitigate the paralysis afflicting many of our domestic policy debates. As further discussed in chapter 7, that paralysis results in part from the failure of both parties to contend with contemporary problems and offer coherent twenty-first-century agendas. A battle of dueling nostalgias makes no room for substantive compromise. A battle of substantive agendas suited to today's circumstances would actually allow for more such room, as each party would have a better idea of what it wanted and what its priorities were, and therefore a better sense of where it could and could not compromise.

30. One promising recent example of such thinking on the Left is Nick Hanauer and David Rolf, "Shared Security, Shared Growth," *Democracy: A Journal of Ideas*, Summer 2015.

31. One promising recent example of such thinking on the Right is Reihan Salam and Scott Winship, "The Leaner Welfare State," *National Review*, August 30, 2010.

32. The evolution of the Medicare debate in recent years is an instructive example along these lines. The program is a federal entitlement, and therefore not an instance of a private market with a public provider, but the introduction of competing private coverage options (through Medicare Advantage) a decade ago launched an experiment that has been proving the viability of both private competition for the provision of a public benefit and competition between a public provider and private providers. Conservatives now propose making Medicare Advantage the default Medicare option and having the public-provision fee-for-service insurance program function as just one of the (otherwise privately provided) options on the menu seniors may choose from. Though many Democrats continue to resist this evolution, Medicare is plainly moving toward a premium-support system in which

a defined benefit would be given to seniors (with its size based on provider bids) to then use to choose an insurance plan; a federally run fee-for-service insurance option would compete with private insurers for those seniors' business. We are thus seeing the emergence of a private-options / public-option experiment at the very heart of the liberal welfare state—a sign of things to come.

33. The importance of this point is easy to overlook. For some of the most thoughtful progressives I've encountered, it is absolutely central: they implicitly believe that most local (public and private) American institutions are thoroughly infested with racism and elite class animosities, so that decentralization involves handing over power to institutions that can't be trusted with it because they are structurally oriented in favor of the maintenance of privilege, rather than, as conservatives incline to think of them, better situated to understand and attempt to address social problems at a personal level. Some on the Left therefore see the national government as the one American institution uniquely capable of rising above such animosities, and especially racism. In opposing decentralization and arguing for more centralized (and therefore unavoidably more technocratic) management of public policy, they often understand themselves to be arguing for justice—not so much for a certain way of solving practical problems, but for a way of avoiding the entrenchment of privilege. Falling back onto this view seems at times to be a way of avoiding an explicit acknowledgment of some epistemological premises about technical and social knowledge, but it is surely also (and above all) genuinely felt and believed. It seems to me that this view of local institutions in contemporary America is highly anachronistic, ill informed, and unfair, but it does seem to be widely held, at least implicitly, among serious and well-meaning people on the Left.

34. There is, of course, some serious tension between the argument that our mediating institutions should provide social services and the argument that our mediating institutions must be left free of government constraint and interference. If they are to be given a role in social policy, they will need to be accountable to some public standards and limits, and in some respects perhaps also to rules regarding inclusion and nondiscrimination intended for public institutions. This tension will require thought and engagement from legislators and from institutions that desire to compete for a role in providing publicly supported assistance to the needy and vulnerable. But the complex questions this tension will unavoidably raise do not amount to a sufficient case against engaging civil society in the kind of ongoing, incremental experimentation with policy solutions that will be required to make a meaningful difference in the lives of those now too often short of opportunities for mobility. The problem can hardly be denied, but the exclusion of private actors from the provision of social services is no solution.

Chapter 6: Subculture Wars

1. An instructive recent example is the reasoning of Supreme Court Justice Anthony Kennedy in his majority opinion in *Obergefell v. Hodges*, which asserted a

constitutional right to same-sex marriage in 2015. Kennedy's opening words were: "The Constitution promises liberty to all within its reach, a liberty that includes certain specific rights that allow persons, within a lawful realm, to define and express their identity." Two decades earlier, in the 1996 case *Planned Parenthood v. Casey*, Kennedy famously asserted an even bolder form of this view, writing: "At the heart of liberty is the right to define one's own concept of existence, of meaning, of the universe, and of the mystery of human life." Both statements imply a far-reaching, almost Gnostic, belief in the capacity of each individual to bend reality to his will by defining his particular identity. Such explicit expressions of this view are rare, but more implicit evidence of its reach and influence is everywhere apparent. This point will be discussed further in chapter 7.

2. Kurt Andersen, "You Say You Want a Devolution?" *Vanity Fair*, January 2012.

3. This point is well made by Moises Naim in his book *The End of Power: From Boardrooms to Battlefields and Churches to States, Why Being in Charge Isn't What It Used to Be* (New York: Basic Books, 2013).

4. On this point, see Francis Fukuyama, *The Great Disruption: Human Nature and the Reconstitution of Social Order* (New York: Free Press, 1999), 90–91.

5. For a thoughtful discussion of the myths and realities of the sharing economy on this front, see Noam Scheiber, "Silicon Valley Is Ruining 'Sharing' for Everybody," *New Republic*, August 13, 2014.

6. No one has yet improved on Alexis de Tocqueville's penetrating description of this peculiar democratic mix of coercion and freedom and its deep connection to individualism. See, for instance, *Democracy in America*, vol. 1, part 2, chapter 7, and vol. 2, part 2.

7. All figures are from the National Center for Health Statistics, maintained by the Centers for Disease Control and Prevention ("Unmarried Childbearing," CDC, www.cdc.gov/nchs/fastats/unmarried-childbearing.htm). Out-of-wedlock birth statistics are marked by vast differences by race, but the upward trend has been consistent for all races for decades.

8. Raj Chetty and Nathaniel Hendren, "The Effects of Neighborhoods on Intergenerational Mobility: Childhood Exposure Effects and County-Level Estimates," Equality of Opportunity Project, May 2015, www.equality-of-opportunity .org/images/nbhds_paper.pdf.

9. The extensive overlap between traditionalists in the liberal society and Christians in the postmodern West is not a coincidence, of course. Far from it. Liberalism from its earliest incarnations has presumed and relied upon the existence of a far-reaching moral consensus in society regarding the basic premises of the Christian worldview. It has also, throughout that time, undermined these premises, and so undercut the preconditions for its own success. It has persisted despite that self-destructive tendency because the denizens of most liberal societies (and Americans, in particular) have always been less liberal and more Christian than they have claimed (and perhaps believed). To say that this is decreasingly the case in our time

is just another way to describe our contemporary condition. To better understand this facet of that condition, one could do worse than reading the collected works of the great social and political philosopher Pierre Manent.

10. Gregory Smith, *America's Changing Religious Landscape* (Washington, DC: Pew Research Center, 2015).

11. These data are from the General Social Survey conducted by the National Opinion Research Center at the University of Chicago. All data are available at http://www3.norc.org/GSS+Website.

12. Gallup's summary of these findings, in Frank Newport, "Four in 10 Report Attending Church in Last Week," Gallup, December 24, 2013, www.gallup.com /poll/166613/four-report-attending-church-last-week.aspx, is worth recounting:

> The most religious era of the past 74 years—at least based on this measure of weekly church attendance—was from the mid-to-late 1950s into the early 1960s, when, at some points, almost half of American adults said they had attended religious services in the past seven days. During this era, marked by the high fertility rates and family formation that was the foundation of the baby boomer generation, the percentage who reported that religion was important also reached high points, and almost all Americans identified with a religion.
>
> Since the early 1960s, weekly church attendance has settled down, generally to a range between 40% and 45%. But self-reported church attendance has been marked by year-to-year fluctuations. For example, less than 40% of Americans reported attending church in 1996 and in 2008. But church attendance was as high as 44% in 2000 and 2004. Americans' self-reported church attendance since 2008 has averaged 39%, down only slightly from the overall average of 42% since 1939.

13. Ed Stetzer, "Survey Fail—Christianity Isn't Dying," *USA Today*, May 15, 2015.

14. Russell Moore, "Is Christianity Dying?" May 12, 2015, www.russellmoore .com/2015/05/12/is-christianity-dying.

15. Ibid. Some Christian intellectuals have been making versions of this argument for decades, perhaps most notably Stanley Hauerwas in his book with William H. Willimon, *Resident Aliens: Life in the Christian Colony* (Nashville, TN: Abingdon Press, 1989).

16. Richard John Neuhaus, a Lutheran-turned-Catholic priest and an important intellectual leader of American social conservatism in the latter decades of the twentieth century, could see this process coming in his 1984 book *The Naked Public Square* (New York: Eerdmans, 1984), and unlike Moore, he did not welcome it. He wrote:

> In recent decades, "pluralism" has become something of a buzzword. It is variously employed. Often it is used to argue that no normative ethic, even of the vaguest and most tentative sort, can be "imposed" in our public life. In practice this means that public policy decisions reflect a surrender of the normal to the abnormal, of the dominant to the deviant. Indeed it is of more than passing

interest that terms such as abnormal or deviant have been largely exorcised from polite vocabulary among the elites in American life. The displacement of the constitutive by the marginal is not so much the result of perverse decision makers as it is the inevitable consequence of a polity and legal system in which the advantage of initiative lies with the offended (p. 146).

17. *New York Times* columnist Ross Douthat put this point well in 2015, writing, on April 28, 2015, in "The Wild Ideas of Social Conservatives" (http://douthat .blogs.nytimes.com/2015/04/28/the-wild-ideas-of-social-conservatives):

In the late 1960s and early '70s, the pro-choice side of the abortion debate frequently predicted that legal abortion would reduce single parenthood and make marriages more stable, while the pro-life side made the allegedly-counterintuitive claim that it would have roughly the opposite effect; overall, it's fair to say that post-Roe trends were considerably kinder to Roe's critics than to the "every child a wanted child" conceit. Conservatives (and not only conservatives) also made various "dystopian" predictions about eugenics and the commodification of human life as reproductive science advanced in the '70s, while many liberals argued that these fears were overblown; today, from "selective reduction" to the culling of Down Syndrome fetuses to worldwide trends in sex-selective abortion, from our fertility industry's "embryo glut" to the global market in paid surrogacy, the dystopian predictions are basically just the status quo. No-fault divorce was pitched as an escape hatch for the miserable and desperate that wouldn't affect the average marriage, but of course divorce turned out to have social-contagion effects as well. Religious fears that population control would turn coercive and tyrannical were scoffed at and then vindicated. Dan Quayle was laughed at [for criticizing the celebration of single motherhood] until the data suggested that basically he had it right. The fairly-ancient conservative premise that social permissiveness is better for the rich than for the poor persistently bemuses the left; it also persistently describes reality.

18. W. Bradford Wilcox, "Don't Hold a Funeral for Marriage Yet," *The Federalist*, May 19, 2015, http://thefederalist.com/2015/05/19/dont-hold-a-funeral-for -marriage-yet.

19. Garry Wills, "The Day the Enlightenment Went Out," *New York Times*, November 4, 2004. Tucker Carlson is cited in Dick Meyer, "The Anatomy of a Myth," *Washington Post*, December 5, 2004.

20. See, for instance, Matthew Dowd, "The Facts: Gay Marriage Didn't Tilt the 2004 Election," *Huffington Post*, December 9, 2012, and the Pew Forum's "Religion and the 2004 Election: A Post-Election Analysis," February 3, 2005, www.pewforum .org/2005/02/03/religion-and-the-2004-election-a-post-election-analysis.

21. The religious liberty debates in question arose from a decision by the administration to require all insurance plans (and therefore all employers providing such plans) to include coverage for some contraceptive and abortive drugs. This coverage

was not required by the statute, but was an exercise of the administration's discretion in its enforcement. That decision set up high-profile fights between the government and some employers (like the Hobby Lobby chain of stores and an order of Catholic nuns called the Little Sisters of the Poor) who did not want to be compelled to support abortion. The resulting fight allowed both sides to understand and portray themselves as the victims of aggression—with the employers claiming they were denied the right to run their business or nonprofit in accord with their religious convictions, and their opponents claiming (far less plausibly, to be sure) that employers were denying women access to contraception. This is just about the most disadvantageous possible form of the religious liberty debate for religious employers, and it was carefully arranged as such by the administration. It is a public debate that certainly tells us something about the state of American attitudes toward religion, but it is also a debate that would not have happened under a more conservative president.

22. The pattern evinced by the same-sex-marriage debate was not entirely a function of strategic and tactical choices by advocates on various sides. There is something of an internal logic to public arguments about traditional institutions in our kind of society. The structure of liberal politics pits individual rights against a public morality, so in the absence of a powerful social consensus around that morality individual dissenters can create a massive crisis likely to end with victory for individualism. The only way out of that pattern is subsidiarity—a pluralism of communities.

23. Louise Melling, "ACLU: Why We Can No Longer Support the Federal 'Religious Freedom' Law," *Washington Post*, June 25, 2015.

24. Benjamin Domenech and Robert Tracinski, "Welcome to Culture War 4.0," *The Federalist*, July 6, 2015, http://thefederalist.com/2015/07/06/welcome-to-culture-war-4-0-the-coming-overreach.

25. Liberal education may seem out of place on this list, but in fact it is entirely at home on it. The appeal of living alternatives in a society like ours is not limited to churches or religious communities. Even as cloistered minorities in otherwise barren universities, devoted teachers of the liberal arts and humanities can create little countercultural communities that help lost souls find direction, and assist searching, intelligent young Americans who long to discover those truths that modern life obscures from our view. The increasing isolation of genuine liberal learning in enclaves of the academic world is, in this sense, another example of specialization at work in ways that can seem like retreats but might function as advances. They can strengthen our liberal, market society in some of the same ways that cohesive religious communities can: by showing us what our democratic capitalism too easily misses or ignores and by helping us attain the moral prerequisites for life in such a free society.

26. Anyone who doubts that such communities exist should consider, among many other examples, the work of the Center for Neighborhood Enterprise around the nation in the past several decades, the many communities it helps and highlights, and the writings of its director, Robert Woodson.

27. Alasdair MacIntyre, *After Virtue: A Study in Moral Theory* (Notre Dame, IN: University of Notre Dame Press, 2007), 243.

28. See, for instance, Rod Dreher, "Benedict Option," *American Conservative*, December 12, 2013.

29. Rod Dreher, "We Are Not Going to the Hills," *American Conservative*, September 22, 2015. Alan Jacobs, a distinguished scholar of the humanities at Baylor University and a leading American Christian intellectual, has sought to emphasize this element of Dreher's approach in "Life in the Garrison," *American Conservative*, June 10, 2015:

> The Benedict Option recommends increased attentiveness to local communities, to the formation of Christians (young and old) in the traditional practices and habits (of thought and action) of the Church. Though what this might look like has yet to be clarified and codified, there are already a good many people describing it as a regrettable withdrawal from "the world." . . .
>
> What do the critics . . . mean by "the world"? . . . [F]or them "the world" is inside the Beltway, and in the *New York Times* and *Washington Post*, and on Politico and HuffPost, and the tweetstreams of politicians and policy wonks, and on our biggest TV networks. But I would like to suggest that the building of a healthy society might depend on people who are willing to say that those vast public edifices—some made of stone, some of pixels—are not the world, that the world lies much closer to hand.

30. See, for instance, Alexis de Tocqueville, *Democracy in America*, Harvey Mansfield and Delba Winthrop, trans. (Chicago: University of Chicago Press, 2000), 424.

31. Michael Brendan Dougherty, "Why Social Conservatives Shouldn't Despair—Even If Liberals Win the Culture War," *The Week*, June 25, 2015, http://theweek.com/articles/562589/why-social-conservatives-shouldnt-despair—even-liberals-win-culture-war.

32. On this point, see William Schambra, "Conservatism and the Quest for Community," *National Affairs*, Summer 2010.

33. Here again, Alexis de Tocqueville can offer us guidance. His reflections on this point, especially in vol. 2, part 2, of *Democracy in America*, are in a sense always pertinent to American life, but they are perhaps particularly pertinent now, more than at any time since Tocqueville wrote in the fourth decade of the nineteenth century, as the place of individualism in our national life is more central and significant than it has been since that time.

34. The experience of many hundreds of local, faith-based initiatives to help those struggling with addiction, reentering society after incarceration, working to heal broken families, or otherwise turning shattered lives around amply confirm the power of moral community in this regard. The work of the Center for Neighborhood Enterprise in the past several decades is highly instructive, among many other examples.

35. It can hardly escape our notice today that individualism, in both its progressive and libertarian forms, is linked to cosmopolitanism, while communitarianism is almost inherently populist.

Chapter 7: One Nation, After All

1. For a useful summary of Gallup data on declining trust in institutions, see "Trust in Government," www.gallup.com/poll/5392/trust-government.aspx.

2. Peter Schuck, *Why Government Fails So Often: And How It Can Do Better* (Princeton, NJ: Princeton University Press, 2014), 411.

3. See, for instance, Francis Fukuyama, *Political Order and Political Decay: From the Industrial Revolution to the Globalization of Democracy* (New York: Farrar, Straus and Giroux, 2014). It is worth noting that Fukuyama's bold and comprehensive book is about much more than US public administration. It is a history of the practice of political order since the late eighteenth century, and my references here are to its concluding discussion of the contemporary state of US public administration.

4. Thomas Mann and Norman Ornstein's book *It's Even Worse Than It Looks: How the American Constitutional System Collided with the New Politics of Extremism* (New York: Basic Books, 2012), is characteristic of this genre of diagnosis.

5. David Brady and Hahrie Han, "Our Politics May Be Polarized, But That's Nothing New," *Washington Post*, January 26, 2014.

6. Tocqueville noted this same pattern with regard to social inequality more generally. See Alexis de Tocqueville, *Democracy in America*, Harvey Mansfield and Delba Winthrop, trans. (Chicago: University of Chicago Press, 2000), 513.

7. For a sense of what this would involve on the Right, in particular, see, for instance, the work of the Conservative Reform Network and affiliated scholars, and especially their 2014 book *Room to Grow: Conservative Reforms for Limited Government and a Thriving Middle Class*, available at http://conservativereform.com/room togrow, or the archives of the quarterly journal I edit, *National Affairs*.

8. For an illuminating discussion of potential reforms of the presidential nominating process, in particular, along these lines, see Jeffrey Anderson and Jay Cost, "A Republican Nomination Process," *National Affairs*, Summer 2013.

9. The second of the three charts presented toward the end of chapter 4, which traces party polarization in Congress over the past century, helps to demonstrate this point.

10. Such reforms would involve, for instance, allowing committees more direct access to the floor of each house and enabling Congress's support agencies, and especially those charged with scoring the fiscal effects of legislation, to reinforce the work of looser networks of members rather than block it.

11. Political scientist John DiIulio of the University of Pennsylvania has written insightfully on this point. See, for instance, his essay "Facing Up to Big Government," *National Affairs*, Spring 2012.

12. As the historian Wilfred McClay put it in "The Federal Idea," *Continuity: A Journal of History*, Spring 1988:

> We have been too easily convinced, I think, by the reflexive argument that the federal idea is useless to us today because we cannot return to nineteenth-century institutions. This is to mistake one expression of the federal idea for

the idea itself, and to imagine that the federal principle cannot permit growth or development, or find expression in other ways. It is to forget the fact . . . that federalism is not a closed, finished system, but is by its very nature dynamic and adaptive. If we can begin to understand this sense of federalism, as an idea rather than a fixed set of immutable relations, and moreover as an idea that is designed to balance and reconcile the competing claims of competing goods, then our debates over the promise of federalism may take on a new vitality and plausibility. The federal idea may then win more general acceptance as an idea whose time has come—again.

13. Tocqueville, *Democracy in America*, 491.

14. *Planned Parenthood of Southeastern Pennsylvania v. Casey*, 505 US 833 (1992).

15. Barack Obama, "Inaugural Address by the President," January 21, 2013, https://www.whitehouse.gov/the-press-office/2013/01/21/inaugural-address-president-barack-obama.

16. As Friederich Hayek put it, in *The Constitution of Liberty* (Chicago: University of Chicago Press, 1960), "liberty in practice depends on very prosaic matters, and those anxious to preserve it must prove their devotion by their attention to the mundane concerns of public life and by the efforts they are prepared to give to the understanding of issues that the idealist is often inclined to treat as common, if not sordid" (p. 7).

17. Among many instances of conservative politicians advancing an expressly communitarian conservatism, a particularly notable one is Ronald Reagan's most prominent 1976 presidential campaign speech (known as the "Let the People Rule Speech"), in which Reagan said, "I am calling also for an end to giantism, for a return to the human scale—the scale that human beings can understand and cope with; the scale of the local fraternal lodge, the church congregation, the block club, the farm bureau. It is this activity on a small, human scale that creates the fabric of community." Among contemporary examples, the most notable may be Utah senator Mike Lee, whose rhetoric and policy proposals explicitly highlight the fundamentally communitarian character of conservatism.

18. Peter Berkowitz, "The Long Rise of the Secular Faith," *Mosaic*, August 24, 2015, http://mosaicmagazine.com/response/2015/08/the-long-rise-of-the-secular-faith.

19. James Madison, "Report on Resolutions of the House of Delegates, 1799–1800," in Gaillard Hunt, ed., *The Writings of James Madison*, vol. 6 (New York: G. P. Putnam, 1906), 352.

20. Tocqueville, *Democracy in America*, 485.

21. Robert Nisbet, *The Quest for Community* (Wilmington, DE: ISI Books, 2010), 262.

INDEX

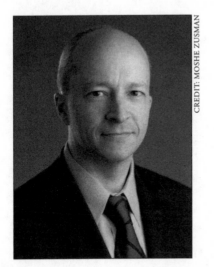

Yuval Levin is the editor of *National Affairs* and the Hertog Fellow at the Ethics and Public Policy Center. He is a contributing editor to *National Review* and the *Weekly Standard*, and his writings have appeared in numerous publications, including the *New York Times*, the *Washington Post*, the *Wall Street Journal*, *Commentary*, and others. He holds a PhD from the Committee on Social Thought at the University of Chicago and has been a member of the White House domestic policy staff (under President George W. Bush) and a congressional staffer. He lives in Maryland.